Ipsative Assessment and Personal Learning Gain

Gwyneth Hughes
Editor

Ipsative Assessment and Personal Learning Gain

Exploring International Case Studies

Editor
Gwyneth Hughes
UCL Institute of Education
University of London
London, United Kingdom

ISBN 978-1-137-56501-3   ISBN 978-1-137-56502-0 (eBook)
DOI 10.1057/978-1-137-56502-0

Library of Congress Control Number: 2016951316

Cover illustration: © Cultura RM / Alamy Stock Photo

Printed on acid-free paper

This Palgrave Macmillan imprint is published by Springer Nature
The registered company is Macmillan Publishers Ltd.
The registered company address is: The Campus, 4 Crinan Street, London, N1 9XW, United Kingdom

ACKNOWLEDGEMENTS

I wish to thank all the authors who have contributed to this collection for their enthusiasm and willingness to give up their time to write and revise their chapters. I also acknowledge all the people who have recently shared their views on ipsative assessment and personal learning gain with me at various events at Bedfordshire, Greenwich, Roehampton and York Universities as well as my own institution UCL, Institute of Education. Finally, I wish to thank Wendy Smith for helping with proof reading the manuscript and for her tireless encouragement.

Contents

LIST OF FIGURES

LIST OF TABLES

Introducing Ipsative Assessment and Personal Learning Gain: Voices from Practitioners and the Themes of the Collection

Gwyneth Hughes

INTRODUCTION TO THE COLLECTION

We expect educators all over the world to care about their students' learning and most teachers aim to motivate all their students, not only the highest achievers. But in a world of financial instability, dwindling resources, meritocratic ideals and pressure on individuals to be the agents of their own success, learners become motivated by externally appointed grades and marks. They are highly tuned to their ranking in comparison to others. 'Winners' and 'losers' are very visible in published results and, even if marks are not made public, students know where they are in the marking hierarchy and whether or not they are a 'good' student. Assessments are high stakes and used for selection of students through qualifications and entry into jobs and employment (Broadfoot 1996). But, such competitive assessment can compromise self-esteem so that students who do not easily

G. Hughes (✉)
UCL Institute of Education, UCL, London, UK
e-mail: Gwyneth.hughes@ucl.ac.uk

© The Author(s) 2017
G. Hughes (ed.), *Ipsative Assessment and Personal Learning Gain*,
DOI 10.1057/978-1-137-56502-0_1

accumulate rewards or good grades can become demotivated, set their sights low or give up (Dweck 1999). Others may take an instrumental approach to learning and focus on what they perceive is required to pass the tests. Teachers may collude in such narrowing of the curriculum despite their best intentions to encourage learning.

But, there is a radically different approach: ipsative assessment (Hughes 2014). The difference here is that a learner's work is compared to their own previous work rather than to external criteria and standards. An ipsative approach to assessment is captured in concepts such as personal learning gain, personal best and progress reports. Like a 'personal best' in athletics an ipsative assessment can be motivational for all learners, not only high achievers, because all students can make progress and achieve a personal goal, at least most of the time. Think of the delight of a novice swimmer who swims from one end of the pool to the other unaided for the first time. In a truly ipsative assessment scheme, those starting from a low base would not be at a disadvantage because it is progression towards individual targets and possibly self-directed goals that matters, not only reaching external standards.

This edited collection is aimed at educational practitioners who are interested in new methods of assessment that motivate and empower a diversity of learners – the strong and the weak, the privileged and the disadvantaged, beginners and more advanced learners. It is a companion text to the editor's book published by Palgrave Macmillan *Ipsative Assessment: Motivation through marking progress*. The collection is written by teachers and lecturers from different parts of the world and from different levels of education. Their practice is presented through exciting and innovative case studies of ipsative assessment and its relationship with measurement of learning gain, diagnostic assessment and self-directed improvement. These bold visions of assessment attract critics and the collection will address the challenges of implementing ipsative assessment and personal learning gain as well as showcasing the benefits. But, first I shall present some definitions of key terms.

Ipsative Assessment: A Name for Making and Marking Progress

Although the term ipsative assessment was first used by psychologists in the 1940s, it is not commonly used today. This may be because the practice is uncommon so a name is not needed, but it may also be that a lack of a familiar word inhibits recognition of practice and possibly the practice itself. I strongly believe that the naming of the concept needs to be better established in educational circles so that ipsative assessment can be theorised and evidence of ipsative practice and its benefits made visible. A name also enables critics to voice their concerns about ipsative practices. A link between ipsative assessment and diagnostic assessment also needs to be identified. For example, an ipsative scheme may begin with a diagnostic test or learning self-evaluation so that personalised goals can be agreed and progress recorded.

Furthermore, ipsative assessment fits well with the idea of assessment *for* learning (Hughes 2014) that is formative and developmental, but the term can also refer to assessment *of* learning requiring a measurement or judgement of learning gain at the end of a period of study – in other words a summative assessment (Hughes 2014, 2011). The collection covers both formative ipsative feedback and ipsative summative assessment which includes personal learning gain.

For the objectives of this book ipsative assessment is an umbrella term for a collection of practices that have in common the learner's progression from an earlier position as the key attribute of the assessment *and these practices have a purpose for directly enhancing learning from the learner perspective*. Ipsative assessment practice might include measuring personal learning gains that are recorded for other purposes, but the data will be available and comprehensible to the learner who can use the information to set goals and plan learning with the guidance and support of teachers.

Learning Gain: A Definition and an Example

Learning gain or learning growth or value-added measurements are used widely in the United States and in the UK as part of measuring both teacher and school effectiveness (Sammons 2012). The gain may be in a broad range of skills and a generic definition of learning gain is:

> ... the 'distance travelled' by students during their studies, demonstrable by an improvement in knowledge, skills, work-readiness and personal development between two points in time. (Higher Education Funding Council for England 2015)

Learning gain is not the same as learning output. For example, a post-compulsory education teacher described her class on ICT skills for a mixed group of students with special educational needs. By the end of the session one student with autism had learnt how to use a publishing software package to produce a newsletter, while another student with Down's syndrome had mastered double clicking of the mouse to open programmes and documents. Both demonstrated considerable learning gain, but it would be nonsensical to compare the outputs of these students. Here is a somewhat extreme example of the inappropriateness of comparing learning outcomes for different students and the importance of recognition of learning gain.

Measuring Learning Gain

Learning gain measurements are used in large scale evaluations of educational institutions and this topic forms the basis of Chap. 2. The rationale behind such evaluation is a discourse of educational improvement that aims to promote high standards. Student exit performance data such as examination results are commonly used to judge and compare the effectiveness of a college, school or university. But examination results alone do not give a full picture of educational effectiveness or teaching excellence. Including learning gain or value-added information alongside examination results can help recognise the achievement of institutions which have a disadvantaged student intake and cannot be judged fairly alongside institutions with a privileged intake. But although we shall see in Chap. 2 that there are some advantages of measuring learning gain rather than judging institutional quality only on examination outputs or other proxies for teaching effectiveness, there is something else missing. Data on learning gain of individual students collated by governments, managers and policy makers are aimed only indirectly at benefiting students through improving teaching methods. I shall propose that because information about individuals is not accessible to students and their educators, there is a missed opportunity for students to be motivated and guided by individual learning gains. It is the personal level of learning gain which can be used for ipsative assessment but is largely hidden in conventional assessment systems that is the main concern of this book.

Voices from Practitioners

While examples of research and experimentation in new assessment methods are well covered in the academic literature, authentic examples of practitioners developing contemporary practice are always useful for wider education audiences – especially in a newly forming landscape of ipsative assessment and learning gain. Now that the terms 'ipsative assessment' and 'personal best' have been theorised in my previous book the terrain is ready to be explored.

The aim of the collection is to provide real-world examples or case studies of practice in using ipsative feedback and/or personal learning gain information for assessment purposes. Case studies that bring alive the practice of ipsative assessment and learning gain measurement will provide a stimulus for others to either advance their own ipsative assessment schemes or to begin to include ipsative assessment and measurements of personal learning gain in their repertoire of assessment practices.

Each case study will not only provide an example of practice, but will also consider evidence for the benefits of ipsative assessment in motivating students to learn. Some chapters are research-based and include data collection, others are reflections on practice. Some chapters are theoretically developed while others are less so. Nevertheless, the accounts are both critical and self-reflective: critical in that innovations in assessment will not be presented as unproblematic, and reflective in that the authors will openly and honestly discuss the challenges that they have overcome in implementing or attempting to implement their novel ideas.

The case studies can also be more conventionally categorised in terms of the type of assessment, the sector or level and the characteristics of the students. This chapter will finish with an overview of the case studies to help readers select which case studies to read and in which order (the case studies are presented in a random order in the book).

The authors of the case studies are all advocates of ipsative assessment in some form and this may detract from the impartiality of the accounts. The practitioner case studies inevitably vary in methodologies and degrees of research rigour and it may be that a single case study is not very convincing on its own. In addition, the case studies mostly present early work on ipsative assessment and learning gain and do not yet constitute an established body of knowledge. However, through multiple case studies that generate some similar findings, the collection will contribute to a robust set of evidence for the benefits of ipsative assessment and the challenges that may arise in a variety of contexts so that the body of knowledge can being to grow.

This chapter will next present four themes that I have used for a meta-analysis of the cases. As I take each theme in turn, I shall illustrate the discussion with examples from the case studies to give a preview of each one. These themes will raise many questions. Not all the questions will be answered in depth in the cases studies as some will need further research to be undertaken, but the final chapter of the book will revisit the themes drawing on evidence so far to provide a vision for the future.

THEMES OF THE COLLECTION

I have previously claimed that ipsative assessment can be motivational, particularly for learners who do not usually succeed (Hughes 2014). But, for ipsative assessment to be taken seriously as an assessment method, especially for high stakes assessment, it must offer reliability in the same way that conventional standards, criteria and marking need to provide reassurances to students that the assessment is fair. But, given the emphasis on qualifications and exit performance in selective education, there may be tensions between traditional assessment and ipsative assessment of progress leading to some practical challenges. I have previously identified that ipsative assessments may not have the same status as externally referenced assessment (Hughes 2014) and the relationship between ipsative and more conventionally marked assessment that leads to credentials also needs exploring. Building on these ideas here are four themes that I will use to introduce the case studies:

1. Enhancing learning through ipsative feedback
2. Advantages of measuring personal learning gain
3. Practical challenges of implementing ipsative assessment and measuring personal learning gain
4. Combining ipsative assessment with criteria-referenced summative assessment or examinations

THEME 1: ENHANCING LEARNING THROUGH IPSATIVE FEEDBACK

The question 'How can ipsative assessment enhance student learning over time?' was addressed by many of the case studies and ipsative feedback features largely in these accounts so enhancing learning is a major theme.

There are many ways of developing learning and to appreciate these we need to explore what enhancing learning through feedback might mean and how ipsative feedback that is visible and explicit might encourage students to engage enthusiastically in learning.

Feedback as Social Learning

There are different types of academic learning, which Bloom et al. (1956) categorised as knowledge, understanding, application, synthesis and evaluation. Enhancing academic learning could mean an increase in rote learning of a series of facts, but from a social constructivist perspective, higher order learning moves from recall through application to evaluation and requires a learner to build their own knowledge and skills from their current position. Learning in this way requires social interaction with peers or teachers and/or engagement with online or print resources (Laurillard 2012; Luckin 2010). But, social learning is not only about sharing knowledge with others; it necessitates some form of developmental feedback that has an important function in enabling learners to adjust their thinking and advance.

There are many definitions of feedback, some which may view feedback narrowly as something 'given' to learners, but a useful and comprehensive definition that includes a notion of feedback as also 'received' by learners to produce change is given by Molloy and Boud (2013):

> Feedback is a process whereby learners obtain information about their work in order to appreciate the similarities and differences between the appropriate standards for any given work, and the qualities of the work itself, in order to generate improved work. (p. 6)

I gave evidence in Hughes (2014) that ipsative feedback is likely to be the most common form of ipsative assessment. We might expect that qualitative information about progress would be part of a teacher, peer or self-commentary on learning with a view of feedback as generating improved work as in the definition above. It might also be expected that feedback that informs learners of areas of progress or lack of progress by comparing a current piece of work with previous ones would be commonplace. Certainly ipsative feedback might occur informally and verbally where students are reassured by teachers that they are 'getting the hang of it' or have improved their writing since the last piece of work. Written feedback may also contain ipsative content, but a feedback analysis that I undertook at a research-intensive UK university suggested that such self-referential feedback is rare and that feedback is more often in the form of critique or praise in relation to external standards (Hughes et al. 2015). However, the research has also demonstrated that ipsative feedback could be easily included on the feedback menu and that doing so was motivational for students and helped them to plan their learning (Hughes 2014; Hughes et al. 2014).

Feedback is a complex topic, but although there are many views on what constitutes effective feedback, there are some points of growing consensus. Firstly, feedback can focus on the strengths and weakness of the current piece of work, for example, through correcting factual mistakes, but feedback can additionally guide a student towards the next developmental steps through advice and questioning (Orsmond and Merry 2011). This is sometimes termed feed forward. Praise or error correction without some explanation and/or feed forward on next steps is not usually very helpful for students.

We could also argue that developmental feedback or feed forward that informs learners of next steps (Hattie and Timperley 2007) is ipsative in that it anticipates future progress. However, I assert that feed forward is ipsative only if a follow-up by students is recorded in a systematic manner so that there can be a comparative process. We shall see some examples of this in the case studies. I would not apply the term ipsative feedback to feed forward that is transmitted to a student in advising them what to do next, but has an unknown influence on the student. In such cases there is no comparative judgement about any personal learning gain.

Secondly, once assessors have given students feedback they may believe that the job is done but feedback that is one directional from the assessor to the student is not necessarily useful. The student may not understand or welcome the feedback. Educators such as Nicol (2010, 2013) and Hattie and Timperley (2007) have argued that for feedback to influence the learner there must be some form of dialogue. Students must find out why something was wrong and why a new course of action is recommended and this means asking questions to assessors and of themselves. Effective education encourages students to question themselves and so become self-critical and self-regulatory in their work over time (Nicol and Macfarlane—Dick 2006). Only then can 'giving feedback' become effective.

Thirdly, feedback can originate from peers as well as from oneself and there are some very good reasons for encouraging this. Molloy and Boud (2013) have explored how teacher-centred assessment where teachers are the main source of feedback does not necessarily enable learning and may produce teacher dependency rather than student autonomy. Meanwhile, students engage fully with feedback and assessment processes when they become assessors themselves. Comparing many sources of feedback develops self-regulation in student-centred models of feedback and peer and self-review come highly recommended as methods to help students develop assessment skills for themselves (Nicol 2010). However, peer and self-review do not slot comfortably into competitive and high stakes assessment environments and can be greeted with scepticism from both assessors and students. Meanwhile slower burning cumulative assessment schemes are much more conducive (Hughes 2014).

The chapters in this collection support these theoretical views. Gwyneth Hughes, Denise Hawkes and Tim Neumann in Chap. 6 explore how the use of digital technology to capture feedback can support self-reflection on feedback in higher education. Chapters by Jiming Zhou and Jie Zang, Emanuela Tilley and Kate Roach, as well as Julie Rattray (Chaps. 3, 7 and 8) consider the benefits of reflection on feedback, including peer feedback, during extended group activities. Kit McIntyre in Chap. 5 also explores how self-reflection can be linked to self-efficacy in young children when reflections are ipsative and made in a non-competitive environment. These cases also illustrate how ipsative feedback differs from more conventional feedback.

Differences Between Ipsative and Conventional Feedback

It is also generally agreed that feedback should be relevant in that it addresses transparent assessment criteria and standards (Gibbs and Simpson 2004; O'Donovan et al. 2004) and this is where a subtle difference between ipsative and conventional feedback occurs. Conventional feedback addresses how well a student has met the published (or tacit) criteria and to what standard or level. Feedback is conventionally used to addresses a gap between where the learner is now and the externally set goal (Sadler 1989). Such feedback is orientated towards possibly unrealistic future learning gain. By contrast explicitly ipsative feedback focuses on the student's actual learning gain or progress which can be viewed in a context of the external goal such as a pass/fail threshold, or a goal set by the learner themselves. In other words any future learning gain projection is built on past learning gain and should be achievable. For example, in Chap. 4, Carrie Winstanley discusses the use of cumulative assignment coversheets which emphasise the student learning journey rather than a performance gap. Staff and students can write comments about improvements since the previous assessment on the cumulative coversheet, which is then submitted with successive assessments. But, ipsative feedback could also highlight inadequate or zero progress towards a threshold or agreed standards, although we would hope that such stagnation of learning would not occur without a good reason and there are no examples in this book.

Another key element of explicitly ipsative feedback is that a starting position of the learner must be known so that it can be compared to the current level. This makes ipsative feedback quite challenging because it is not only the learner's current performance that is being judged but also a previous performance. A purposeful diagnostic assessment may be used to identify a learner's needs and this can then be compared with a later performance. However, the information for such comparative judgements may not be readily available, or the previous performance may have occurred a considerable time ago. Making comparisons is especially problematic if past records are concealed in institutional assessment systems or would be time consuming for the assessor to access. The assessor could rely on recall of a previous performance, but although appraising progress using memory alone may be fine for individual supervision or small classes, it is not appropriate for large group of undergraduates who may in any case be deliberately anonymised with the aim of reducing marking bias.

Keeping Records of Progress

An obvious solution to the problem of comparative judgement is to keep electronic records of previous goals and feedback that can be checked. In Chap. 6, Hughes, Hawkes and Neumann explore record keeping in more detail through adapting a virtual learning environment so that it captures every student's feedback history throughout their programme of study. Asking students to identify their goals (perhaps drawing on previous feedback that is stored electronically) and then giving feedback on how well students have addressed the feedback (or not) is quite easy for assessors to do as in Winstanlsy's coversheets. Digital video recording is another approach that can be used for performing arts, for example, Mathieu Boucher, Francis Dubé and Andrea Creech give an example of guitar students' use of video recordings of their playing to compare present and past performances and for setting future goals in Chap. 10. These examples support the premise that for ipsative feedback to be useful it must be cumulative over time so that once one goal is met the next one is agreed. Progress must also be visible.

Engaging Students in Feedback

We could ask a question about student motivation to engage in feedback. Different forms of feedback may motivate – or de-motivate – learners in different ways. There is a motivational problem with focusing on Sadler's gap between performance and a desired goal because the learning gain required may be large and drawing attention to the gap is dispiriting. Is it better for one's self-esteem to focus on distance travelled and next achievable steps for that learner in a personalised ipsative feedback approach than to focus on distant and seemingly impossible goals? Chapter 7 by Tilley and Roach provides evidence that self-reflection on progress motivated group work in engineering and McIntyre's school children in Chap. 5 also found an ipsative rather than a competitive approach engaging.

The Problem of Qualitative Comparative Judgements

Ipsative feedback from a human assessor usually means judgements that are qualitative and to be taken seriously such judgements must stand up to scrutiny and be justified. For example, if a learner is informed that her or his academic writing has improved this is only helpful if we know which aspects of academic writing are under discussion: paragraph construction, referencing, critical thinking, etc. and we would need some evidence of improvement. In other words the same depth of evidence is needed to judge progress as is required for evidence of meeting (or not meeting) external standards. Even more detail may be needed because ipsative feedback considers the situation 'before' and 'now' and not just 'now'. Rattray in Chap. 8 addresses the specificity of ipsative judgements through examining a particular 'threshold concept' – in this case criticality in higher education–that students must master by passing through a temporary liminal or confused state.

Comparative decisions are dependent on human interpretation of records of past and present performance and the problem of making a reliable judgement of progress should not be easily dismissed. Sometimes there will be demand for an objective measure of the learner's distance travelled or learning gain. Marks derived from robust schemes, criteria and standards can be turned into quantitative measures of learning gain at the individual or personal level. This takes us to the second theme of the book collection.

THEME 2: ADVANTAGES OF MEASURING PERSONAL LEARNING GAIN

Ipsative assessment might never extend beyond the enthusiast's local application unless there is a systematic and robust method for measuring personal learning gain that can be applied across disciplines and institutions. So, what are the advantages of measuring personal learning gain?

The most obvious advantage of measuring personal learning gain rather than personal achievement is that those who are not usually the top performers can shine, and this could well be the large majority of students. In my previous book (Hughes 2014), I proposed that highly competitive assessment systems make it very clear which students are successful, but for those who attain mediocre or low marks, competitive assessment can be very dispiriting. Many students equate low performance with low ability and such assessment damages self-esteem and self-belief (Dweck 1999). However, the tables are turned if the marks are for progress and it is learning gain rather than learning outcome that is measured. Now the traditionally lower achievers can demonstrate potential and develop mastery or a growth mentality as well as those few who are outstanding as summarised in the statement:

> Most of the time, most people will not achieve perfection or excellence, but most people can make improvements most of the time. (Hughes 2014, p. 1)

Ghandi in Chap. 11 supports this view in her studies of using a 'Compete with Yourself' method for personalising the learning of primary school children. The method motivates pupils to work on very specific topics that need attention with very visible signs of making progress. The method also produced some impressive impacts on a cohort's average performance in standard tests.

But, learners who are accustomed to excelling may find it more difficult to demonstrate progress from an already high starting point and there is a risk that highly competitive students may not agree with learning gain measurements and may complain bitterly if they feel that their advantages have been taken away. On the plus side, if learning gain measurement is taken seriously then this could stimulate high achievers to aim even higher and may discourage complacency or over-confidence. But, mixing the very different conventional and learning gain assessments implied here may be problematic as I will explore in the final theme.

Cohort Learning Gain

Learning gain measurements at scale can provide indicators of enduring learning in key skills and attributes or act as a warning about temporary learning that does not last beyond the test. We shall see in Chap. 2 how Arum and Roksa (2011) used learning gain data in higher education to identify limited learning in key graduate and employment skills such as critical thinking, problem-solving and communication. Similarly information about a cohort's progress or lack of progress over time is very useful for teachers to estimate how much learning is retained beyond formal assignments, tests and examinations. Just because a student demonstrates a particular skill or attribute at one assessment point does not guarantee a repeated performance. Indeed performance may well decline after the formal testing has ended and this could have serious consequences if knowledge or skill from one assessment needs to be re-applied for future learning and assessment. Hui-Teng Hoo and Hughes in Chap. 9 illustrate how learning gain scores in cultural conflict resolution increased during a formal testing period, but fell off a few weeks after the final test.

Cumulative curricula make the assumption that certain skills or knowledge will accumulate rather than deteriorate after a formal assessment. However, although teachers may be very aware that students have peaks in performance and then forget some or all of what they appeared to have learnt, such detailed information about what happens to learning in the longer term is not often readily available because it would be difficult to collect after the main event and is not a priority.

Hoo and Hughes's case study was originally designed as pedagogic research to compare teacher-led and student-led formative assessment and demonstrates how learning gain data can be useful for research purposes – in this case to show that both methods are equally effective in the short term. With greater information about learning gain and learning decline, can teaching be adapted to encourage retention of key skills and knowledge and to discourage 'forgetting'? Learners armed with learning gain or learning decline information can more readily keep their learning 'finely tuned', practised and up to date. But, seeking out the 'holy grail' of measurement of enduring learning rather than one-off event learning raises many questions as we shall see next.

THEME 3: PRACTICAL CHALLENGES OF IMPLEMENTING IPSATIVE ASSESSMENT AND MEASURING PERSONAL LEARNING GAIN

When two or more performances are compared at different points in time to measure a personal learning gain, three pressing questions arise.

Are the Tests of Performance Equivalent?

Firstly, to measure learning gain the same skill or attribute must be measured at different points. This presents a huge challenge. One solution is to set the same test twice, but then there may be learning gains from repetition and practising the test leading to a false positive. For example, a student may remember a previous answer and this gives more time to spend on other answers resulting in a better score. Such effects are hard to predict and making allowances may not be possible.

If the tests are not identical then statistical methods can show whether or not one test is easier than another, but this requires large numbers and a comprehension of statistics that is not expected of students and many teachers. Students may compare successive grades to see if they are improving without knowing whether or not these comparisons are valid or useful because the grades or marks may be for different skills or the level of difficulty may have changed.

Assessor reliability is also a tricky issue and it is difficult to ensure that two or more human assessors will provide the same verdicts. Computer marking, carefully designed mark schemes and moderation of assessors can provide some assurance that marking is consistent between tests. But, even when there are formal assessment criteria, this is a huge challenge (Bloxham et al. 2011). Assessors have their own idea of what they are looking for and their judgements will depend on external factors such as marker fatigue. In the Hoo and Hughes study the assessor re-graded a 10 % sample of the work to check for marking consistency: a time-consuming practice which is necessary for research purposes, but not practical for most teaching situations.

Having a greater number of comparisons may make the learning gain measurement more meaningful. If there are only two measurements a learner might have had an 'off' day and underperformed in one of the tests. If there are a series of measurements then a learning trajectory can be plotted and any anomalies can show up. This takes us to a second question.

How Can Learning Gain Measurements be Presented Meaningfully and Reliability to Learners?

One method of introducing students to the idea of learning gain is to combine a robust learning gain measurement with ipsative self-review that helps the learner to see where the gains have been made and what steps to take next. This was the basis of a portfolio assessment for taught doctoral students explored by Hughes, Neumann and Hawkins in Chap. 6. At the end of a taught programme, students with low grades were interviewed by the programme leader for suitability for progression to the thesis research and writing stage using a combination of information on progress from a self-review and learning gain (or lack of gain) in grades. But self-review requires a good level of student investment in the learning process taking us to a third question.

Which Strategies Encourage Investment in Ipsative Assessment in Practice?

We have seen that recording a personal learning gain measurement requires an input of time and effort on the part of the learner and/or the teacher. Both will need to be convinced of the benefits of tracking a learning journey if they are to invest in this process alongside other forms of assessment. The case studies are early explorations of ipsative practice – very much dipping a tentative toe in the water – but there is enough here to illustrate with real-life examples that once ipsative assessment is introduced, students of all ages begin to appreciate that this new approach can be very worthwhile.

Nevertheless, I concede that competitive selection of students, whether for further study, for employment or as a requirement for a professional qualification, is likely to remain in place for the foreseeable future. Therefore investing in an ipsative process is likely to be in addition to high stakes outcomes-based assessments that, for example, determine degree results. The balance between the two methods of assessment will need careful attention otherwise ipsative assessment could be side-lined. In my previous book I suggested that ipsative assessment phases should be kept apart from competitive assessment phases as far as possible to avoid such marginalisation (Hughes 2014). This leads us to the final theme that will be explored in this collection.

THEME 4: COMBINING IPSATIVE ASSESSMENT WITH CRITERIA-REFERENCED SUMMATIVE ASSESSMENT OR EXAMINATIONS

Authors in this collection recognise that the relationship between ipsative assessment methods and orthodox competitive assessment can be problematic and that the key role of assessment for selection and for demonstration of professional qualification requirements is likely to continue. Zhou and Zang in Chap. 3 agree that ipsative assessment will not replace externally referenced assessments in the near future. However, ipsative assessment could be combined with traditional methods to give richer and more helpful information about learners and their potential in the workplace or other contexts. From the case studies some tensions arising from combining the very different assessment paradigms include the following:

- maximising learning versus maximising outcomes
- balancing long-term and short-term learning gains for students
- distinguishing and then weighting ispative and externally referenced assessments.

The tension between maximising learning processes and maximising learning outcomes is not new. Freire challenged the 'banking' model of learning which assumes that chunks of knowledge are laid down in the brain in the same way that sums of money are deposited in a bank (Freire 1973). Assuming there is no financial crisis, money will accumulate in a bank account and not deplete. No so with learning. Forgetting or losing skills that are not practised is an accepted part of being human and this is why many professions insist on continuing professional development to maintain and update professional knowledge. But much academic learning is demonstrated through a single, clearly defined assessment event and learning trajectories before or after the event are not important to those involved. This encourages students to put effort into maximising their performance in the one-off event or examination which at its most instrumental extreme results in teaching to the test (Ecclestone 2007; Stobart 2008). Investment in learning gain may not seem so attractive to students who are mainly judged by formal assessment outcomes. While the case studies all represent attempts to shift the balance away from learning outcomes to celebrate learning processes, the scope is somewhat limited by formal educational contexts.

For example, Winstanley describes in her chapter how ipsative grades were eventually discontinued because of an incompatibility with the university's assessment regulations.

Closely related to the tension between learning process and outcome is the balance between long-term and short-term learning gain. Investing in a long-term learning gain trajectory is difficult to achieve when the next high stakes assessment is on the horizon and demands immediate attention. Although, not all learners are extrinsically motivated and many are interested in longer term intrinsic goals, in a culture of performativity and measurement and where learning contexts are juxtaposed with many competing demands from employers, families etc., it will not be unexpected if ipsative processes are hidden or undervalued in a context of high stakes credentials.

However, when tests and formal assessments are not the main motivator, longer term views of learning gain may be easier to promote at all levels of education. McIntyre (Chap. 5) illustrates how culturally diverse school pupils were motivated by an emphasis on their personal learning gain rather than competition with others using Feuerstein's Instrumental Enrichment Programme. The engineering undergraduates in Tilley and Roach's Chap. 7 were able to document development of non-assessed group working skills more easily than their development of formally assessed outputs. Those studying at doctoral level are highly skilled and motivated by their research topic and Hughes, Neumann and Hawkes in Chap. 6 explore how these students were easily persuaded to monitor their own progress over a year through reflections on feedback.

Ipsative assessment, therefore, works well when it is somehow kept apart from high stakes summative assessment. I have proposed a dual system of assessment as a method for enabling assessment of externally set outcomes and ipsative assessment to coexist, but in separate phases (Hughes 2014). In the ipsative phase progress is recognised and learners set their own goals. Maximising performance in the short-term is not attractive or necessary and the focus is on longer term learning plans. An example of this phase is when students undertake self-defined project work or research over a set period of time. Reliability of assessments in this phase is not essential and so peer and self-assessment can be employed without too much controversy. Tilley and Roach give an example of what can be achieved in group work through a series of peer and self-assessed review meetings with a tutor, followed by an external teacher-marked assessment that brings this work together in the second phase.

Nevertheless, at some point a reliable summative measurement will be required in most academic programmes. In an externally assessed phase, students will prepare for an assignment or examination with pre-arranged criteria and standards and will be marked or graded for the work in the usual way. The PhD submission of a thesis and viva would be an example of this phase. The stakes are high and so reliability needs to be demonstrated as far as possible through some form of moderation – in this case an external examiner.

Is it possible for summative assessment also to be ipsative? Winstanley gave an example of ipsative criteria included in high stakes assessment alongside externally set criteria, but the weighting of the ipsative contribution was low to minimise any concerns over equity or reliability. The alternative is an ipsative only summative assessment and Gandhi in Chap. 11 presents us with a vision for replacing all competitive assessment by ipsative assessment or 'Compete with Yourself' at primary school level before the onset of public examinations.

OVERVIEW OF THE CASE STUDIES

The case studies in this book are varied and emerge from different levels of education and disciplinary perspectives. What they all have in common is that they are voluntary and practitioner-led and not directed by institutional or state educational monitoring processes. To aid the reader in appreciating the range of case studies, I have categorised each case study in Table 1.1 according to the type of ipsative assessment:

- ipsative feedback on progress (from self, peers or teachers)
- self-recording of personal learning gain information
- teacher or peer recording of personal learning gain information.

I distinguish self and teacher/peer assessment of learning gain because although many of the case studies cover both, there are several in which one or other is the main feature. The table also indicates the level and sector and level of study and the student background such as ethnicity or nationality, if known.

Table 1.1 Overview of case studies

Case study chapter	Explicit ipsative feedback	Self-recording of personal learning gain	Teacher or peer recording of personal learning gain	Sector and level	Student nationality and background
3. Using Ipsative Assessment to Enhance Self-regulation in Chinese College English Classrooms (Zhou and Zang)	Y	Y	N	Undergraduate	China
4. Supporting Student Learning with Cumulative Cover Sheets (Winstanley)	Y	Y	Y	Undergraduate	UK university with mixed selectivity and mixed ethnicity
5. Raising Self-Efficacy through Ipsative Assessment and Feuerstein's Instrumental Enrichment Programme (McIntyre)	N	Y	Y	Secondary school	New Zealand school with mixed ethnicity
6. Use of Digital Technology to Capture and Support Student Progress across a Taught Postgraduate Programme (Hughes, Hawkes and Neumann)	N	Y	Y	Postgraduate doctorate	UK and International
7. Ipsative Learning: a Personal Approach to a Student's PBL Experience within an Integrated Engineering Design Cornerstone Module (Tilley and Roach)	Y	Y	Y	Undergraduate	UK

(continued)

Table 1.1 (continued)

Case study chapter	Explicit ipsative feedback	Self – recording of personal learning gain	Teacher or peer recording of personal learning gain	Sector and level	Student nationality and background
8. Assessing Liminality: the Use of Ipsative Formative Assessment during a Postgraduate Taught Induction Programme to Support the Development of Criticality (Rattray)	Y	Y	N	Postgraduate professional learning	UK
9. Use of Learning Gain Data to compare Teacher-Centric and Student Centric Feedback (Hoo and Hughes)	N	N	Y	Undergraduate	Singapore
10. The Effect of Video Feedback on the Self-assessment of a Music Performance by Pre-university Classical Guitar Students (Boucher, Dubé and Creech)	N	Y	N	Post-compulsory education	Canada
11. Compete With Yourself (CWY): Maximizing Learning Gain in Schools (Gandhi)	N	Y	Y	Primary school	Iceland, India and UK

Y, Yes; N, No.

CHAPTER SUMMARY

This chapter has explored the rationale for the collection and defined the key terms. It has introduced an innovative collection that explores a range of practitioner applications of ipsative feedback and/or measurement of personal learning gain. All levels of education are represented in the case studies from many different countries and the case studies are far from identical in style and methods. To help make sense of this variety, the chapter has introduced four themes that build on theory from the editor's previous work: the benefits of ipsative feedback; the advantages of measuring learning gain; the challenges of both these approaches and the integration of these innovations in assessment into mainstream practice. These themes and an overview of each case study should enable readers to select the most relevant case studies to pursue. Some requirements for ipsative assessment are already emerging and to be successful the assessment must be:

- recorded and visible to learners
- consistent in the comparisons made with earlier work
- successfully combined with conventional assessment.

The themes and these conclusions will be revisited in the final chapter. But, before the case studies the next chapter teases out the relationship between the concepts of ipsative assessment and personal learning gain in more depth and in a broader educational context.

REFERENCES

Arum, R., & Roksa, J. (2011). *Academically adrift: Limited learning on college campuses.* Chicago & London: University of Chicago Press.

Bloom, B. S., Engelhart, M. D., Furst, E. J., Hill, W. H., & Krathwohl, D. R. (1956). *Taxonomy of educational objectives: The classification of educational goals. Handbook I: Cognitive domain.* New York: David McKay Company.

Bloxham, S., Boyd, P., & Orr, S. (2011). Mark my words: The role of assessment criteria in UK higher education grading practices. *Studies in Higher Education, 36*(6), 655–670.

Broadfoot, P. (1996). *Education, assessment and society.* Buckingham: Open University Press.

Dweck, C. (1999). *Self-theories: Their role in motivation, personality, and development.* Philadelphia: Taylor & Francis.

Ecclestone, K. (2007). Commitment, compliance and comfort zones: The effects of formative assessment on vocational education students' learning careers. *Assessment in Education: Principles, Policy & Practice, 14*(3), 313–333.

Freire, P. (1973). *Pedagogy of the oppressed*. 2nd edition. London: Penguin.

Gibbs, G., & Simpson, C. (2004). Conditions under which assessment supports students' learning. *Learning and Teaching in Higher Education, 1*(1), 3–31.

Hattie, J., & Timperley, H. (2007). The power of feedback. *Review of Educational Research, 77*(1), 81–112.

Higher Education Funding Council for England. (2015). *Invitation to submit expressions of interest in piloting and evaluating measures of learning gain*. http://www. hefce.ac.uk/pubs/year/2015/CL,042015/. Accessed July 2015.

Hughes, G. (2011). Aiming for personal best: A case for introducing ipsative assessment in higher education. *Studies in Higher Education, 36*(3), 353–367.

Hughes, G. (2014). *Ipsative assessment: Motivation through marking progress*. Basingstoke: Palgrave Macmillan.

Hughes, G., Smith, H., & Creese, B. (2015). Not seeing the wood for the trees: Developing a feedback analysis tool to explore feed forward in modularised programmes. *Assessment & Evaluation in Higher Education, 40*(8), 1079–1094.

Hughes, G., Wood, E., & Kitagawa, K. (2014). Use of self-referential (ipsative) feedback to motivate and guide distance learners. *Open Learning: The Journal of Open, Distance and e-Learning, 29*(1), 31–44.

Laurillard, D. (2012). *Teaching as a design science: Building pedagogical patterns for learning*. London: Routledge.

Luckin, R. (2010). *Redesigning learning contexts: Technology-rich, learner-centred ecologies*. London: Routledge.

Molloy, E., & Boud, D. (2013). Changing conceptions of feedback. In D. Boud & E. Molloy (Eds.), *Feedback in higher and professional education: Understanding it and doing it well* (pp. 11–23). London: Routledge.

Nicol, D. (2010). From monologue to dialogue: Improving written feedback processes in mass higher education. *Assessment and Evaluation in Higher Education, 3*(5), 501–517).

Nicol, D. (2013). Resituating feedback from the reactive to the proactive. In D. Boud & E. Molloy (Eds.), *Feedback in higher and professional education: Understanding it and doing it well* (pp. 24–49). London: Routledge.

Nicol, D., & Macfarlane-Dick, D. (2006). Formative assessment and self-regulated learning: A model and seven principles of good feedback practice. *Studies in Higher Education, 31*(2), 199–218.

O'Donovan, B., Price, M., & Rust, C. (2004). Know what I mean? Enhancing student understanding of assessment standards and criteria. *Teaching in Higher Education, 9*, 325–335.

Orsmond, P., & Merry, S. (2011). Feedback alignment: Effective and ineffective links between tutors' and students' understanding of coursework feedback. *Assessment & Evaluation in Higher Education, 36*(2), 125–126.

Sadler, D. R. (1989). Formative assessment and the design of instructional systems. *Instructional Science, 18*, 119–144.

Sammons, P. (2012). Methodological issues and new trends in educational effectiveness research. In C. Chapman, P. Armstrong, A. Harris, D. Muijs, D. Reynolds, & P. Sammon (Eds.), *School effectiveness and improvement research, policy and practice: Challenging the orthodoxy* (pp. 9–26). London: Routledge.

Stobart, G. (2008). *Testing times: The uses and abuses of assessment.* Abingdon: Routledge.

Gwyneth Hughes is Reader in Higher Education at UCL, Institute of Education, London, UK. She leads and teachers on Masters programmes in higher education and supervises doctoral students. She is on the editorial board for the journal London Review of Education. She has researched and published widely on learning and teaching in higher education and she specialises in both assessment and e-learning. She is co-author of *Learning Transitions in Higher Education* (Palgrave Macmillan, 2014). Her latest book *Ipsative Assessment: Motivation through marking progress* was published by Palgrave Macmillan also in 2014. She is a Senior Fellow of the Higher Education Academy.

CHAPTER 2

Exploring the Relationship Between Ipsative Assessment and Institutional Learning Gain

Gwyneth Hughes

Overview

This chapter explores in more detail how the concepts of ipsative assessment and personal learning gain are related to macro-level learning gain measurement, yet are largely absent from current educational discourse. While learning gain has currency as part of institutional monitoring, evaluation and ranking, the action of an individual learner in capitalising on information about their learning gain – for example through an ipsative assessment – is neither encouraged nor visible in competitive and selective assessment systems and schemes. As we have seen in the opening chapter, a fully ipsative approach, which rewards progress or learning gain as much as achievement for all levels and backgrounds of learners, would require considerable assessment reform. However, that is not to say that there are not countless small steps towards this vision being undertaken in educational institutions across

G. Hughes (✉)
UCL Institute of Education, UCL, London, UK
e-mail: Gwyneth.hughes@ucl.ac.uk

© The Author(s) 2017
G. Hughes (ed.), *Ipsative Assessment and Personal Learning Gain*,
DOI 10.1057/978-1-137-56502-0_2

the globe. This chapter provides a conceptual and wider contextual basis for the book to support the professional evidence base for encouraging ipsative assessment in schools, colleges and universities.

The first section examines why learning gain measurements for schools and universities are collated and how these provide a more just and equitable indication of teaching effectiveness than exit performance data alone. The limitations of learning gain measurement at scale will then be explored to include the difficulty of standardising tests and questions about data reliability alongside consideration of the desirability and value of national and global institutional performance rankings that can perpetuate elitism. Other related concepts that will be briefly covered include the discourse and practice of continuous improvement and use of learning gain data for research in learning and teaching.

The second section of the chapter considers how not only similar but also different concerns confront the assessor of individual students. Using ipsative marking or measurements has an equalitarian purpose to motivate all learners, but that means it is problematic for credential-based systems of selection because it gives those with more to gain rather than top performers an advantage. Employers might also need convincing to accept ipsative credentials. The challenges of comparing two or more assessments will persist for learning gain at the individual level. Nevertheless, ipsative assessment might encourage high achievers to raise their game further so that the resistance from an educational elite can be tempered.

The range of purposes for gathering learning gain data will then be mapped out for the different learning gain audiences along a micro-level to macro-level continuum. The chapter ends with an explanation of why, despite increasing recognition of learning gain as a concept, ipsative assessment is underused and largely invisible.

Exploring the Discourses and Practices of Large-Scale Learning Gain Measurement

Exit performances of students are measured, averaged and widely used for comparing teaching effectiveness in schools and colleges. The data can also be used to produce rankings or comparative league tables of institutions and made publically available. In the UK, performance assessment arising from government-led inspections and end of course examinations is freely available online and influences school popularity and status. Meanwhile, international rankings of universities are gathered and published by a range of bodies such as QS World University Rankings and the Times Higher Education World University Rankings, which are also made public.

However, institutions which are selective or which have a greater proportional of academically and socially advantaged students will predictably outperform those which are less advantaged. Use of learning gain or value-added data may enable a more equitable comparison.

Advantage of Using Learning Gain Rather Than Exit Performances for Institutional Evaluation and Ranking

A teacher with engaged and capable, independently working students is likely to obtain good outcomes unless the teaching is extremely inappropriate. Meanwhile, dedicated teachers are unlikely to get all-round excellent results with more challenging students who struggle to spend time and effort on learning for whatever social and psychological reasons. Learning is complex business that cannot readily be captured by outcomes alone given that there are so many influences from students' broader social learning contexts: family, previous education, leisure pursuits etc. (Bloomer and Hodkinson 2000). Exit performances do not necessarily give a good picture of teaching effectiveness.

Whether competition is global or local, institutional rankings tend to favour the elite. For example, the prominence of knowledge production and research in higher education rankings means that research-intensive institutions invariably sit at the top of the tables, although the growing range of ranking categories, such as breaking down data into disciplines, means that many institutions can strategically highlight areas in which they do well (Marginson 2009). The value of these rankings has been widely critiqued, yet rankings continue to be supported by those institutions which top the charts and less prestigious institutions aspire to improve their national and global ranking and reputation. University rankings are often given high national priorities (Hazelkorn 2015).

However, lower performing institutions can demonstrate effectiveness through the value that they add for students. Recording learning gain has an advantage over using one-off exit performances for evaluation of teaching and learning because measuring a growth in performance can make allowances for teachers in schools which have high numbers of students who start from a lower base (Liu 2011; Steedle 2012). The baseline can be factored in so that a school or college with a low achieving intake could demonstrate a higher than expected improvement – indicative of successful teaching – without necessarily producing high outcomes. Such 'value-added' is a type of learning gain measurement made when predicted outcomes based on the first measurement are compared with actual outcomes. Improvements added by different teaching methods or schools are then comparable – although only schools at the extremes of high and low performance tend to show meaningful effects (Goldstein et al. 2000).

Although learning gain and value-added have been mainly applied to schools, the idea of measuring learning gain or learning growth as part of quality monitoring is taking root in higher education. There has been growing interest by governments, educational leaders and educators in improving student engagement with learning at their institutions and in methods of benchmarking effective institutional teaching practice (Coates and McCormick 2014). At present, indirect and questionable proxies are used as measures of teaching quality such as staff – student ratios, contact hours, completion rates or student evaluations of teaching, while learning gain might provide a more direct and meaningful measure of teaching quality (Higher Education Funding Council for England [HEFCE] 2015). Nevertheless, the UK and many other countries do not yet use measurement of learning gain to compare different departments or institutions as part of an accountability system. Perhaps research-led elite institutions oppose more robust measurements of teaching quality which might shift rankings in favour of 'teaching' institutions. Such resistance could be exacerbated by a lack of standardisation of qualifications. In the UK, for example, there are many ways of making decisions about boundaries between first-, second- or third-class achievements, and so degree performances are difficult to compare across the higher education sector, whereas at the secondary level, where there are national examination systems, comparisons can be more robust.

Measuring Learning Gain in Higher Education – A Need for Standardised Tests

Two systems from the United States that could be used to overcome the lack of standardisation in higher education are the grade point average (GPA) system and the Collegiate Learning Assessment (CLA).

A grade point average (GPA) system might provide more reliable comparison of learning gain between institutions. GPA is exactly what it sounds like – an average of all grades a student obtained on a programme of study. GPA is the method of classification of degrees in the United States and is widely recognised internationally and is being explored as an eventual replacement for the degree classification system in the UK (Higher Education Academy 2015). However, a GPA is not equivalent for different disciplines where different skills are being assessed and so would not be a valid measure for comparing institutions with a range of disciplines – this would require a generic standardised test.

There are standardised tests for undergraduates available which students can sit on entry and on exit of their course so that their learning gain can be measured. These tests are not discipline specific and instead measure a more general range of graduate attributes. Although exactly which skills a graduate should have can be readily disputed, there is broad agreement that all higher education aims to develop critical thinking as well as communication skills (speaking, reading and writing). The CLA was developed in the United States and differs from other general ability tests like the Scholastic Aptitude Test (SAT) as it measures broad discipline-independent competencies such as critical thinking and problem solving in real-world contexts.

What Learning Gain Data Can Potentially Reveal about Student Learning

Use of learning gain data for quality assurance can backfire if there is the possibility of revealing large-scale inadequacies in an educational system. For example, Arum and Roksa (2011) analysed large amounts of data from the CLA and, after making allowance for prior experience, used the data to claim that the majority of US students do not show significant learning gains in key graduate skills in the first two years of college, and are unlikely to gain much in the following two years. Students are, they say, 'academically adrift':

> Many students come to college not only poorly prepared by prior schooling for highly demanding academic tasks that ideally lie in front of them, but – more troubling still they enter college with attitudes, values, norms and behaviours that are at odds with academic commitment. (p. 3)

After taking account of school and social backgrounds, Arum and Roksa (2011) used learning gain CLA data to suggest that time spent on study, for example, reading for more than 40 hours per week, predicts a high learning gain especially while working alone. They argue that many students are distracted by the social and networking aspects of college life, which may well have benefits and instil confidence, but which also take away time from study. Even group work, which has become a popular way of engaging learners in study, may give students social opportunities rather than provide academically demanding work. Nevertheless, the significance of these results may be overplayed. Being side-tracked from study is nothing new; meeting friends and partners has long been an important aspect of university life for full-time students; and balancing family and work commitments has long posed challenges for part-time and professional learners.

Arum and Roska concede that there are wide variations in learning gain even within institutions, demonstrating that the factors which enhance learning are highly complex. They argue that because a minority of students do develop the expected higher order skills this indicates that the CLA provides some useful comparative measurement. But 'before and after' standard tests have limitations: because of the many variables and possible unknown factors, all learning gain and value-added measurements are subject to unreliability.

Reliability and Validity of Learning Gain Measurements

Learning gain measurement for high stakes purposes such as evaluating and comparing institutional performance needs sophisticated statistical methods and models because there are many variables that might influence the results. For example, the growth rate of those starting from a low base is not necessarily equivalent to the growth rate of those starting from higher up: it could be that starting low means that there is more to gain. Alternatively, those who are already advantaged from the start may progress more than those who are disadvantaged. Previous teaching and learning experience may influence measured learning growth as might class size, the selectivity of the institution or the resources available to learners. Although statistical methods can compensate to some extent for these variables using covariate and multivariate statistical models (Anderman et al. 2015; Liu 2011), the uncertainty over reliability suggests that learning gain measurement should be used with caution as different statistical methods of measuring learning gain can produce very different results. To improve reliability, it is generally better to have many cycles of gain rather than one wave. Combining statistical models with other qualitative methods such as self-assessment against planned learning outcomes, standardised tests, skill audits, personal development portfolios, student evaluations and graduation or persistence rates also helps (Anderman et al. 2015; McGrath et al. 2015; Steedle 2012).

Others question the validity of CLA measurements and other generic systems and argue that the range of skills that are being tested is limited and not necessarily helpful. Critics have argued that the CLA test is not related enough to the specific knowledge taught in degree courses, is too generic and in any case measures prior learning rather than learning gains at university (Lodge and Bonsanquet 2014). The generic higher order skills may be discipline dependent and so the CLA is not necessarily a good proxy for overall learning. For example, those taking a philosophy course might develop critical thinking more readily than applied sciences students irrespective of teaching quality. As Hazelkorn (2015) has identified, there is a trade-off between measuring what is easy and measuring what is meaningful.

It could be that learning gain is more valuable as an aspirational rather than a reliable measure of teaching quality. Such an aim to enhance or improve performance is also captured in discourses of continuous improvement and quality enhancement in which institutions self-monitor their performance. There are some useful points to be made next by locating learning gain within the concept of continuous improvement as well as some more caveats.

Learning Gain as Continuous Improvement – Raising the Bar Too Quickly?

Learning gain measurement is part of a wider discourse of continuous improvement. Continuous improvement started in the 1930s and uses data on outputs, originally mainly statistical, to identify how a system is functioning and how the performance of the system can be improved (Dew and Nearing 2004). Continuous improvement can apply to a range of organisations from manufacturing to health and education. For example in education, performances of departments from student evaluations can be recorded over time with the aim of demonstrating year on year improvement in performance. Such continuous quality improvement or quality enhancement can take place at the micro-level as small changes, or these changes can have a multiplication effect so that large-scale institutional shifts occur.

One example of continuous improvement from a micro-level practitioner perspective is action research. It consists of a cycle of planning for change, taking action, observation and reflection leading to another cycle of improvement (McNiff and Whitehead 2006). Historically it has been practitioners who led action research with a dual aim to improve practice and contribute to knowledge (Norton 2008). Educational action research is also manifest in terms and approaches such as 'teacher-as-researcher' and 'reflective practitioner' (Schön 1991).

However, we might argue that maintaining the status quo is enough of an ambition for an educational organisation and that continuous improvement whether through quality outcomes measures or action research may be unachievable especially if external conditions are unfavourable. For example, my institution has recently undergone a merger with a larger university and a reversal or halt in continuous improvement trends is expected during a period of instability. Inflexible continuous improvement for teachers or even individual students could be equally problematic and for me produces a certain amount of unease.

Learning and improvement for an individual seem on the surface to be tautologous. If there is no improvement how has learning taken place? Nevertheless, applying the concept of continuous improvement to an individual may not always be desirable or possible. Always aiming for a new personal best in a particular skill or learning outcome may be unrealistic and learning may sometimes be better viewed as keeping up a level of achievement as circumstances shift or even deteriorate. For example, an elderly person may experience reduced physical or mental capacity and maintaining independence may require considerable effort and learning. A student may encounter a limit to time and resources available for learning as a consequence of illness or increased demands from the workplace or family. For such a student, temporarily preserving the status quo may be a challenging enough goal (Hughes 2014). But, it is implied in commonly used terms such as 'continuing professional development' and 'teaching excellence' that teachers should strive to develop their teaching throughout their careers in response to external changes. For example, emergence of new technologies alongside a continual pressure for greater efficiency has fuelled the mantra 'do more with less'. Continuous improvement as an aspiration may motivate both staff and students, but at times simply standing still may be enough, and institutional leaders need to apply brakes to unrealistic upward trajectories of achievement.

Yet at the same time students or teachers who are underperforming for whatever reason do need to be identified and supported. Thus, there is a distinction between recording an absence of continuous improvement that is to be expected because of shifts in external circumstances, and recording lack of improvement which is not expected and warrants intervention or further action. Viewing learning gain as an aspiration for individual or collective continuous improvement illustrates further that the interpretation of learning gain measurements is highly context dependent and this point is well illustrated next by the use of learning gain data in pedagogic research.

Educational Research and Learning Gain

A final and rather different use of learning gain data is for educational research. Some educational practitioners and researchers use learning gain measurements to compare the effectiveness of teaching methods. For example, learning gain measurements in medical education in Australia were used to compare a small group who completed a task together as a unit and a group where the task was divided into sub-tasks with peer teaching of each sub-task to the remainder of the group. Results indicated that the latter produced a greater and more lasting learning gain (Kooloos et al. 2011).

Another study in Hong Kong used self-reported learning gain measurements to demonstrate that higher education students showed learning gain not only in subject knowledge, cognitive and intellectual skills, but also in personal, social and cultural matters (Tam 2004). Results indicated that those who engaged most with peers and teachers demonstrated most learning gain, which is not surprising for developing social and personal skills. But, these findings do not complement those of Arum and Roksa (2011) mentioned earlier who argued that social contact alone is not sufficient for development of high-level intellectual skills and that independent study and time spent on task are the key factors. However, given that the contexts of these studies are different we might expect different findings. There is also a question here about the reliability of self-reporting.

Because pedagogic studies like this are often localised, small-scale and highly context dependent, they may have a limited effect on enhancing teaching and learning more generally. Furthermore, many busy teachers may not have time to gather and scrutinise their own learning gain data and adjust their teaching accordingly. Learners have even less access than their teachers to quality personal learning gain data as part of assessment processes as we shall see next.

IPSATIVE ASSESSMENT AS PERSONAL LEARNING GAIN

So far the discussion has been mainly of learning gain measurements in the hands of governments, accountability bodies and managers who monitor school and university and teacher performances to identify underachievement so that it can be rectified, or to showcase and benchmark excellence. While learning gain data may have some advantages over learning outcome measurements in helping governments monitor education to assure that it delivers value for money and is fit for purpose, there is no guarantee that any data gathering exercise will improve teacher performance and/or school effectiveness. Critics have questioned how far quality control over education is desirable and empowering for teachers who are caught up in the machinery of accountability and performativity which at times may seem divorced from educational goals and the professionalism of teachers (Ball 2013). But could learning gain be of more use at the individual level?

Learning Gain Monitoring for Teachers and Students: From Large-Scale Data Sets to Personal Learning Gain

Measurement of learning gain for comparative and quality monitoring purposes synthesises and averages out data from often very large numbers of learners. Such methodologies using data analysed by statistical modelling are not accessible to learners and may not provide sufficient granularity to help individual teachers or students. That the large-scale methods of measuring learning gain do not usually provide personal data for learners that can motivate and help them plan their learning is I suggest a missed opportunity.

But, learning gain information does not have to be linked to the management of education if teachers and students themselves can identify what I term 'personal learning gain' through comparing individual marks or achievement of learning outcomes over time as part of an assessment process. There are other forms of qualitative personal learning gain information such as ipsative feedback on progress for self-improvement that individuals could also use. However, this kind of grass roots personal learning gain or ipsative activity is not usually recorded in educational reports or institutional data. We shall explore later why personal learning gain is hidden. First, we need some discussion about the acceptability of ipsative summative assessment using personal learning gain information.

Ipsative Marking – Is It Feasible?

Ipsative summative assessment occurs when a high stakes measurement of personal learning gain is recorded. It is more controversial than measuring learning outcomes and is at present unlikely to be used at any level of education where the main purpose is to measure attainment for a qualification. This is because professional and government agencies who manage qualifications require standards and criteria that are absolute; in this way assessment can be selective and competitive (Broadfoot 1996). If the learner's journey or progress were to be the basis of a qualification there would likely be concern that those who progress from a lower base have the advantage over high fliers because they have 'more to prove' and this could upset selection based on the ideal of meritocracy. Professions such as medicine also have non-negotiable requirements, for example, that patient safety standards are met. In addition the problems of standardisation of learning gain measurements identified earlier will apply to any assessments made at two or more points in time.

Employers are also unlikely to be convinced that ipsative assessment will help them identify suitable candidates for jobs and they tend to seek out those who have already attained qualifications rather than those with learning potential. I have argued that this attitude perpetuates inequality because the disadvantaged can rarely catch up even if they make huge strides in the right direction. Giving at least some recognition for distance travelled could go some way towards equitable forms of assessment and might provide useful information for educators and employers alike. For example, professional knowledge needs to be regularly updated and what matters is an employee's ability and willingness to do this alongside realistic goal setting.

In the opening chapter I hinted that it might be possible to satisfy both the personal learning and measurement goals of assessment. I have previously suggested that a dual system that combines an ipsative regime with a standards and outcomes-based regime might be feasible (Hughes 2014). This already happens when students undertake supervision such as for a doctorate. Here there is a developmental phase where progress is monitored and recorded that is separate from a final submission phase – the viva voce – where a conventional summative grade or thesis pass is given.

From the above discussion we can see that there is a real possibility of including assessment of an individual's progress as part of an assessment regime. Learning gain information at the personal level – both qualitative and quantitative – could be made available to learners to form the basis of ipsative assessment and feedback. But such a view of learning gain has different methods and audiences from learning gain conducted at scale and a summary will be presented next.

Mapping the Relationship Between Ipsative Assessment and Learning Gain Measurement

Table 2.1 summarises the different purposes of ipsative assessments and learning gain measurements with examples, the different methodologies and the different audiences.

EXPLAINING THE INVISIBILITY OF IPSATIVE ASSESSMENT AND PERSONAL LEARNING GAIN

Table 2.1 might imply that all things are equal along the micro-level to macro-level learning gain continuum, but that is far from the current reality. There are a number of reasons why ipsative assessment is underused and personal learning gain measurements are largely invisible to learners and

Table 2.1 The purposes of measuring or capturing learning gain

Personal learning gain		↔	*Learning gain at scale*
Ipsative feedback about progress to enhance learning	Ipsative assessment as a measure of personal learning gain	Learning gain measurement used in practitioner research or for continuous improvement	Measurement of learning gain for comparison or benchmarking between classes, cohorts, programmes or institutions
E.g. teacher, peer or self-assessment of progress	E.g. individual progress scores	E.g. comparing the effectiveness of different methods of group work	E.g. measures of school or university effectiveness
Qualitative	Qualitative or quantitative	Quantitative sometimes combined with qualitative data	Quantitative but could be combined with qualitative data
Student audience	Student and teacher audiences	Researchers and teachers as main audiences	Audience is educational managers, policy makers and accountability monitors

teachers alike with only a few exceptions. First, ipsative assessment based on learning gain is not usually part of the formal assessment of students, although there are some possible options. Second, although formative assessment is widely practised, it tends to be carried out on a short-term basis and a longer term ipsative approach is not easy to establish. Third, ipsative assessment may be undertaken verbally in informal tutorial and classroom settings and is therefore unrecorded. Invisibility means missed opportunities for assessors and learners alike and it is worth exploring each of these points in a little more detail.

Formal assessments and examinations usually measure achievement of pre-defined criteria with standards judged using a marking scheme or rubric. The assessment stands alone and is considered independently of previous work and credit is not given for progress. Any deterioration in standards is likewise not visible. As maximising the objectivity of marking is the aim, information on the learner's past history may be viewed as creating preconceptions of learners and consequently a bias to the assess-ment process. But in an attempt to minimise marking bias, the opportu-nities are lost for using progress to motivate and assist planning, or for using lack of progress as a warning.

One well-established exception to this is the recording progress in port-folio assessments. In a portfolio, a learner collects evidence of their practice and provides a narrative to demonstrate learning that has taken place. Sometimes a learner may be asked to showcase their 'best' work such as in creative disciplines while at other times a learner may be asked to capture a developmental journey, for example, in teaching or other professional prac-tice. There may be ipsative processes going on in portfolio construction, but that does not necessarily mean that the overall assessment recognises process and the final mark may only be for the quality of the content. In such cases, ipsative assessment may be sidelined in comparison to criteria and standards-based assessment and largely invisible unless there are clear assessment criteria that refer to development work and a learner's progress.

Second, we have already encountered the idea in the opening chapter that developmental or formative assessment is potentially ipsative because it helps learners establish goals and next steps based on current levels of work. However, such goals are often short-term – addressing the next piece of work – and thus do not address longer term goals or review the distance travelled as part of a learning trajectory. Short-term goal setting processes for monitoring achievement may stunt growth. For example, learners may respond to feedback with an action plan for improvements or

correct their errors, but be unaware of whether or not they have implemented recommendations. Given that students have choice over when and
how to respond to feedback, it is difficult to isolate and measure student
responses to feedback (Price et al. 2010). Learners may repeat the same
errors or ignore the more challenging aspects of intended feedback, especially if this is peer feedback (Walker 2015). But over time, judgements of
progress in response to feedback, whether from self or others, could be
very helpful in revealing when feedback has had negligible impact and for
beginning to ask why.

Students need time and support to become self-regulating and learn how to
manage feedback (Nicol and Macfarlane–Dick 2006). But while a longitudinal
or programme level approach to assessment could enable students to identify
repeated unhelpful behaviour, this is not easy with modularised curricula that
are not very coherent (Hughes et al. 2015). Without a visible and systematic
approach, formative assessment which is potentially developmental in the
longer term may go unnoticed by students and teachers. Formative assessment
might, therefore, benefit from defining and establishing ipsative approaches to
tracking the longitudinal development – or personal learning gain – of learners
and we shall see some good examples later in the book.

A third reason for the invisibility of ipsative assessment is its association
with verbal feedback, perhaps used as a motivational device. Progress may
be discussed informally in the classroom or in a tutorial, but when such
feedback is spoken there is usually no permanent record and agreed learning
goals may be easily forgotten. Even when discussion of progress is captured
for a formal progress review, the outcome is likely to be very general – for
example, in the ipsative phase of doctoral supervision a tutorial or review
might record overall progress on a thesis as either satisfactory or unsatisfac-
tory. A more nuanced perspective in which personal learning gain can be
compared for a range of skills and attributes is then missed. This begs the
question of how the clarity and precision with which standards are articulated in supposed 'good assessment practice' can be replicated for measurement of personal learning gain. But for reliability to even be an issue,
ipsative assessment must first be given more status and recognition.

CONCLUSION AND SUMMARY

Learning gain defined is simply the difference between two (or possibly
more) measurements of achievement, and is usually collated for large
numbers of students; ipsative assessment occurs when a student's present

and past (and possibly future) performances are compared over time as a personal learning gain. The chapter has briefly reviewed the burgeoning use of learning gain data at the macro-level to monitor and compare institutional and teacher performance and introduced some of the debates that are relevant to the collection. Commentators on the use of large-scale data sets for comparing institutional performances tend to view such data gathering as valuable if only the data analysis quality could be improved. Yet performance monitoring, however thorough, is not necessarily a desirable or helpful activity for teachers and learners.

This book is not directly concerned with the wider politics of educational evaluation and government control; it explores instead examples of teachers and students using ipsative assessment and personal learning gain information voluntarily as part of their practice with educational and emancipatory aims. But, despite the growing worldwide practice of measuring learning gain or value-added for quality monitoring at scale, ipsative qualitative judgement and measurement of personal learning gain are not routinely used as part of the assessment strategy for individual students to guide and assist their learning. If such practices exist then they lack visibility. Giving weight to personal learning gain is very likely to be controversial because it may mean unsettling the status of top performers – a theme that will reoccur in this book.

To begin to rectify this situation, the collection offers case studies of practice which explore the benefits and challenges of different methods of ipsative assessment and individual learning gain measurement in a variety of educational contexts.

References

Anderman, E. M., Gimbert, B., O'Connell, A. A., & Riegel, L. (2015). Approaches to academic growth assessment. *British Journal of Educational Psychology, 85*, 138–153.

Arum, R., & Roksa, J. (2011). *Academically adrift: Limited learning on college campuses.* Chicago & London: University of Chicago Press.

Ball, S. J. (2013). *The education debate.* 2nd edition. Bristol: Policy Press.

Bloomer, M., & Hodkinson, P. (2000). Learning careers: Continuity and change in young people's dispositions to learning. *British Educational Research Journal, 26*(5), 583–597.

Broadfoot, P. (1996). *Education, assessment and society.* Buckingham: Open University Press.

Coates, H., & McCormick, A. C. (2014). Introduction: student engagement-A window into undergraduate education. In H. Coates & A. C. McCormick (Eds.), *Engaging university students: International insights from system-wide studies* (pp. 1–12). Dordrecht: Springer.

Dew, J. R. & Nearing, M.M. (2004). *Continuous quality improvement in higher education*. Westport: American Council on Education/Praeger.

Goldstein, H., Huiqi, P., Rath, T., & Hill, N. (2000). *The use of value added information in judging school performance*. London: Institute of Education, University of London. http://www.bristol.ac.uk/cmm/team/hg/value-added-school-performance.html. Accessed July 2015.

Hazelkorn, E. (2015). *Rankings and the reshaping of higher education: The battle for world-class excellence*. 2nd edition. Basingstoke: Palgrave Macmillan

Higher Education Academy. (2015). *Grade point average: Report of the GPA pilot project 2013–14*. New York: Higher Education Academy.

Higher Education Funding Council for England [HEFCE] (2015). Invitation to submit expressions of interest in piloting and evaluating measures of learning gain, http://www.hefce.ac.uk/pubs/year/2015/CL,042015/. Accessed July 2015.

Hughes, G. (2014). *Ipsative assessment: Motivation through marking progress*. Basingstoke: Palgrave Macmillan.

Hughes, G., Smith, H., & Creese, B. (2015). Not seeing the wood for the trees: Developing a feedback analysis tool to explore feed forward in modularised programmes. *Assessment & Evaluation in Higher Education, 40*(8), 1079–1094.

Kooloos, J., Klaassen, T., Vereijken, M., Van Kuppeveld, S., Bolhuis, S., & Vorstenbosch, M. (2011). Collaborative group work: Effects of group size and assignment structure on learning gain, student satisfaction and perceived participation. *Medical Teacher, 33*(12), 983–988.

Liu, L. (2011). Value-added assessment in higher education. A comparison of two methods. *Higher Education, 61*(4), 445–461.

Lodge, J. M., & Bonsanquet, A. (2014). Evaluating quality learning in higher education: Re-examining the evidence. *Quality in Higher Education, 20*(1), 3–23.

Marginson, S. (2009). The knowledge economy and higher education: Rankings and classifications, Research metrics and learning outcomes measures as a system for regulating the value of knowledge. *Higher Education Management and Policy, 21*(1), 31–46.

McGrath, C. M., Guerin, B., Harte, E., Frearson, M., & Manville, C. (2015). *Learning gain in higher education*. Cambridge: Rand Corporation. http://www.rand.org/content/dam/rand/pubs/research_reports/RR900/RR996/RAND_RR996.pdf. Accessed July 2015.

McNiff, J., & Whitehead, J. (2006). *All you need to know about action research*. London: Sage.

Nicol, D., & Macfarlane-Dick, D. (2006). Formative assessment and self-regulated learning: A model and seven principles of good feedback practice. *Studies in Higher Education, 31*(2), 199–218.

Norton, L. S. (2008). *Action research in teaching and learning: A practical guide to conducting pedagogical research in universities.* London: Routledge.

Price, M., Handley, K., Millar, J., & O'Donovan, B. (2010). Feedback: All that effort, but what is the effect?. *Assessment & Evaluation in Higher Education, 35*(3), 277–289.

Schön, D. (1991). *The reflective practitioner: how professionals think in action.* 2nd edition. Aldershot: Arena Ashgate.

Steedle, J. T. (2012). Selecting value-added models for postsecondary institutional assessment. *Assessment & Evaluation in Higher Education, 37*(6), 637–652.

Tam, M. (2004). Using students' self-reported gains as a measure of value-added. *Quality in Higher Education, 10*(3), 253–260.

Walker, M. (2015). The quality of written peer feedback on undergraduates' draft answers to an assignment, and the use made of the feedback. *Assessment & Evaluation in Higher Education, 40*(2), 232–247.

Gwyneth Hughes is Reader in Higher Education at UCL, Institute of Education, London, UK. She leads and teachers on Masters programmes in higher education and supervises doctoral students. She is on the editorial board for the journal London Review of Education. She has researched and published widely on learning and teaching in higher education and she specialises in both assessment and e-learning. She is co-author of *Learning Transitions in Higher Education* (Palgrave Macmillan, 2014). Her latest book *Ipsative Assessment: Motivation through marking progress* was published by Palgrave Macmillan also in 2014. She is a Senior Fellow of the Higher Education Academy.

CHAPTER 3

Using Ipsative Assessment to Enhance First-Year Undergraduate Self-Regulation in Chinese College English Classrooms

Jiming Zhou and Jie Zhang

INTRODUCTION

Educational assessment is on the innovative agenda in many countries. In China, the move towards formative assessment has been launched to enhance English language education in universities. In the assessment change discussed in this chapter, classroom assessment evaluating higher level learning skills was embedded in an English curriculum innovation at several universities in Shanghai, China. Tutors were recommended to implement peer assessment and give more learning-facilitating feedback.

Assessment is arguably the most resistant aspect in educational change (Gibbs 2006); changing assessment practices in the dominant testing

J. Zhou (✉)
Fudan University, Shanghai, China
e-mail: jmzhou@fudan.edu.cn

J. Zhang
School of Foreign Studies, Shanghai University of Finance and Economics, Shanghai, China
e-mail: zhang.jie@mail.shufe.edu.cn

© The Author(s) 2017
G. Hughes (ed.), *Ipsative Assessment and Personal Learning Gain*,
DOI 10.1057/978-1-137-56502-0_3

43

culture is particularly difficult (Medland 2012). Among many factors influencing the effectiveness of assessment innovation, student self-regulation is a crucial aspect. Assessment is likely to facilitate learning when students understand the learning goal, compare their current work against this goal and take action to improve (Sadler 1989). While learning goals are usually set by change initiators or teachers, it is students themselves who take the initiative in terms of whether they aspire to the learning goals and how to work towards them (Brookhart 2012). Competition and misalignment between different stakeholders' perceptions can lead to ineffectiveness of an educational change (Timperley and Parr 2005).

Hughes (2014) proposes an ipsative approach to assessment and feedback which compares students' current performance with their previous performance. The idea that students learn at their own pace and do not need to be compared with external criteria is theoretically appealing. The feasibility of ipsative assessment, however, warrants further examination. Previous studies indicate a collectivist feature in Chinese students' learning goals: they work hard not only to achieve their own goals but also to meet the external goals set by the group to which they belong (Salili 1996). Littlewood (1999) makes a distinction between two levels of self-regulation: proactive autonomy, whereby learners establish a personal learning agenda, and reactive autonomy, whereby students take action to attain external-set goals. Chinese learners are perceived to demonstrate a tendency towards reactive autonomy.

On the other hand, epistemological beliefs aligned with ipsative assessment can be found in some studies in Chinese contexts. One of the Chinese national award-winning English tutors in Zhou and Deneen's (2015) study said that he helped students work out their own progress plans. This tutor believed 'student self-assessment should be combined with this progress plan, rather than being used in isolation in some fragmented language ability exercises' (p. 8). In the curriculum innovation examined in this chapter, the faculty leader believed that 'the degree of student progress should also be counted in their final grades'. These perceptions resonate with the principles of ipsative assessment, although the interviewees were not aware of this term. There were some tensions between tutors' aspiration to evaluate students based on their progress and students' collectivist-oriented learning goals and reactive self-regulation. The aims of this chapter are, therefore, to look for evidence of ipsative assessment in English language classrooms, to explore in what way ipsative assessment relates to student self-regulation and to critically discuss the benefits and challenges of its implementation in contexts where exam-oriented education dominates.

LITERATURE REVIEW

Ipsative Assessment

Ipsative assessment shares some similarities with concepts like formative assessment (Wiliam 2010), assessment for learning (Assessment Reform Group 2002) and learning-oriented assessment (Carless 2007), that is, the purpose of assessment is to enhance student progress, and students are encouraged to self-assess their progress or lack of progress. Ipsative assessment, however, differs from these forms of assessment in that students' current performance is compared with a previous performance, rather than with the required or desired standards (Hughes 2011). In other words, self-referenced criteria differentiate ipsative assessment as a radical approach to assessment. Hughes (2014) argues that self-referenced criteria direct students' attention to their own progress and the next move forward, and that self-adjusted goals enhance students' self-regulation.

While the feature of self-referenced criteria makes ipsative assessment special and appealing, it impairs its feasibility in this era of accountability. With competitive assessment and its effects lingering in the background (Hughes 2014), ipsative assessment sounds more like a utopia. Hughes (2014) provides two examples to illustrate how ipsative assessment can be implemented in small steps within the established assessment regime. First, in her study, written ipsative feedback was given to students in online modules, and in a second example students' progress was considered as one criterion when final grades were given. The two examples suggest that students are more motivated to take further action after their progress has been confirmed. Challenges in implementing ipsative assessment include: maintaining the coherence between different assessment tasks so that students have opportunities to take action in response to ipsative feedback; the online mode reduces opportunities for tutor – student dialogue over feedback; and the extent to which criteria are allowed to be set as self-referenced in an institution's assessment policy.

Assessment and Student Self-Regulation

The current perspective of student self-regulation conceptualises it as a dynamic and developmental process during which student identity unfolds and emerges through classroom interactions (Kaplan and Flum 2009). The present study adopts such a developmental conceptualisation and draws upon Zimmerman's (2002) model of student self-regulation consisting of three phases: forethought, performance, and self-reflection.

Zimmerman's model is adopted mainly because its sub-processes relate to the three fundamental dimensions of assessment: where the learners are, where they need to go and how best to get there (Assessment Reform Group 2002). In the forethought phase, students set goals and plan their strategies. The mastery or performance orientation of learning goals affects student motivation. Self-efficacy, that is, students' personal beliefs about their capability to reach their outcome expectations, is an important construct in this phase. In the performance phase, students employ certain strategies and observe their own performance. In the self-reflection phase, students self-evaluate their performance, analyse the attributing factors in their success or failure and take defensive or adaptive reactions. The three phases in this model are not linear, rather, constructs in which different phases interact with each other dynamically.

There are substantial connections between assessment activities and student self-regulation, especially in terms of learners' goal setting, strategic planning and self-efficacy. With respect to learning goals, Sadler (1989) points out that the external standard or reference level becomes the learner's goal only 'when it is desired, aimed for, or aspired to' (p. 129). A learner's decision to ignore or reject an external goal may undermine self-regulation. Students do not necessarily share with tutors the same degree of commitment to external academic goals (Hattie and Timperley 2007). Instead, their learning goals are to a large extent framed by assessment (Gibbs 2006). The content, means, weight and feedback of assessment influence student perceptions of what is important in the discipline.

Assessment also affects student learning strategies. Gibbs (2006) describes the phenomenon of 'faking good' in many universities: students present themselves and their work for the purpose of maximising grades. Such a performance-oriented learning goal tends to lead students to employing a superficial approach (e.g. memorising) to learning (Gibbs 1992). Although research shows that memorisation can occur in conjunction with the intentions and practices of deep learning (Kember 2000), the learning goal of applying knowledge in tertiary education requires students to adopt other strategies.

Gan, Humphreys and Hamp-Lyons (2004) compare the learning attitudes, strategies and motivation of nine successful and nine unsuccessful second-year EFL students in two Chinese universities. Unsuccessful students demonstrated an incremental/quantitative approach, that is, viewing English as a collection of linguistic bricks. In addition to the strategy of learning English words by rote, successful learners reported a greater variety of strategies, and they were able to sustain their work towards a learning goal at their own pace. Classroom interaction was found to stimulate progressive development among successful students, but regressive coping efforts among unsuccessful students because the latter believed their teachers' feedback was not supportive. Hattie and Timperley (2007) argue that teacher feedback targeting student self-regulation helps students to self-evaluate, to analyse the attributions for success or failure and to take next steps. Students are found to be more open to small-scale assessment innovation if the rationale for change is clear, and they can feel cognitive gains and affective satisfaction or motivation (Carless and Zhou 2015).

Self-Regulation of First-Year University Students

Existing literature has documented perceptual gaps between first-year university students and their tutors with respect to expectations for academic study (Yorke 2005), assessment tasks (Williams 2005) and assessment criteria (Nulty 2011). Perceptual gaps may result in students' lack of self-regulation and failure to assimilate themselves into the university academic culture.

Such gaps partly derive from the unsophisticated reflective skills of first-year students. Learners' capacity for self-reflection and self-evaluation is essential to their self-regulated learning, but first-year students are found to demonstrate fewer well-developed skills than students in later university years (Cassidy 2007; Van Hattum-Janssen and Lourenço 2006). It is unfair, however, to interpret students' lack of skills as a justification for excluding them from relevant tasks (Nulty 2011; Williams 2005). Tutors need to develop strategies to foster student self-regulation and nurture students' willingness to participate (Nicol 2009). Previous studies provide evidence of the role of formative assessment tasks in clarifying expectations and building up student self-confidence and self-control over learning (Asghar 2010; Yorke 2005).

The transitional period of the first year of university is crucial and difficult for Chinese learners, too. The high-stake university entrance examination functions as a watershed between school and university education in the Chinese education system (Zhou and Deneen 2015). Tutor and student perceptions of education compete with each other, evolve during the change process and mutually shape the practices of classroom assessment. How assessment fosters and sustains student regulated-related beliefs and actions in this process warrants a better understanding.

Context of Assessment Change

This chapter is part of a larger project that examined Chinese tutors' and students' perceptions and practices of assessment in a college English language curriculum change. The curriculum innovation was top-down initiated by a municipal steering committee in Shanghai. A framework document was issued to guide the innovation implementation, but individual institutions need to work out their own institutional changing plans. The change initiators hoped that the aim of improving undergraduates' academic English language capacities would serve as a nucleus to promote a more coherent connection between curriculum, instruction and assessment.

In response to the change initiative, tutors organised an innovation team to collectively plan classroom assessment and select reading materials. Individual interviews with tutors indicated that before the current change, explaining vocabulary and the text was a major component of classroom English teaching. After the change was initiated, students were required to read authentic English materials and search for relevant information before class. In class, students first shared their synthesised information within groups and then collaboratively discussed comprehensive questions given by their tutors. The results of group discussion and synthesis were orally presented to the whole class or written into reports. Tutors believed that classroom assessment provided opportunities for developing and evaluating higher level learning abilities, such as information-searching, synthesising, applying and collaborating, and students needed to learn vocabulary by themselves before class. This chapter reports findings related to the information-rich case of a teacher given a pseudonym Mei. Mei was the only tutor who had received systematic training in language assessment research and extensive experience in test-development practices. The ipsative assessment and feedback detected in her classes had practical and theoretical implications.

METHOD

Data Collection

This chapter draws upon four sets of data in the larger research project. The first set of data related to students' perceptions of the current assessment change, their learning goals and their learning strategies. Six groups of students (four to five students in each group) were interviewed at two different times over one academic year. Each interview lasted approximately one hour and was transcribed verbatim. The second data set was composed of field notes and audio records of Mei's English classes. Four units of Mei's English teaching (24 sessions with a total length of 1080 minutes) were observed, audio-recorded and selectively transcribed. To triangulate the interview and observation data, students were invited to write learning journals reflecting on their learning experience at the end of the academic year. The fourth data set consisted of Mei's perceptions elicited from interviews and her own reflexive essay. Mei was individually interviewed twice during the academic year. She also provided her critique of the feasibility and challenges of ipsative assessment in the process of writing this chapter.

Data Analysis

Content analysis procedures (Merriam 2009; Miles and Huberman 1994) and constant comparative analysis (Strauss and Corbin 1990) were applied to interview transcriptions. Along with intensive coding, students' and tutor's perceptions were constantly compared in order to identify conceptual patterns and generate abstract categories. After several rounds of open coding, the core categories that emerged from the open and axial coding processes were: students' 'learning goals orientation', 'learning strategy', and 'self-efficacy of evaluating abilities'. The relationship between codes was further validated against the data.

With regards to classroom observation data, a selective transcription strategy (Strauss and Corbin 1990) was adopted in this study. Classroom extracts were selected because the classroom observation scheme and field notes indicated that they could be put at different points along the formal-informal classroom assessment spectrum (Rea-Dickins 2001). These classroom assessment activities were assigned numerical identification codes; teacher and student discourse was transcribed; and a database of classroom assessment was constructed. Involving the case teacher's reflections helped provide reflexivity in this study.

FINDINGS

Findings are organised around three major themes: student perceptions at the starting point, Mei's classroom assessment and feedback and student perceptions in the second semester.

STUDENT PERCEPTIONS AT THE STARTING POINT

This section reports findings related to student self-regulation emerging from the focus group interviews at the beginning of the innovation. These findings constituted a baseline against which changes in student perceptions could be traced and links between student self-regulation and classroom assessment could be established.

Nearly all the students agreed that if they could fulfil all the tasks as required by the tutors, they would improve a lot. However, they mentioned 'laziness' and 'lack of motivation' as the reasons for their failure to fulfil assessment tasks in and outside the English classroom. One student elaborated:

> In the changed assessment framework, we are not faced with high-stakes exams, nor are we controlled by some regulations. We find our current English proficiency is sufficient to do in-class discussion.

Underlying the reason of 'laziness' was students' disagreement with tutors on learning objectives. Two quotations illustrate students' viewpoints:

> What do we learn English for? Mainly for passing the CET tests. Do we need to summarize the content and take notes when we answer the reading comprehension items in these tests? Obviously not. That's why I think these skills are utterly useless.
>
> Those skills and standards stressed by teachers are not congruent with the standards of good English in my opinion. I think we learn English in order to communicate with foreigners fluently.

Taking into account all the interview data collected at the first time point, we concluded that the innovative classroom assessments were not in line with the external high-stakes test. For those students with performance-oriented learning goals, assessment activities unaligned with test items were 'useless'. Second, there were perceptional gaps between tutors and students with regard to the indicators of 'good English'. One student drew an analogy between evaluating advanced skills and building castles in the air, and pointed out that he believed vocabulary was the foundation of the castle. A large repertoire of vocabulary and fluent communication in daily scenarios were two indicators mentioned most frequently by students, in contrast to those generic skills valued by tutors, such as skills of evaluating, reflecting, information searching and synthesising.

In line with the perceived importance of vocabulary, students mentioned that they were accustomed to English learning strategies such as looking up the meanings of words in a dictionary, memorising word meanings and doing grammar and word exercises. They also reported their unwillingness to use learning strategies recommended by university tutors, such as searching for information and synthesising it before class. The following quotation is representative:

> I miss the experience of doing English exercises in my secondary school. It gave me a concrete feeling that I was learning English.

Peer assessment was implemented in order to develop students' evaluative ability. Students generally distrusted their own or their peers' evaluating competence and expressed doubts about the legitimacy of students being assessors:

> I don't think I have the ability to stand on a higher platform and to evaluate others.
> Classmates' English ability was roughly at the same level. We are not in the stance to criticize others' problems. However, teachers are different. They have higher proficiency, and could kindly remind us of our problems.

To sum up, there were perceptional gaps between tutors and students regarding English language learning goals. Students' learning strategies were influenced by their understandings of good English language standards and their perceptions of learning English as accumulating vocabulary. They harboured doubts over their personal competence and legitimacy to conduct peer and self-assessment.

Classroom Assessment and Feedback

It's not because students are lazy. It's not knowing how to learn that leads to student low engagement. (Mei)
Once they know how to do the task and how to do it well, they will be more engaged. (Mei)

Tutor Mei believed that students' low engagement resulted from their insufficient knowledge about how to learn. She believed tutors should create opportunities for students to attempt to learn on their own, and give students targeted and timely feedback.

Although the basic content and forms of classroom assessment activities were collectively designed by the innovation team, two patterns distinguished Mei's assessment implementation from that of other tutors. The first difference was that Mei designed several assessment tasks for students to reflect on their former learning strategies, which were absent in other tutors' classrooms. Through these reflective activities, Mei had access to students' former learning conditions and, therefore, was able to deliver ipsative feedback focusing on student progress. The second pattern was a degree of internal consistency in Mei's classroom assessment, and students had the opportunities to act on tutor feedback in the assessment that followed. Although Mei had not heard of the term 'ipsative assessment', the two patterns suggested there was evidence of ipsative assessment in her class. The following part gives two examples of how ipsative assessment and feedback was used to enhance student learning and student self-regulatory capacity.

Example 1: Changing Student Text-Reviewing Strategies

In the second week of the first semester, Mei asked students to discuss within their groups (four to five students per group) how they reviewed English texts outside class, and to reflect on the pros and cons of their learning strategies (assessment Task 5). In her feedback, Mei confirmed the effectiveness of the strategies mentioned by students (e.g. consulting a dictionary and memorising word meanings) but said that these should be combined with new strategies:

These traditional methods are helpful but not enough for college study. What I recommend is you use the traditional way to memorize those words. Besides this, you need to paraphrase the long sentences in your own words....You also need to search on the internet for background knowledge....I think you should combine traditional learning strategies with these new ways.

The learning strategies recommended by Mei included learning vocabulary before class and sharing vocabulary knowledge within groups in class; searching for background knowledge related to the themes of the reading materials; noting down keywords or drawing graphs of the essay structures; using one sentence to synthesise the main idea and so on. A variety of classroom assessments were designed to evaluate the effectiveness of student preparation. Mei explained in her feedback that she had noticed students' success or failure in making progress in changing their strategies. For example, in assessment Task 6, a reading comprehension task, she reminded students that they should search for information and collect solid evidence for their in-class discussion. In assessment Task 13, she confirmed students' progress and suggested how they could improve:

> As I looked around, I found most of you have done an after-class research thoroughly. Very good research on the background information of this article in *The Economist*. You should also synthesize these pieces of information and figure out what factors lead to this company's success.

In each unit, one group of students would orally present information about the new English words on the podium. In the peer teaching session in Unit 1, students picked out almost all the new words and quickly briefed their peers on the Chinese meanings. Mei suggested that they 'focus on fewer words but learn in depth'. Students used this feedback in their peer teaching in Unit 5. Mei gave the following feedback:

> I think this group has done very well by choosing appropriate words to present. If I were them, I'd chose exactly the same words and expressions. This group covered fewer words than the group in Unit 1, but they deepened and widened their vocabulary learning by mentioning the derived words and usage. There are lots of things you can learn from their group presentation. When delivering the presentation, you should consider what kind of explanation will help most of your peers to understand the words, rather than reading what you have copied from dictionary. It would be better if this group had compared the usage of some synonyms.

Example 2: Developing Student Synthesising Ability
in Interlinked Assessment

This curriculum innovation aimed to develop students' skills of higher order thinking and their capacity to use English in an academic context. Mei reflected that she 'broke down the overall goals to smaller and attainable objectives'. Take, for example, the capacity to synthesise information. Mei highlighted the internal connection between the assessment activities:

> It is with a clear sense of the targeted abilities of each assessment task that I was able to link different tasks that have seemingly different foci and objectives. By referring back to the related tasks, which share a target ability, I could reinforce the strategies and, at the same time, help students understand the integrated nature of language use.

The internal linkage between some classroom assessment activities is illustrated in Fig. 3.1. In assessment Task 7, Mei gave students four versions of a synthesis of an English article and asked them to decide within groups the best version and give the reasons. The good attributes of a synthesised version listed by students included: clear internal logic, a topic sentence at the beginning, evidence to support the argument and a clear conclusion. Mei summarised these features and related them to the students' oral presentation performance:

> I observed that in the previous presentations, most of you just began your presentation by reading your notes without a clear introduction and conclusion. The point is you should not only enumerate the main ideas, but also present them logically in a coherent paragraph. This is what you need to learn in your own writing and presentation.

The above advice given in assessment Task 7 was adopted by students in their oral presentation in Task 10. The student group started their presentation with a clear introduction and ended it with a conclusion and Mei praised them, saying that 'by doing so, the audiences may feel it easier to follow your presentation'. She further suggested students' use of linking expressions to connect their argument to the supporting examples. Assessment Task 20 was a listening task. Mei led students in listening to the beginning part and in guessing what content would follow. She reinforced the benefits of beginning writing or oral products with a proper

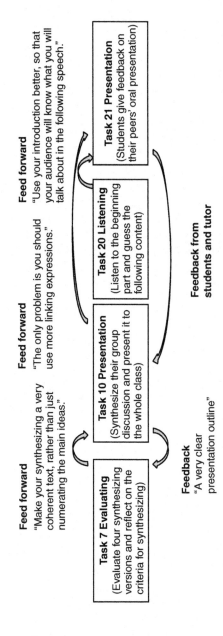

Fig. 3.1 Developing synthesising ability in interlinked assessment (adapted from Hughes 2014, p. 82)

synthesis, and explained that the next step for students was to 'use your introduction better, so that your audiences will know what you will talk about in the following speech'. Mei broke down the broader goal of developing students' synthesising skills into a series of small goals. Students not only gradually developed synthesising skills but also built up a self-belief in their evaluative ability and learned the discourse necessary to comment on the learning products. In Task 21, Mei invited students to give peer feedback on an oral presentation. The merits mentioned by student assessors included: the existence of an introduction and a conclusion, and the use of transitive expressions to connect the argument and the supporting details. The disadvantage mentioned by students was that the introduction did not summarise the presentation topic very well.

Mei's feedback, as shown in Fig. 3.1, could be considered ipsative in that it confirmed students' remedial action and suggested how they could improve. Similar internal linkage between different assessment tasks was not observed in the other tutors' classrooms. Mei's own reflection suggested that in her 7 years' study in the field of language testing, she had developed an awareness of the need to build abilities to meet assessment criteria over several assessments.

Student Perspectives Revisited

The same students were interviewed in focus groups in the middle of the second semester and were invited to write reflexive essays about their English learning experience over the whole academic year. Students' learning goals had gradually changed, as illustrated in the following excerpts:

> I feel 'knowledge' is not as important as it was for me in the first semester. The confidence in communicating with others and expressing myself is more important.
>
> I think we are accepting the change from transmitting knowledge to developing our learning strategies and academic skills.
>
> Before entering university, we had learned English for nearly twelve years. Most students' passion for English has been extinguished in all kinds of exams. Variations in assessment are likely to rekindle our passion for English learning.

Students related their changes in learning strategies to classroom assessment. With regard to their previous learning strategies, one student said:

We know too well how to deal with the traditional way of assessment. We would recite some words and paragraphs, and recited those 'knowledge points' before the final exam. This preparation would normally reward us with high scores.

With reference to the current classroom assessment, students said that Mei 'did not play her cards in the traditional way.'

You need to rely on your real English abilities, such as your daily accumulation and your efforts in reading those extended reading materials. It's not very easy to get a high grade. We make more effort.

I learned a lot through preparing and discussing the reading materials outside and in class. I really want to understand the essays, and I'm willing to search for relevant information for our group discussion.

In Mei's class, students were more willing to comment on their peers' performance than in others. The following excerpt was selected from one student's comment on their peers' oral presentation in Task 21:

I think their presentation is well-organized. First, they defined what e-commerce is. Second, they explained the reasons for the quick development of e-commerce in China. I think I learned a lot. I think the only weakness is that the presenter is not passionate enough.

Several features of this feedback illustrate students' improvement. First, the feedback was referenced to the criteria which had been reflected on by students in Task 7 and reinforced by teachers in Task 10 and Task 20 (see Fig. 3.1). Second, although Mei said 'again I give you the opportunity to be the "good guy". You only need to point out some good points', this student also mentioned a weakness. A greater degree of student engagement in assessment activities and willingness to give critical feedback was observed in this class compared to other classes that did not adopt this pedagogy. Last but not least, the feedback itself was a coherent text, conforming to the criteria agreed among tutor and students.

DISCUSSION

In the assessment change examined in this chapter, the case teacher, Mei, engaged her students in self-reflection on their accustomed learning strategies. She also gave feedback targeted at student progress and implemented interlinked assessment tasks for students to take action on feedback. The following sections analyse why these strategies can be perceived as ipsative assessment, trace how ipsative assessment enhances student self-regulation and discuss the practical implications for its implementation.

Interpreting Mei's Assessment from the Perspective of Ipsative Assessment

Mei's assessment and feedback are different from the examples given by Hughes (2014) in several ways. First, she was unaware of the term ipsative assessment, whereas in Hughes' study, tutors were trained to give ipsative feedback, and students were asked to reflect on the criteria of personal progress. Second, this case study examined the oral feedback delivered in classroom settings, while written ipsative feedback in Hughes' study was delivered through an online module. Third, in the first example of this chapter, Mei targeted students' learning strategy rather than their performance in specific assessment tasks.

We interpret the examples discussed in this chapter as ipsative assessment spontaneously emerging from an assessment change. In the top-down initiated assessment, the teaching and learning objectives were to improve student academic English abilities. Mei realised the huge gap between student learning conditions and the external goals and believed that students' lack of knowledge about how to achieve the goals dampened their engagement. She, therefore, tried to translate the broad goals into more concrete and achievable goals. The departing point was student self-reflection (e.g. students reflecting on their text reviewing strategy in Example 1) or the tutor's observation of students' previous performance (e.g. Mei observing the lack of coherence in student presentation in Example 2). The small steps forward taken by students were confirmed by the tutor (e.g. Mei confirming students' usage of a clear presentation outline in Example 2). More importantly, how to progress further was described very clearly (e.g. in Example 1, Mei suggesting that students focus on fewer words but explain them in depth in the peer teaching of vocabulary; and in Example 2, Mei suggesting that more linking expressions and an informative introduction would make the presentation more coherent). Face-to-face feedback increased the likelihood of dialogue between tutor and students. However, the verbal ipsative feedback delivered in informal classroom settings might be difficult to record, and consequently, it might be hard for students to keep track of their progress.

Links Between Ipsative Assessment and Self-Regulation

The findings provided some evidence of students' improved self-regulation in terms of learning goals, strategies, and self-efficacy. How do these findings inform us about the interplay between teacher classroom assessment and student self-regulation? The emerging linking constructs included 'motivation for change', 'strategies for change', 'abilities to change' and 'outcomes of change'.

Ipsative assessment fosters students' intrinsic motivation for change. Transitional difficulties observed among first-year undergraduates in previous studies (e.g. Yorke 2005) were also found from the first round of focus group interviews in the present study. As Gibbs (2006) has argued, a test informs students what to value. Students either described classroom assessment inconsistent with external tests as 'useless' or believed that their current English proficiency was 'sufficient' for the low-stakes classroom assessment. Resonating with Sadler's (1989) and Hattie and Timperley (2007) aspiration to nurture student commitment to learning goals, self-reflection activities were implemented in class. Reflection on the pros and cons of the traditional English learning strategy allowed students to realise the inadequacy of their English proficiency. The need to change was not imposed on them by external requirements but was the intrinsic motivation emerging from a self-awareness process.

Ipsative feedback scaffolds students with the necessary strategies for change. The Chinese undergraduates' obsession with vocabulary learning resonates with the findings of Gan et al. (2004) study in that students' perceived learning English as building up a castle with word bricks, and they subsequently selected memorising as the primary learning strategy. In contrast to students' attributing their lack of self-regulation to 'laziness', Mei believed the real reason lay in the lack of knowledge about how to change. Information about how to change was important, especially after students realised that the tutor was 'playing her cards in a different way', and that the traditional 'faking good' strategy did not work well. As the findings suggested, Mei's feedback boosted student confidence, directed their efforts and attention to particular learning strategies and helped them to analyse the reasons for success or failure.

Ipsative feedback confirmed student's changes over time, and boosted their self-efficacy in their learning abilities. Visible outcomes enabled students to feel cognitive gains and emotional satisfaction (cf. Carless and Zhou 2015). The unsuccessful Chinese undergraduates in Gan et al.'s study (2004) tended to adopt regressive coping efforts after they had received 'unsupportive' tutor feedback. The tutor's confirmation of the learning progress is valuable, especially for first-year undergraduates in a changing context. In line with Hughes (2014), ipsative feedback in this chapter developed into continued dialogues due to the internal connection between assessment tasks. Students gradually acquired the confidence and discourse to evaluate their peers' work.

In summary, a socio-cognitive perspective is helpful in understanding the interplay between ipsative assessment and learner self-regulation. The self-regulatory processes discussed in Zimmerman's research (2002) do not take place in a social vacuum. As indicated in Salili's (1996) and Littlewood's (1999) studies, Chinese university students' learning goals and strategies are hardly a purely personal agenda but are greatly shaped by the broader educational contexts. When educational innovation is promoted, and learning goals and strategies are expected to change, the self-referenced criteria and feedback centralised in the notion of ipsative assessment are able to bridge the gap between students' current learning condition and the expected outcomes.

Implementing Ipsative Assessment in China: Benefits and Challenges

The core concepts encapsulated in the framework of ipsative assessment are to some extent familiar in the discourse of assessment for learning. Setting individualised learning goals, confirming students' progress and delivering self-referenced feedback have been discussed in the worldwide move towards using assessment to facilitate learning. Ipsative assessment goes a step further by framing these concepts within a coherent theoretical framework. This relatively radical approach is useful in raising tutors' and students' awareness of the prioritised status of learner and learning. Such an awareness is of great value in this era of accountability, when tutors are expected to use assessment to meet multiple requirements. In this sense, ipsative assessment is not only beneficial to student learning but also very useful for tutors reflecting on their classroom assessment and for change initiators planning the themes of professional development.

The findings described in this chapter are evidence that implementing low-stakes ipsative assessment in Chinese classroom settings is feasible and valuable. Through translating the broad and abstract curriculum goals into concrete and individual-tailored goals, ipsative assessment is likely to maintain a balance between meeting external requirements and catering for individuals' current learning levels. In this study, Mei was found to deliver ipsative feedback without her realisation. This fact has some practical implications for implementing assessment changes. As Allwright and Bailey (1991) argue:

> Classroom research is all about gaining a better understanding of what good teachers (and learners) do instinctively as a matter of course so that ultimately all can benefit. (pp. xv–xvi)

Other tutors without sufficient assessment literacy might feel it too challenging to set the self-referenced criteria and goals, and to deliver self-referenced feedback to students. In disseminating and scaling up ipsative assessment and feedback, it might be worthwhile recording the concrete and smaller goals and criteria in a systematic way (e.g. using portfolio) so that the majority of tutors can be equipped with the discourse of ipsative assessment and use it flexibly.

However, there are perceptional and administrative barriers to implementing high stakes summative ipsative assessment. In the Chinese context, the results of summative assessment are often used to serve some non-academic functions like selecting, competing or rewarding. The extent to which self-referenced criteria could be incorporated is questionable. The introduction of this chapter describes the faculty leader's aim to take into account student individual progress when giving their final grades. This aspiration was not fulfilled in reality. Tutors were worried that the presence of 'self' in summative assessment might be perceived as unfair by students and university administrators. Exploration of this challenge is beyond the scope of this chapter, but it would be a robust topic for future studies.

References

Allwright, D., & Bailey, K. M. (1991). *Focus on the language classroom: An introduction to classroom research for language teachers.* Cambridge: Cambridge University Press.

Asghar, A. (2010). Reciprocal peer coaching and its use as a formative assessment strategy for first-year students. *Assessment & Evaluation in Higher Education, 35*(4), 403–417.

Assessment Reform Group. (2002). *Assessment for learning: 10 principles.* http://www.aaia.org.uk/content/uploads/2010/06/assessment-for-Learning-10-principles.pdf. Accessed 25 August 2015.

Brookhart, S. M. (2012). Teacher feedback in formative classroom assessment. In C. F. Webber & J. L. Lupart (Eds.), *Leading student assessment* (pp. 225–239). Netherlands: Springer.

Carless, D. (2007). Learning-oriented assessment: conceptual bases and practical implications. *Innovations in Education and Teaching International*, 44(1), 57–66.

Carless, D., & Zhou, J. (2015). Starting small in assessment change: Short in-class written responses. *Assessment and Evaluation in Higher Education*. http://dx. doi.org/10.1080/02602938.2015.1068272.

Cassidy, S. (2007). Assessing 'inexperienced' students' ability to self-assess: Exploring links with learning style and academic personal control. *Assessment & Evaluation in Higher Education*, 32(3), 313–330).

Gan, Z., Humphreys, G., & Hamp-Lyons, L. (2004). Understanding successful and unsuccessful EFL students in Chinese universities. *The Modern Language Journal*, 88(2), 229–244.

Gibbs, G. (1992). *Improving the quality of student learning*. Bristol: Technical and Educational Services.

Gibbs, G. (2006). Why assessment is changing. In C. Bryan & K. Clegg (Eds.), *Innovative assessment in higher education* (pp. 11–22). London: Routledge.

Hattie, J., & Timperley, H. (2007). The power of feedback. *Review of Educational Research*, 77(1), 81–112.

Hughes, G. (2011). Towards a personal best: A case for introducing ipsative assessment in higher education. *Studies in Higher Education*, 36(3), 353–367.

Hughes, G. (2014). *Ipsative assessment: Motivation through marking progress*. London: Palgrave Macmillan.

Kaplan, A., & Flum, H. (2009). Motivation and identity: the relations of action and development in educational contexts – An introduction to the special issue. *Educational Psychologist*, 44(2), 73–77.

Kember, D. (2000). Misconceptions about the learning approaches, motivation and study practices of Asian students. *Higher Education*, 40, 1, pp (99–121).

Littlewood, W. (1999). Defining and developing autonomy in East Asian contexts. *Applied Linguistics*, 21(1), 71–94.

Medland, E. (2012). Assessment in curriculum change. In P. Blackmore & C. B. Kandiko (Eds.), *Strategic curriculum change: global trends in universities* (pp. 92–108). Abingdon: Routledge.

Merriam, S. B. (2009). *Qualitative research: A guide to design and implementation*. San Francisco: Jossey-Bass.

Miles, M. B., & Huberman, A. M. (1994). *Qualitative data analysis: An expanded sourcebook*. 2nd edition. Newbury Park, CA: Sage.

Nicol, D. (2009). Assessment for learner self-regulation: Enhancing achievement in the first year using learning technologies. *Assessment & Evaluation in Higher Education*, 34(3), 335–352.

Nulty, D. D. (2011). Peer and self-assessment in the first year of university. *Assessment & Evaluation in Higher Education, 36*(5), 493–507.

Rea-Dickins, P. (2001). Mirror, mirror on the wall: Identifying processes of class-room assessment. *Language Testing, 18*(4), 429–462.

Sadler, D. R. (1989). Formative assessment and the design of instructional systems. *Instructional Science, 18*(2), 119–144.

Salili, F. (1996). Accepting personal responsibility for learning. In D. A. Watkins & J. B. Biggs (Eds.), *The Chinese learner: cultural, psychological and contextual influences* (pp. 85–105). Hong Kong: CERC & ACER.

Strauss, A., & Corbin, J. (1990). *Basics of qualitative research: Techniques and procedures for developing grounded theory.* Newbury Park, CA: Sage.

Timperley, H. S., & Parr, J. M. (2005). Theory competition and the process of change. *Journal of Educational Change, 6*(3), 227–251.

Van Hattum-Janssen, N., & Lourenço, J. M. (2006). Explicitness of criteria in peer assessment processes for first-year engineering students. *European Journal of Engineering Education, 31*(6), 683–691.

Wiliam, D. (2010). An integrative summary of the research literature and implications for a new theory of formative assessment. In H. L. Andrade & G. J. Cizek (Eds.), *Handbook of formative assessment* (pp. 18–40). New York: Routledge.

Williams, K. (2005). Lecturer and first year student (mis)understandings of assessment task verbs: 'Mind the gap'. *Teaching in Higher Education, 10*(2), 157–173.

Yorke, M. (2005). Increasing the chances of student success. In C. Rust (Ed.), *Improving student learning 12: Diversity and inclusivity* (pp. 35–52). Oxford: Oxford Centre for Staff and Learning Development.

Zhou, J., & Deneen, C. (2015). Chinese award-winning tutors' perceptions and practices of classroom-based assessment. *Assessment and Evaluation in Higher Education.* http://dx.doi.org/10.1080/02602938.2015.1066306.

Zimmerman, B. J. (2002). Becoming a self-regulated learner. *Theory into Practice, 41*(2), 64–70.

Jiming Zhou is a lecturer at Fudan University, China. Her research interests include assessment and learning, educational innovation and English language teaching. Her articles about classroom-based assessment and assessment changes appear in the journal of *Assessment and Evaluation in Higher Education.* Financial support for this study was provided in part by the National Social Science Foundation of China (grant #016BYY027F), the Key Research Projects of Philosophy and Social Science of Ministry of Education of China (15JZD048), the MOE Project of Key Research Institute of Humanities and Social Sciences at Universities in China (15JJD740007) and the research project of College English Teaching Center at Fudan University, China.

Jie Zhang has been teaching at School of Foreign Studies of Shanghai University of Finance and Economics since 2009. She obtained her PhD degree in language testing from Guangdong University of Foreign Studies, China. Her research interests include rater variability and rater training in performance assessment and the use of integrated writing tasks for academic writing assessment.

CHAPTER 4

Supporting Student Learning with Cumulative Coversheets

Carrie Winstanley

INTRODUCTION

Ipsative assessment is practised in this case study through cumulative coversheets. These are used to track student progression; record dialogue with the tutor; track improvement and development over the course of a module; and help students reflect on their responses to tutor commentary. In this chapter, the use of cumulative coversheets is discussed, explaining the 'why, what and how', and sharing the challenges, benefits and general outcomes of ipsative assessment used in this manner.[1]

Cumulative coversheets using ipsative measures have been used on a stand-alone module for more than a decade. They have gone through various iterations, and a number of developments have arisen, including dialogue via the cumulative coversheets; ipsative feedback on the coversheets; verbal ipsative feedback in open tutorials; a change in the spread of assessment across the module; and the deliberate adoption of a friendlier and more personal style of interaction with students.

C. Winstanley (✉)
Roehampton University, London, UK
e-mail: C.Winstanley@roehampton.ac.uk

© The Author(s) 2017
G. Hughes (ed.), *Ipsative Assessment and Personal Learning Gain*,
DOI 10.1057/978-1-137-56502-0_4

These measures were introduced in order to help students become more conscious of their progress and of how effectively they were understanding and applying tutors' suggestions for improvement. To an extent this aim was realised successfully with many of the students. In some cases, students still appreciated the support and even if they did not see immediate grade improvements, they noted a change in how they made use of feedback across their degree and reported a greater sense of understanding and appreciation of tutor comments. A further unexpected outcome of the ipsative assessment techniques was a shift in tone on the module in general. As the conversations with students deepened, a more frank and friendly style of communication emerged which seemed to be an additional significant factor in helping the students improve their work.

WHY USE IPSATIVE ASSESSMENT? MEETING STUDENTS' NEEDS

The story in this chapter is of assessment undertaken with Year Two undergraduates on an elective module, taught over one twelve-week semester to one or two groups of twenty five students enrolled on a three-year BA Education degree.[2] It has been running for fifteen years to date, with around 530 students having participated in total. The module includes four off-campus visits to museums, galleries and places of outdoor education, so students may critically review the learning opportunities these offer through four short (1000 word) assessed written papers. In some years the assessment has made use of ipsative measures in a bid to improve student engagement and achievement. Ipsative assessment has been combined with other criterion referenced summative assessment in order to comply with university regulations around summative assessment and feedback, so this can be defined as a 'dual regime' (Hughes 2011, p. 3).

In terms of their journey through a degree programme, second-year undergraduates on three year programmes are often vulnerable, entering a period known as 'the second year slump' (Thompson et al. 2013). The honeymoon period of the first year is over and the final graduation ceremony seems too far away to be realistic. This 'slump' is amplified for students from complex backgrounds who may struggle to remain motivated, and applies to the students in this case study who originate from a range of diverse backgrounds. Most are female and many are mature students with multiple caring responsibilities, which often impact negatively on available time and ability to focus on studies. A large percentage of students are from minority ethnic backgrounds and most are first-generation Higher Education students, many whose dominant language is not English. A significant minority have additional learning needs and whilst only some are part-time, many have employment to manage alongside their university life. As widely acknowledged (Higher Education Funding Council for England (HEFCE) 2013; Tinto 1993), these cohorts constitute students within the widening participation agenda and such that they are at a higher risk of failing to complete their degree. They tend to come to university with a reluctance to share their concerns for fear of being judged by tutors and peers. Discussions around such students and their needs have become increasingly nuanced and recent studies have criticised the tendency to presume that all students under the umbrella term of 'non-traditional' have similar concerns (Teaching and Learning Research Programme (TLRP) 2009, p. 20). The term:

> ...inadequately describes the rich diversity of students that we teach. Furthermore, teaching based on this deficit view of students tends to overlook the different knowledge, skills and experiences that students now bring. (TLRP 2009, p. 20)

As a Higher Education Funding Council for England (HEFCE) report recognises, fostering engagement is vital for retention and success and 'the prime location for nurturing participation and a sense of belonging is the academic domain' (Higher Education Funding Council for England (HEFCE) 2013, p. 57). It is therefore the responsibility of the tutor to adjust assessment and teaching to cater to their students. In this case study, the use of both cumulative coversheets and ipsative assessment was not sudden; it came about via a few different attempts to address various problems on taught modules that are relatively common with the cohorts described. These concerns were addressed as follows:

1. Engagement and attendance – having cumulative components that build upon one another helped students appreciate the coherence of the module, seeing how reading, assessment and experiences connect.
2. Reading feedback – when students know they will get credit and/or comments for responding to suggested changes highlighted in their feedback, they are more likely to read and engage with tutor comments.

3. Understanding feedback and deciphering what is said – this is done by setting direct goals for improving writing, and reinforced via face-to-face tutorials with the tutor.[3]

As well as the cumulative approach, ipsative elements in the assessment process are helpful, since they help maintain motivation and engagement through recognising individual positive qualities in the student's work and building on these for general improvement. A wide range of factors influence learning and academic engagement, including 'race, gender and class' as well as 'differences in age, family background and situation, prior education, work and life experiences' (TLRP 2009). The ipsative approach helpfully presupposes that students already have something worthwhile as a starting point, as well as a genuine capacity to improve and to hone their skills and ideas.[4] The use of cumulative coversheets aims to help students and tutors to maintain and record a dialogue about these developments and also to encourage reflection.

WHAT WAS DONE USING CUMULATIVE COVERSHEETS AND WHY?

In the module, four papers are submitted, and each one is assessed with:

1. a numerical grade
2. written marks on the text
3. an overall comment on the coversheet

Each submission is graded to ensure that all students submit something, but the first component is lightly weighted at only five or ten per cent of the final mark and treated as a trial paper to help students find their feet on the module. When submitting the next paper – on a related, but different theme – students are invited to respond to the written comments for the previous paper, logging the aspects they have specifically worked on perfecting. Feedback on this second, subsequent paper consists of comments on this new work, but also includes remarks about the improvements. Comments are made about the extent to which the improvements the students claim to have made are actually evident in this new submission. Some years, they also received a numerical grade for this ipsative element. This ipsative grading and the ipsative comments are discussed in more detail below, but they need to be understood in the context of other more general supportive and constructive explanatory feedback.

Additional General Group Feedback for Information

After the first submission, in addition to the personalised comments on the coversheets, generic feedback is provided to the entire group via an oral presentation from the tutor accompanied by a written sheet with all the relevant information listed, such as examples of common grammatical errors and reminders about accurate referencing. This also includes short sample passages demonstrating the difference between descriptive and analytical writing, to show students how to be more critical, for example. This supplementary feedback supports the more bespoke comments and frees the tutor and student from only focusing on the more generic elements, allowing instead a more directed approach where individualised increments of progress are more easily managed.

Tutorials and Feedback to Improve Assessment Literacy

Following the presentation of generic information to the group, individual feedback on this first submission is provided face-to-face with the tutor and an Academic Learning Advisor (support tutor) also present, providing useful groundwork for any subsequent support meetings.[5] In this discussion, the written ipsative aspects are used to help the student identify goals for improvement and the tutors use the discussion to evaluate how well the students understand feedback and how 'usable' they are finding the written comments. This helps prepare the students to make the most of future written feedback.

Through talking with the students, a series of questions was used to establish their levels of understanding and confidence and since these were posed to all in an open environment, students were able to see that many peers faced the same concerns and they felt less isolated. Comments and responses can then be tailored to each individual, making each person more likely to engage with future written comments. The questions asked were as follows:

1. How do you think you did on this paper?
2. With which parts of your work were you happiest?
3. Which comments on the text make the most sense to you?
4. Have you had these kinds of comments on previous work? What have you done to address them?
5. Which comments don't really make sense, or are surprising to you?
6. Let's look at the first section – see what is said here … how could you avoid getting that comment on your next paper?

Following this detailed discussion, the students were able to identify concrete areas for improvement. They started to develop the short-hand habit of asking themselves to reflect by considering: 'What was good, tricky and useful about x or y today?' These strategies were introduced once it became clear through the ipsative assessment that students were not always acting on the written feedback, even when such information was very detailed. Having had a face-to-face meeting, subsequent written communication seems easier. Student comments include:

> I felt better about emailing and asking questions after we had the talk.
> I wasn't so embarrassed at asking things – it was like a conversation on the coversheet so I looked forward to the comments and not just getting the grade.
> I have kept my coversheet as a record of how I have improved. It's got your comments and mine like sort of messages back and forth and I prefer that to an online trail; it's got more personality and meaning.

Through the dialogue, students are developing 'assessment literacy' (Hughes 2011, p. 136) making use of feedback '... in different ways including enhancing motivation, enhancing learning, encouraging reflection and clarifying their progress' (Crisp 2007, p. 573). This dialogic approach is the key. 'While the quality of the comments is important, the quality of the students' interaction with those comments is equally, and perhaps more, important' (Nicol 2010, p. 503).[6] Similarly, Higgins et al. observe that 'for formative assessment to work in practice, feedback must 'connect' with students' (2002, p. 54) and this is easier to achieve if the students have opportunities to discuss the feedback with tutors and peers.

Tutor comments on work are only helpful if they are understood by the students. Students can be unfamiliar with the 'disciplinary discourse' on their programme.

> Every act of assessment gives a message to students about what they should be learning and how they should go about it. Assessment messages are coded, not easily understood and are often read differently and with different emphases by staff and by students. (Boud 1995, p. 39)

It has long been known that if the comments are too deeply coded they cannot be deciphered (Sadler 1989, p. 121) and students 'may fail to understand the taken-for-granted academic discourses which underpin assessment criteria and the language of feedback' (Higgins et al. 2002, p. 56). For example:

> ...feedback comments may be ambiguous (e.g. 'poor effort, could do better'), too general or vague (e.g. 'you've got the important stuff'), too abstract (e.g. 'this essay is not sufficiently analytical'), too cryptic (e.g. 'why?'). (Nicol 2010, p. 507)

Markers need to be aware of students misinterpreting academic discourse (Weaver 2006) and Chanock has also focused on this problem, clearly demonstrating the disparity between tutor meaning and student understanding (2000). Furthermore, as Walker identifies, feedback is only useful if it helps students to address the disparity between what they are presenting and what they could be achieving if they were to improve their work:

> It can be argued that, to be usable by the student, a tutor's comment must do more than simply point a gap out; it must be designed to help the student to reduce or close the gap. (Walker 2009, p. 3)

On the module discussed in this chapter, because the students were being graded and evaluated on their efforts to incorporate developmental feedback into their subsequent papers, they were more determined (and perhaps courageous) when it came to finding out precisely what the tutor meant by any particular comment. Together with the open tutorial session, an atmosphere developed in which asking for clarification and detail was expected and encouraged. This helped to break down the (vestigial) habit of normative assessment, in which students compare themselves with one another, rather than focusing on their own improvements. Tutors, of course, make use of different types of comments, with varied purposes, not all directly usable to make improvements, but perhaps to serve as praise or positive reinforcement (see Brown and Glover 2006, for an interesting inventory of comments). Walker identifies the most readily usable category as concerning:

> ...skills development – that is, comments about the structure of the answer (whether text, diagram or mathematical argument), about whether the

question has been properly addressed, about the student's communication skills, etc. (Walker 2009, p. 76)

Tutor comments need to be carefully explained however or they can become a kind of checklist used for a kind of cosmetic redrafting that can be done relatively simply without taking the developments fully on board. To avoid such an instrumental approach on this module, students were required to apply the comments to subsequent papers and not allowed the option of resubmitting existing work. The focus was firmly on applying what is learnt to a new paper, rather than revising an existing one. This worked well for this module and is consistent with constructivist learning, encouraging deep rather than surface or strategic learning (Marton and Säljö 1976; Biggs 1993; Lublin 2003). It is important that the application of change and improvement is done in a thoughtful manner and this can be encouraged through:

> ... comments which include an element of explanation of why the student's answer is incorrect, incomplete or inappropriate and of why what the tutor is suggesting is more acceptable. This is bringing a constructivist perspective to bear on commenting. (Walker 2009, p. 68)

Ipsative feedback practice using coversheets and tutorials allows tutors to see the extent to which students are understanding and applying the feedback and helps teachers in getting to know their students. This encourages tutors to reflect more fully on the quality of their feedback and to understand better the impact of their approach to assessment and make improvements.

Ipsative Feedback on Cumulative Coversheets

Cumulative coversheets with ipsative elements can be presented in various ways, but always require students to 'review the developmental aspects of past feedback and state how they [had] addressed each of the points raised in the current piece of work' (Hughes et al. 2014, p. 37). The focus on this module has been mostly on qualitative commentary since grading for improvement has not been able to sit easily with university regulations and has had to be abandoned for now.

The coversheets in this module were divided into different-sized sections to allow dialogue on each submission, incorporating space for both tutor and student comments to be recorded. The first and final assessments had the most space for commentary. As the module progressed, comments and grades for each submission were written in turn by the tutor and student. The sheet, therefore, serves as a record of student progress and development, as they also note how they have responded to the tutor suggestions for improvement. Generally, the first comment links directly to the published module criteria. Subsequent submissions are then marked in relation both to these criteria, with the addition of one more requirement – to demonstrate explicitly where the previous feedback has been acted upon. The dialogue tends to focus around the first three submissions with a view to improving writing style and content. The comments for the final paper are usually more summative, except for the years when there has been a grade for the ipsative elements. Here follow some illustrative examples of dialogues from the coversheets:

> Tutor [Paper 1]: Try and back up your personal view of the museum with a theorist who has said something similar. Student [Paper 2]: I have used Hein to back up my view that the 'fire' exhibit encourages discovery learning.
> Tutor [Paper 1]: Analyse, don't just describe – why is it effective? (Don't just describe what you see) Student [Paper 2]: I explained why the gallery is good for creative writing (the way the pictures are hung not like you would expect). Tutor [Paper 2]: Ok – can you find a quotation to support the point you are making? Try the Falk article. Student [Paper 3]: This time I backed up the view and remembered to explain why and not just describe. Tutor [Paper 3]: Great! Can you do these things again for the final paper?

Students are required to craft their own essay titles and even with a great deal of support, this task often proves very challenging. Feedback on student work has therefore been focused on refining the task itself, as well as the content, style and tone of the critical review. On progressing from first-year modules, students tend to be adept at responding to tutor-led assessment, but less well-equipped to delineate the parameters of their own work by framing their own enquiries. Such a skill is essential in shaping more substantial research questions, such as those they needed for final-year dissertations, for example. It is a worthwhile exercise to spend time and effort on thinking about writing clear, answerable questions and so the ipsative assessment has sometimes included feedback on the development of the titles as well as the content.

IPSATIVE GRADING

As Hughes et al point out, 'ipsative feedback is less controversial than ipsative grading' (Hughes et al. 2014, p. 24) and Orr declares that 'ipsative assessment is deemed unacceptable in the academy because its focus on individual student learning journeys challenges the concept of national standards' (2007, p. 653). On this module, students were generally less keen on numerical grades for ipsative aspects of their work than on the qualitative comments.

During the life of the module, when ipsative grading was used, criteria were published for how effectively the student had applied the recommendations for ameliorating their writing. Scores were given on a scale of zero to five from 'no discernible improvements', through 'some clear improvements' up to 'significant improvements demonstrated'. In some instances, this was relatively simple to assess, such as suggestions to 'include more references to literature from peer-reviewed journals' or 'make better use of paragraphs; one clear point discussed fully in each'. However, looser comments such as 'adopting a more scholarly tone' were trickier to evaluate 'cleanly'.

The percentage of the final grade for each component and for the ipsative element has changed over the years. This is in response to various factors including: programme regulations; requirements to align practice with other programme tutors; the adoption of electronic submissions with pre-designed formats; and also due to students with specific additional needs. At its height, the ipsative grading element was worth twenty per cent of the final mark, but this has dropped to zero in the last two years due to university requirements to streamline assessment styles and reduce the number of components on grade sheets. Ipsative assessment is now used for formative feedback and feed forward.

In some years the ipsative grade was a percentage added to the submission grades in the final total and in other instances points were added to each submission grade depending on the ipsative score for each paper. One year, students were invited to resubmit the paper that had the lowest grade together with a reflective summary of how they had enhanced their original. Unfortunately, these methods have proved unwieldy when pitted against university procedures, and difficult to harmonise with some rather rigid quality assurance measures. It is hoped to reintroduce a weighting for the ipsative element at some point, but even if this cannot be achieved, the impact of the process has been helpful in making feedback more meaningful to students.

EVALUATING THE PROCESS: BENEFITS AND CHALLENGES OF CUMULATIVE COVERSHEETS

Better Assessment Experiences All Round

Student grades and satisfaction with module both improved following the changes in assessment. With the most recent modules (for the last four years), the only fail grades have been from non-submission; all students who engaged with the process of reflecting on their progress have passed the module, even those who failed the first essay (worth only five of ten per cent of the final mark). Following the first and second submissions, students were more likely to attend sessions with Academic Learning Advisors as they had specific questions to ask and particular targets to attain. Students who reported long essays as an overwhelming experience appreciated having the shorter papers with more focused feedback, stating that this made things more manageable because they had directed advice on what to improve.

The structure of the cumulative worksheet also made the discussion with tutors simple to manage. It was possible to have a key meeting after the submission of the first component and then follow this up with very brief meetings as the course progressed, since the main work had already been undertaken.

Focused Individual Comments

Personalised ipsative feedback was seen as a benefit by all students who expressed an opinion. Students are provided with a series of subheadings for writing the first few papers, in order to help them focus on content rather than structure. The headings also guide students to separate analysis from description and facts from personal experience, which is commonly difficult for students, yet important (as highlighted by Chanock 2000). Comments can, therefore, be very tightly directed, which is appropriate for this cohort. For example, students may be good at presenting facts and information but less good at tying the theory in with their observations, or using references to support an argument. Concentrating on this, with constructive and direct feedback can helpfully direct a student's attention, making change more manageable.

Other students struggle with presenting information concisely for example, and the ipsative comments in this instance might be targeted at helping them write succinctly and clearly within the word limit. The comments could also encourage the use of appendices, or recommend specific texts. Grammar and spelling are highlighted but remain the focus of the group generic feedback and were less used for the individual ipsative grades to avoid the feedback being used merely as a kind of checklist.

A Concern: Students Failing to Progress

The main limitation surfaced with students who did not improve grades or those who were unable to usefully address the concerns raised. In some instances, the areas they aimed to improve were too nebulous or too ambitious and became impossible to fulfil. Help with identifying clear, realistic enhancements was appreciated in these cases. In some instances, they felt demoralised by the sheer number of comments and by the amount of work they felt was needed.

Spreading the Workload

By breaking assessment into smaller components, each with dedicated feedback, students were able to see that the tutor was responding to their needs for spreading out their workload and making coursework as manageable as possible. Students had been complaining of bunching of assessments at key points in the academic year, saying that they would prefer to complete several lower stakes pieces of work as they went along, rather than one high-stakes essay at the end of a module. Students tended to undertake the substantial writing of their longer pieces of work in the vacation period at a time when fewer academics were readily available to discuss work. Spreading the work through the module and focusing on steady improvement illustrated to the students that the tutor was genuinely interested in helping them progress, further enhancing the experience of the module.

For tutors, marking as the module progressed had some implications around time management and could prove complex and feel rushed, but there was also the benefit of a smaller pile of papers at the end of the module and improved quality and more focused comments.

A Less Equivocal Result: Perceived Inequity of Ipsative Comments and Grades

Overall, students generally responded well to the grades used for the ipsative element of the assessment process as it helped them chart progress:

It's been a real help – I can see my work improving and it's not just on this module.[7]

I still really want to know my grade but I can also see that the comments can be helpful too; I actually read them more carefully now.

It's a bit like when people actually learn your names; with this grade for improvement it feels like my effort has been noticed and that makes it more worthwhile. It's like someone has actually noticed me.

Ipsative assessment seems to encourage students to aim for deep learning, be intrinsically motivated and focus less on the extrinsic reward, taking pride in their learning and not focusing on the grade alone (Higgins et al. 2002). The conversational style of this also helps develop formative assessment as something done *for* and *with* students, rather than something *'done to'* students (Brown and Knight 1994, p. 38).

Some students, however, found the process unfair. Previous researchers have found that students are disappointed when they have made enhancements to their work, but their overall grade is still lower than they hoped (Hughes et al. 2014), which tends to be a problem with a dual system. This was not a major concern on this module because ipsative grading has been eroded over the years. More of an issue was that some students felt they were required to make more complex improvements than their peers; they perceived the personalised nature of the comments as unfairly weighted in favour of students with weaker work in the first instance:

Grades for improving isn't really fair on those who are already doing quite well. What would happen if I made some deliberate silly mistakes like messing up a few references and then I get marked down like three per cent for the mistake and then get five per cent more for correcting it – do you get me?

Yeah, the better your work, the more sort of fluffy the comments are: 'write more fluently' or 'be more scholarly'. I mean, how do I know if I have got it right?

Some people just have to like, correct their grammar or something simple, and then they get a better grade. I had to include more references which is a much harder thing to do.

Whilst ipsative assessment must also be about comparison with one's previous performance, it can also include maintaining standards that are already high. To the students above it was possible to reassure them that they are graded on their own learning gain. Ipsative assessment can ensure that present performance is compared to past performance, but sometimes 'simply maintaining some levels of activity is a goal worth having' (Brown and Knight 1994, p. 19).

Students also worried about improving one aspect of their writing and then failing to maintain a different aspect that might suffer if they shifted their attention. Ultimately as a tutor, one is aiming to inculcate effective self-regulated learning (Bjork et al. 2013) and so students need to learn to manage multiple aspects simultaneously. Focusing on each element through directed ipsative assessment can help in this regard. With the feedback sheets, a focus on issues beyond the mechanics of writing mentioned earlier was partly in response to this and the more basic issues of English were relegated to the generic feedback sheet.

A Challenge for Tutors

The responsibility for usable ipsative feedback lies with the tutor, who must make each word really count. As Crisp points out:

> For academics, a less comfortable option than blaming students for their apparent ignoring of feedback is to critically reflect on their own practices. Providing information prior to an assignment regarding the criteria for assessment, followed up by written feedback on completed assignments, frequently represents a series of unilateral pronouncements by assessors rather than a dialogue with students. (Crisp 2007, p. 578)

Taking extra care to make comments usable has implications for tutor workload. Over time, the cumulative coversheets seem to 'pay off' as later comments are brief and easy to target, but the initial investment in written and oral comments can be exhausting.

> I appreciate that the face-to-face sessions are helpful, but they are physically and emotionally draining. After that class I need a lie down in a darkened room!'
> The more I use the cumulative coversheets the less inclined I am to use the phrase bank on the electronic system as it seems impoverished. Marking takes longer though; it's not sustainable.

The class sizes in this case study are relatively small, fifty students maximum in some years and so the methods were (mostly) manageable. How scalable such approaches might be is not immediately apparent, but with a restructuring of module delivery, perhaps including peer support and paired work, it could be feasible to preserve the most useful features for a larger group as recommended by Nicol (2010). Training and support for those wanting to try a more ipsative approach will also be time-consuming initially but could pay off in the longer term. Tutors have limited hours allocated for each module and finding sufficient time to concentrate fully on new initiatives is a challenge, so the benefits need to be highlighted to encourage people to engage with the methods.

Increasing Emphasis on Adopting a Positive Tone

Through this experience of adjusting the assessment, it was noted that adopting a compassionate tone in general helped to assure a more positive experience for students. Research has demonstrated that the manner in which the assessment task is expressed also has an impact on how students approach the course from the outset (Harnish and Bridges 2011; Harnish et al. 2011). In producing the module materials, care was taken to use supportive language that assures students that they will progress if they participate fully with an emphasis on helping them to reach their own (progressively complex) targets.

For example, in the course materials the assessment was described as follows (abridged):

> These first three papers are an exciting challenge in which you are invited to choose your own focus to match your personal interests. You will be provided with a useful structure to guide you – follow it closely. For the fourth and final submission, you can choose from a range of set titles and within those, you can pick a specific focal point that capitalises on reading you have already completed for the earlier papers (a bargain!).
>
> We'll discuss the assessment tasks in each session and you are encouraged to ask questions about what you are working on as we go along. You will receive a variety of written, audio and face-to-face feedback on each submission as you progress along the module in order for you to improve your work as you go along.

In earlier iterations module instructions words and phrases were less friendly and more formal, using phrases such as 'the course requirement is...' and 'you will need to....' Following focus groups and evaluations, adjustments were made. Students noted that there was a mismatch between the tone of the formally written module guide and the teaching sessions, evaluated as *'friendly'*. Being approachable 'on paper' as well as 'in the real' has been shown to be positively correlated with higher levels of engagement as explored by Harnish and Bridges (2011, p. 322). They identify characteristics such as 'using positive or friendly language'; 'using humour'; and 'conveying compassion' as helpful tactics (op cit: 321) and suggest:

> Indeed, care should be taken in developing the syllabus with particular attention to its tone, because impressions are made that may facilitate faculty engagement with students. Such impressions, in turn, may set the stage for a more rewarding educational experience for those on both sides of the lectern. (Harnish and Bridges 2011, p. 328)

It is not only the syllabus but also the written feedback itself where tone should be carefully considered (Crisp 2007). This is even more important as the nature of higher education shifts to include larger classes and more blended learning methods.

> The workload of tutors is growing alongside an expansion in the number of students. At the same time, the use of distance learning and new technologies is becoming more extensive. As a result, face-to-face student–tutor contact time is diminishing, leading to a greater reliance on written correspondence (whether paper-based or electronic). (Higgins et al. 2002, p. 54)

Nicol addresses both staff workload and feedback language practically through the use of peer review in order to facilitate 'moving away from a model based on teacher delivery of feedback to one based on the co-construction of feedback' (Nicol 2010, p. 515).[8]

Conclusion

Ipsative assessment has helped focus the attention of both students and tutors on ways of making clear and specific improvements to submitted work and the quality of feedback respectively. It afforded students deep learning about the subject matter and about their own learning, studying and understanding. Cumulative coversheets have provided a structure for recording and developing students' metacognition and self-regulation and documenting their progress. Students self-reported positive impact on tutorials and evaluated the module very highly.

Whilst it required adjustments to working practices and an investment of time and effort in feedback and building relationships, this was put to good effect. The experience of using ipsative assessment had an additional benefit of reminding tutors that getting to know individual learners and responding to their needs pays off handsomely in terms of student engagement and commitment. 'Ipsative marking emphasizes the lecturers' involvement with, and commitment to, the students' development over time' (Orr 2007, p. 653). Finally, in this case study, the adoption of a friendlier and more personal tone over the years seems to have gone hand in hand with better student achievement and resulted in a good atmosphere in class with high levels of participation and engagement.

NOTES

1. Qualitative data in the chapter are drawn from formal university-administered student evaluations and informal, in-class mid-module evaluations. Extracts from seven different focus groups are also included, from discussions held over the life of the module for various formal and informal purposes including: module review; on-going reflective evaluation of teaching methods and curriculum content; trips to museums and galleries; and efficacy of the assessment-feedback loop.

2. The module content and assessment has adapted and changed over time but has always included reviews of the places visited, plus a more general paper about broader issues in museum and gallery education. More typically, assessment for Year Two modules consists of one long essay (4000 words) and so the short-paper format offers variety. Writing multiple short papers brings with it possible benefits as well as potential additional challenges such as developing the flexibility to cope with different assessment styles.

3. An Academic Learning Advisor (ALA) helped to deliver the feedback where possible. This served to maximise the students' understanding of the feedback since having two experienced staff members present allows for more than one explanation of the points being raised. Through extensive one-to-one work with students the ALA has practical strategies to suggest and useful metaphors and analogies to help explain how to make improvements, study more 'smartly', write more clearly, manage time more efficiently and answer the question more fully, yet succinctly, etc.

4. Ipsative assessment chimes with the work of Dweck around the value of cultivating flexible mindsets (Dweck 2012).

5. For the last three years, the face-to-face meetings have also been digitally recorded and emailed to the students following feedback from students that they do not always remember everything that has been said. This has been described as *'the most useful type of feedback that I can replay when it suits me and when I need a blast of motivation'*.
6. For more detail on this, see Nicol who explores this in depth, citing Laurillard's work on dialogue and the 'goal-action-feedback cycle' (2010, p. 503).
7. Being able to transfer what has been understood to other modules is helpful. This can be evaluated through synoptic assessment which enables students to show their ability to integrate their learning and apply it across their programme (QAA 2006, Section 7). For ipsative assessment to be fully of value, it would be worth seeing how well the improvements transfer across all spheres of study.
8. Some peer review has been used on the module, with varying degrees of success, but the material does not lend itself to this style of working as much as other modules. See Nicol (2010) for some useful discussions of pros and cons of peer review particularly in large group teaching.

References

Biggs, J. (1993). What do inventories of students' learning process really measure? A theoretical review and clarification. *British Journal of Educational Psychology*, *83*, 3–19.

Bjork, R. A., Dunlosky, J., & Kornell, N. (2013). Self-regulated learning: Beliefs, techniques, and illusions. *Annual Review of Psychology*, *64*, 417–444.

Boud, D. (1995). Assessment and learning: Contradictory or complementary? In P. Knight (Ed.), *Assessment for learning in higher education* (pp. 35–48). London: Kogan Page.

Brown, E., & Glover, C. (2006). Evaluating written feedback. In C. Bryan & K. Clegg (Eds.), *Innovative assessment in higher education* (pp. 81–91). Abingdon, Routledge.

Brown, S., & Knight, P. (1994). *Assessing learners in higher education*. Oxford: Routledge Falmer.

Chanock, K. (2000). Comments on essays: do students understand what tutors write?. *Teaching in Higher Education*, *5*(1), 95–105.

Crisp, B. R. (2007). Is it worth the effort? How feedback influences students' subsequent submission of assessable work. *Assessment & Evaluation in Higher Education*, *32*(5), 571–581.

Dweck, C. S. (2012). *Mindset: How you can fulfill your potential*. New York: Random House.

Harnish, R., & Bridges, K. R. (2011). Effect of syllabus tone: Students' perceptions of instructor and course. *Social Psychology of Education*, *14*(3), 319–330.

Harnish, R. J., O'Brien McElwee, R., Slattery, J. M., Frantz, S., Haney, M. R., Shore, C. M., et al. (2011). Creating the foundation for a warm classroom climate: Best practices in syllabus tone. *Association for Psychological Science Observer, 24*, 23–27.

Higgins, R., Hartley, P., & Skelton, A. (2002). The conscientious consumer: Reconsidering the role of assessment feedback in student learning. *Studies in Higher Education, 27*(1), 53–64.

Higher Education Funding Council for England (HEFCE). (2013). *Network literature review of research into widening participation to higher education*, conducted by the 'Aimhigher Research and Consultancy'. http://www.hefce.ac.uk/media/hefce/content/pubs/indirreports/2013/Literature,review,of,WP,to,HE/Literature%20review%20of%20research%20into%20WP%20to%20HE.pdf. Accessed May 2015.

Hughes, G. (2011). Aiming for personal best: A case for introducing ipsative assessment in higher education. *Studies in Higher Education, 36*(3), 353–367.

Hughes, G., Wood, E., & Kitagawa, K. (2014). Use of self-referential (ipsative) feedback to motivate and guide distance learners. *Open Learning: The Journal of Open, Distance and e-Learning, 29*(1), 31–44.

Lublin, J. (2003). *Deep, surface and strategic approaches to learning (good practice in teaching and learning)*. Dublin: University College Dublin, Centre for Teaching and Learning.

Marton, F., & Säljö, R. (1976). On qualitative differences in learning – 1: Outcome and process. *British Journal of Educational Psychology, 46*, 4–11.

Nicol, D. (2010). From monologue to dialogue: improving written feedback processes in mass higher education. *Assessment & Evaluation in Higher Education, 35*(5), 501–517.

Nordrum, L., Evans, K., & Gustafsson, M. (2013). Comparing student learning experiences of in-text commentary and rubric-articulated feedback: Strategies for formative assessment. *Assessment & Evaluation in Higher Education, 38*(8), 919–940.

Orr, S. (2007). Assessment moderation: constructing the marks and constructing the students. *Assessment and Evaluation in Higher Education, 32*(6), 645–656.

Quality Assurance Agency (QAA). (2006). *Code of practice for the assurance of academic quality and standards in higher ducation*. Gloucester: Quality Assurance Agency for Higher Education.

Sadler, D. R. (1989). Formative assessment and the design of instructional systems. *Instructional Science, 18*, 119–144.

Teaching and Learning Research Programme (TLRP). (2009). *Widening participation in higher education: A commentary by the teaching and learning research programme*. http://www.tlrp.org/pub/documents/HEcomm.pdf. Accessed June 2015.

Thompson, S., Milsom, C., Zaitseva, E., Stewart, M., Darwent, S., & Yorke, M. (2013). *The forgotten year? Tackling the second year slump* Liverpool John

Moores University/higher education academy. https://www.heacademy.ac. uk/project/7903. Accessed May 2015.

Tinto, V. (1993). *Leaving college: Rethinking the causes and cures of student attrition*. 2nd edition. Chicago: University of Chicago Press.

Walker, M. (2009). An investigation into written comments on assignments: Do students find them usable?. *Assessment & Evaluation in Higher Education, 34*(1), 67–78.

Weaver, M. (2006). Do students value feedback? Student perceptions of tutors' written responses. *Assessment and Evaluation in Higher Education, 31*(3), 379–394.

Dr Carrie Winstanley is Principal Lecturer at Roehampton University, London, UK. She works with undergraduate and postgraduate students and has responsibilities for supporting staff in developing practice. She is interested in pedagogy, and creating challenge, particularly for able learners with learning difficulties, disabilities and disadvantage. Carrie is an Executive Council member of the Philosophy of Education Society of Great Britain. Her monograph *The Ingredients of Challenge* (2010, Trentham Books) investigates ways of providing worthwhile challenge for children in schools. This follows from her co-edited collection considering the role of Philosophy in Schools (Bloomsbury, with Hand, 2008).

CHAPTER 5

Raising Self-Efficacy Through Ipsative Assessment and Feuerstein's Instrumental Enrichment Programme

Kit McIntyre

INTRODUCTION AND RATIONALE FOR THE ROYAL OAK PROJECT

Throughout my teaching career I have always been aware of the effects of standardised tests on the self-efficacy of my students. There were always winners or losers in the standardised methods of assessment. The extraordinary and diverse abilities of my students were often hidden in an assessment system that had quite specific criteria and a timed gateway. Searching for more effective methods of assessment, I first encountered the concept of Ipsative Assessment in Gwyneth Hughes' 2014 publication *'Ipsative Assessment: Motivation through Marking Progress'* and developed a new mindset.

Ipsative assessment is the measurement of an individual's own progress against his or her personal best. It fosters a 'strengths-based'

K. McIntyre (✉)
SENCO (Special Education Needs Co-ordinator) and Teacher School: Woodlands Park School, Titirangi, Auckland, New Zealand
e-mail: eddiemc@slingshot.co.nz

© The Author(s) 2017
G. Hughes (ed.), *Ipsative Assessment and Personal Learning Gain*,
DOI 10.1057/978-1-137-56502-0_5

85

perspective when defining the learning ability of the individual. Ipsative assessment was selected as the best assessment approach for the Royal Oak Project in New Zealand (NZ) because it measured present performance against prior performance for the student. This form of assessment is not concerned with the student's assessment related to his or her peers. I was particularly drawn to the potential for developing a strong self-belief in the students by using ipsative assessment. Albert Bandura, Department of Psychology, Stanford University, has defined self-efficacy as a motivational force. He has found that the more capable people believe themselves to be the higher the goals they set for themselves (Bandura 1991).

At the same time I also encountered the theories of Professor Reuven Feuerstein and began to question how the assessment practices in my classroom should alter. I know that one of the greatest challenges in teaching is the need to recognise the learning barriers our students face if we are to assist progress. This challenge can be even more difficult when assessment is only focused on correct and speedy answers. The learning struggle is necessary for progress and can be seen in the differing cultural perspectives of the East and West. James Stigler, Professor of Psychology at the University of California, Los Angeles, describes the learning struggle as a predictable part of the learning process. This struggle is often viewed by the West as the indicator of a low intelligence whereas in the East the struggle can be perceived as an opportunity to show your prowess in emotional resolve and persistence.

Ahead of his own time, Feuerstein also described this struggle in the 1950s. He viewed the struggle as the most important part of learning because it involved the student's journey of metacognition and his or her perception of success. When self-efficacy is not in place the motivation to learn is missing, students will often withdraw from tasks, avoiding challenges and group participation. A fixed mindset of what they can and cannot do is very entrenched.

These influences led me to the research project at Royal Oak Intermediate School. The overall goal of the project was to develop students who could problem solve before acting and could analyse their tasks and stimuli confidently. This chapter explores the results, the methods and learning journey of the students through their tasks and through their self-assessments and written reflections.

THE PARTICIPANTS OF THE ROYAL OAK PROJECT

The class consisted of academically able students from diverse cultures ranging from Samoan, Tongan, Fijian and Cook Island Maori to a minority group of three Asian and two Russian students. The setting for the project was a classroom in a centrally urban area of Auckland. With the support of the School's Board, Senior Management Team, parents and the students themselves, we embarked on a three month learning journey together. The project was designed to determine if:

1. Explicit teaching of Metacognition through Feuerstein's Mediated Learning Experience (MLE) would increase the academic performance and strategies of the students.
2. Self-efficacy could be enhanced through ipsative assessment.
3. Feuerstein's Instrumental Enrichment (FIE) would transcend cultural barriers to positively impact the academic learning of the Pasifika students in the class.

Feuerstein's Instrumental Enrichment programme provides fourteen instruments; four of these were selected for this project. They were Organisation of Dots, Comparisons, Orientation in Space and Analytic Perception. They provided the students the opportunity to develop self-efficacy, achieve the internalisation of a sophisticated vocabulary and to develop metacognitive awareness.

In this project the students were clear from the outset that they were measuring their own performance and that no one was judging their level of competence. Instead they were encouraged to self-assess their on-going metacognition and measure their increasing confidence in the tasks set. Throughout the three months of the project the students were never given teacher feedback regarding their individual performance, the focus was on developing their self-assessment skills. Interestingly, although the students were only 11–12 years of age, their written reflections provided articulate and insightful comments regarding their own progress and that of their peers. As the project progressed the students corrected errors in their own thinking, either by hearing the concepts explained in another way, experiencing accuracy when working on the instruments, or watching peers explain and demonstrate their alternative strategies at the whiteboard.

BACKGROUND TO THE THEORY AND THE TOOLS USED
IN THE PROJECT

To best understand the purpose of the project it is necessary here to present some background regarding the inspiration for it, the legacy and theories of Reuven Feuerstein.

Reuven Feuerstein was a Cognitive Psychologist, Nobel Prize Nominee, genius, and for the many children he encountered in his life a beneficent 'Pied Piper'. Undeniably a humanitarian, Feuerstein transformed lives. He believed in the achievement of Special Needs children, even when no one else thought their progress was possible. Feuerstein was mentored by Jean Piaget at the University of Geneva. He would later part from Piaget's work and develop his own theories in the 1950s. Feuerstein's altruism was evident when he first encountered the surviving child victims of the Holocaust. These traumatised children were suffering from unimaginable human loss. He was faced with the question: 'How could they now learn and reintegrate into a meaningful life?'

It was very obvious that conventional forms of assessment would not be effective in determining the learning level or emotional needs of these displaced and damaged children. He could see that the traditional methods of assessment were inadequate indicators for the learning propensity and Intelligence Quotient (IQ) of these children. At this time 'Static Testing', which is testing with no intervention from the assessor and a focus on standardised results, was the predominant practice.

In response Feuerstein began to formulate his theory and design a method of assessment which was culturally universal. The Holocaust children had received no mediation of their own culture. The natural transference of family culture from parent to child had been disrupted and as a result their history and family values were now disjointed. Feuerstein knew cultural development can be interrupted or worse not transmitted due to many causes such as poverty, social discrimination and the bias of the dominant educational system. He believed that there was a collision of past, present and future when the parent was not the one to initiate their child into the structure of society. He knew assessment would be more successful if the content was not linked to a specific culture or linguistic system. A focus for the Royal Oak Project was to explore the 'handing down' of culture, or loss of it, with this predominantly Pasifika group.

This class were of particular interest because they were high achieving, motivated Pasifika students, defying a stereotype. Pasifika students are classified as those who have moved to New Zealand (NZ) from Polynesia or identify with a Pacific Island heritage. Statistics record that Pasifika students have been under-performing in the NZ education system (Ministry of Education, NZ (a)).

The students in the Royal Oak Project were clearly able to articulate their progress and identify their learning. It is generally acknowledged that there is a bias in NZ's assessment systems favouring English as the first language and the promotion of a culture historically connected to Britain. Throughout this project, however, the Pasifika students in the class were highly engaged and reflective in the course. This group were already a high achieving cohort of students so their progress was to be expected.

Further time and focus would be needed to ascertain the breadth of impact that Feuerstein's Instrumental Enrichment training could have on long-term academic and cultural goals for this group. I could not gather meaningful evidence in the cultural 'handing down' of cultural practice in this project due to the short timeframe.

I knew from previous experience that Pasifika students are very aware of the needs of the community over self and that this would probably manifest itself in the classroom. In Polynesian culture status has a high priority. For Pasifika students, interrupting an adult or elder when speaking is highly disrespectful. Rules around showing humility in the Polynesian and Maori culture can be enigmatic and misunderstood in the classroom. This misunderstanding can alter a teacher's perception. For example, the lack of shared oral participation in the classroom can be misinterpreted as disinterest. In general the girls' lack of responses in class discussions was apparent, but their written reflections revealed that they were actually fully engaged in their learning. I came to understand that for most of the girls their cultural heritage was manifesting itself in their respectful silence. It is not unusual for Pasifika students to sit silently and listen in class.

Aware of the importance of heritage, Feuerstein believed in adding value to the existing cultural context and not erasing it. I believed that *plural identity* could possibly cause disequilibrium for the Pasifika students in the group and made reference to Polynesian history whenever possible. As a result the class studied the wayfaring skills and ancient knowledge of the Polynesian Navigators, highly acclaimed for their skills. They 'bridged' their new knowledge to ancient Polynesian themes. This included specific knowledge such as the use of Mattangs, which are ancient Polynesian structures for measuring wave movement around an island, how constellations were used as markers in open ocean and the use of compass notches on a canoe. A new pride in the knowledge once held by their ancestors was referred to by some of the students in their summative appraisals.

THE USE OF FEUERSTEIN'S TOOLS AND THEORIES IN THE PROJECT

To remove the cultural bias in assessment, Feuerstein devised a set of tools that provided a platform for teachers to use (Feuerstein et al. 1980). The tools increase in complexity with carefully gradated levels of challenge, this set of instruments was collectively called Feuerstein's Instrumental Enrichment (FIE). Alongside these teaching tools he also developed a method of interactive and mediated learning called the Mediated Learning Experience (MLE). Both tools MLE and FIE were always delivered with the transference of the new knowledge to the curriculum in class. An example of transferring prior knowledge and making a comparison is recorded here by James, an 11-year-old Chinese boy:

> I learnt that the 1, 1, 2, 3, 5, 8, 13...sequence is called the Fibonacci sequence. I notice it is also like the Pascal Triangle.

Another crucial aspect of the project was the decision not to provide individual feedback or critique in the project, instead mediator assessments were class wide and were used to inform the next steps only. This allowed the students an opportunity to focus on their own progress and develop their confidence at their own pace. Self-efficacy increased with the successful completion of each task for the students, evident in their excited responses and requests for more tasks.

MEDIATED LEARNING EXPERIENCE

MLE is an interactive experience for both the Mediator (teacher) and the student. Feuerstein refers to mediation as an intervention that allows the student to access and engage with external stimuli. In this method the Mediator enters into a learning and assessment process with the student that can best be described as a dance.

During the mediation process, the Mediator and student are altered by each other. The Mediator joins into the process of learning and makes simultaneous assessments by inviting the student to explore the environment with prompting, guiding and questioning. The student is asked to do an analysis of the situation and the stimuli using inductive and deductive reasoning and by seeking the logical evidence in his or her responses.

The Principles of MLE

Feuerstein's theories in mediation also include a focus on targeting our Cognitive Functions in three phases, Input (Data gathering), Elaboration (i.e. mental manipulation of the data) and Output (communication of the final product to others). The Royal Oak Intermediate Project focused on how these three phases in the learning process could be enhanced. It quickly emerged that the key mediation foci for this particular class would be around impulsivity, precision and articulation at the output level.

The project had at its core Feuerstein's three principles of mediation:

1. Intentionality and reciprocity: This refers to the intent of the mediator and the receptiveness of the student to the mediated stimuli. As time passed the students began to enjoy the tasks for their intrinsic challenges.
2. Meaning: This refers to mediating the significance and meaning of the stimuli for the student. It was necessary to give the students the terminology first and then connect that terminology to the concept through a matching task. The tasks in the Instruments lead to the conversations that become the most exciting part of the mediation.
3. Transcendence: This refers to the transference of a concept to a new context. The ability of the students to transfer their knowledge to another principle or concept was evident in the majority of their written reflections.

Key mediation goals for developing the student's self-assessment skills were focused on the reinforcement of flexibility in thinking, the ability to recognise and change strategies that don't work, and behavioural self-regulation. The students would voluntarily choose to work in silence during the individual thinking tasks; they concentrated intensely without prompting. After the tasks they were encouraged to discuss and compare discoveries with their peers. They developed the need to give logical evidence in their descriptions and in their answers, reasoning became an important factor in their ability to successfully communicate with each other.

The Need for Labelling

The explicit use of sophisticated vocabulary to inform new concepts was an important part of the dialogic teaching process of the project. As they gained the vocabulary it was easier for the students to assess their own errors and their own progress. It became very apparent that the focus on the 'labelling' of the terms was crucial. Terminology was taught quite explicitly at that start of every session. One or two words were introduced daily and reinforced until the students grasped their meanings. The words were written on the whiteboard, discussed and explained, students would then do a correlating page in their Instrument followed by a debrief session. In time we had gathered a large enough repertoire in Feuerstein's language to effectively converse together.

Our minds generate understanding based on the level of abstraction in words. The need for 'labelling' concepts and terminology in the mediation process was brought home to me when strolling one day hand in hand with my grandson Lucas on a local beach. I had asked him to tell me what colour the shells were on a beach, he immediately looked down and said '*white.*'

I asked him to look again and we crouched down to pick some up. '*Oh!*' he exclaimed excitedly, '*They are orange, black and green too.*'

Feuerstein referred to this as Spontaneous Comparative Behaviour. He believed that the development of thinking skills in children was greatly enhanced by teaching the skills of comparison.

Later I discussed this incident with a Master Trainer from the Feuerstein Institute, Keith Prowell. He asked me if I had told Lucas at the time that we were 'differentiating'.

I replied: '*But he's only three, surely that word is too complex for him to learn?*'

Keith's reply became an embedded focus in my future teaching. He asked '*Did your grandson have the concept of the comparison?*' I replied he had. His response was: '*Then why did you withhold the label that would enhance his understanding?*'

I reflected that I had often over-simplified many concepts for students assuming that was the best approach. With further training in Feuerstein's theories I discovered the importance of labelling. I came to realise that without labels the brain cannot use or manipulate the concepts at a higher level. I no longer withhold the abstract labels, instead I mediate their meaning.

During the project the students became particularly aware of the abstract quality of words and this was evident in Diana's reflection. Diana, a 12-year-old Cook Island Maori girl, understood and demonstrated that the meaning of words can be misinterpreted by an individual due to their own level of perception; she became mindful of this whenever she was communicating with others:

> Today I learnt that people can have many images in the mind when a simple word is written. Although some ideas were similar no one's image was the same.

IPSATIVE ASSESSMENT

In keeping with the philosophy of ipsative assessment I removed all aspects of peer competition from the project. The students measured their progress from task to task against their own increasing awareness and new knowledge. Competition as a motivator was simply not needed in this context, the intrinsic desire to achieve created by the Instruments was enough. The desire to improve in tasks, and thus to feel an increasing sense of competence, was motivational in itself.

In the past I have seen the way competitive learning has the potential to undermine the efforts of the less confident students, they would inevitably lose heart and withdraw interest. They tended not to try again. The continual bombardment of failure in academic results is demoralising. When students are measured against peers it can also have a life-long and crippling impact. It is not that unusual to hear an intelligent and creative adult declare that they are no good at maths regardless of the fact they inevitably employ some form of mathematics on a daily basis and have not experienced mathematics lessons in decades.

Although I acknowledge the value of competition when a student can productively pace themselves against a peer, I found that even the students who saw themselves as the most able had never learned how to fail. This impeded their ability to recognise the value in analysing their mistakes and developing perseverance. Seeking the praise of their teacher was overly important so even impartial critiques were crushing. In my experience well-meaning parental expectations could also hinder the student's progress. Competitiveness in the classroom resulted in a 'fear of failure' mentality and a lack of risk taking by many students. Hughes (2014) reminds us that competitive assessment has a price to pay when many learners are not personally and academically fulfilled.

During the project the students were not aware of their peers' levels of achievement because any individual results were issued privately. This approach allowed them to gauge their own development in tasks and to undertake the Ravens (1936) and e-asTTle Reading Test without performance anxiety. The lack of a competitive focus provided the students with a far greater opportunity to work collaboratively, sharing ideas and strategies for mutual benefit.

DATA GATHERING ACTIVITIES DURING THE PROJECT

During the total period of three months, the students received three 45 minute sessions per week. Assessment data was gathered through the following:

1. Written student reflections and appraisals. Students recorded their feelings of competency and reflected on major learning for 5–10 minutes after each session. Mid-way through the course the students were asked to appraise their satisfaction with the programme and then mark that on a continuum line. They consistently rated themselves between 80 % and 100 % satisfied in their responses.
2. The Ravens IQ Test

This IQ test was selected due to its figural, rather than verbal, content. Accepting 'the limitations of psychometric testing' as outlined by Caroline Gipps (1994), the Ravens Test was selected specifically to assess if FIE mediation could impact student performance and was not implemented to achieve a standardised score. No assistance was provided during the testing, the students worked silently for approximately 30 minutes.

The Ravens Test was administered again eight weeks later after brief exposure to Feuerstein's extension work (Variations 2). These results displayed an increase in performance for 75 % of the students. The results showed an overall 10.6 % increase in the scores of the class as a whole over a 3-month period.

3. E-asTTle Reading Test. The students received Feuerstein lessons in lieu of two thirds of their reading sessions for eight weeks. E-asTTle

Reading tests (Ministry of Education, NZ (b)), administered in many NZ schools, were used as pre and post-test and administered by the school. The results showed significant changes in approach and despite the short time frame an increase in 1–2 sublevels was noted for 67 % of the students tested.

4. A standardised FIE task to determine speed and accuracy. The students were given Page 7 of the 'Organisation of Dots' Instrument as a timed pre – and post-test. The tasks in the Organisation of Dots requires the students to identify and outline within an amorphous cloud of dots, a series of overlapping geometric shapes such as squares, triangles, diamonds and stars (Feuerstein, Falik & Rand 2006, p. 215)

5. Anecdotal information regarding student participation. Impartial observers were requested to view the class in action and record empirical data. Observers remarked on the engagement and the sophistication of the language used by the students.

6. Mediator reflections were gathered in the form of a daily journal and lesson planning.

WHAT THE STUDENTS REPORTED

Recognising Progress Through Comparisons

The students were clear that they were measuring their own performance and their written reflections were astute. For example Helen, a Chinese girl aged 12 years, describes how willing she was to take risks:

Today I was very impulsive because I was nervous and wanted to get a head start. I managed to finish page 7. I realised that it was a lot easier than the first time I did it. I stuck with my plan and it worked throughout the whole page.

I was exceptionally proud of our class test results as we made huge improvement. I can't wait to try a new instrument next week. When I took the first glance at the C-10 question I was clueless. In the end it was a hard choice between 2 answers. Luckily I had a strong confident friend who persuaded me with her logical evidence, and I agreed with it a hundred per cent. We looked at how to compare and contrast. I was a bit afraid to put my hand up, because I have to be really precise. Hopefully I'll be able to take risks more often.

Helen realised that sometimes it can be a challenging choice when there are two answers closely aligned and she needed to compare and differentiate between her choices carefully. She will be able to recognise this again in another context if her self-efficacy remains intact. She was open to the persuasion of a peer based on his logic. She showed that she was perceptually aware of others. Her written reflection allowed me to view rich information about the way she processed external information. Knowledge of MLE enabled me to assess the clues in her responses.

The students were not only self-reflective, but peer mediation also became a natural and productive aspect of learning for these students. Group work changed from the issuing of traditional roles such as leader, scribe, organiser, etc. to an arena where the group actively listened to the person with the 'best' logical evidence.

Slowing Down and Attention to Detail

Planning, finding reference points, the use of comparison and defining a problem were all thinking processes explicitly taught in the FIE programme. Lessons were based on 'bridging' specific concepts to new contexts. In Feuerstein's Instrumental Enrichment Programme the levels of abstraction, complexity and novelty in tasks are planned for. It became apparent there was a need for these students to slow down and search systematically for reference points. They needed to determine the 'novelty' by scanning the differences and similarities to previous work or pages and then analyse exactly what the task was asking of them. For example Rose, a European girl aged 11 years, consistently used the FIE language accurately and formed strategies for her tasks. Rose recognised that by focusing too hard in one area she had missed the big picture.

> Today's focus was all about precision. I realised that I was focusing on just one area and was blocking out all of the other possibilities of the shapes. I then applied 'conservation of constancy' to my strategy and I was able to come up with more shapes. Although I didn't do much, I still feel proud because of my strategy and reflecting during the task.

Mediating an attention to detail for these students meant a focus on accuracy because even when students have success they may not recognise why. Asking the students to explain further, even when they were already correct, helped their metacognition. The students noted that they had improved their e-asTTle Reading Test performance due to their focus on minimising impulsive behaviours; they slowed down when reading instructions and used structural analysis to break down comprehension questions.

Many of the students reflected that the mediation had an effect on how they now approached their summative academic tests in class and their subsequent classwork. Any incorrect answers offered exciting opportunities to back-track and discover which of the cognitive functions was involved. Feuerstein proposed that we do not have to assume that failures are due to a low IQ or lack of understanding around the content, but instead to consider that there was in play a cognitive function which needed to be developed or modified.

As the Mediator I also kept a reflection journal. I appreciated the opportunity to witness the self-efficacy developing in each student so quickly. I was particularly impressed by the way the students were so receptive to the ideas of others. Greta, Samoan girl aged 12 years, demonstrates the confidence to speak up:

Today I learnt the definitions of new vocabulary such as Gestalt, logical evidence, transcendence, and word association. During the 'Variations' pages I could see that James had a different answer to mine so I persuaded him and my group to change using logical evidence and with words like elimination and infer, in the end everyone in my group agreed with me.

Greta developed thinking skills that began with an elimination process first and then developed more effective strategies. She was a quiet girl who became increasingly confident in her ability. Greta found the voice to persuade others and consequentially her self-efficacy and presence in the classroom grew.

I found that teaching metacognition was a very uplifting process because the Instruments generated valuable insights. By the end of the project, I noticed there was an intrinsic desire to 'beat' the challenge of the pages so the student motivation to do the tasks was consistently high. The phrase 'Stop and Think' became a classroom mantra.

In the beginning, some of the students articulated that they were hesitant to raise their hand to give an answer because they knew there would be further, probing questions such as: *'Why is that so?'* or: *'Are you able to give some logical evidence to show that?'*. In time they had confidence in their answers and practised presenting their oral answers in a defined and succinct manner.

For example, Antony, a Samoan boy aged 12 years, displayed quick visual perception. I knew that at a more challenging level this was not always going to work for him and noticed he struggled to give detailed answers in class. To mediate this he was set the task of mindfully reviewing the strategies he was using and then articulating his process to the class. He enjoyed the challenge and over time improved the detail of his replies, altering his language to use more specific terms and vocabulary. He moved from saying *'That thing down there'* when pointing to the whiteboard, to saying: *'I am referring to the black, vertical line which is situated on the far left of the whiteboard, and is south of the equilateral triangle which you have just drawn.'*

Developing Self-Assessment

The goal was always to encourage the students to assess themselves and to acknowledge surpassing their personal best. A developing confidence in his ability is evident in Isaac's reflection below. Isaac, a Russian boy aged 11 years, emerged early in the project as an alternative thinker and a highly intelligent student.

> It was very interesting doing the Analytical Perception page because I like to synthesise the columns together. It was fun talking about Feuerstein in our real life use. I am training my brain to think in a smarter, more systematic way to help me in life. It allows me to think in a higher order way and a lot of the things we learn can help us in tests and other things. I feel as though my IQ has risen just by being here! I know it has helped because I am able to use the language in normal speech and I am able to complete puzzles I couldn't do before.

Isaac's feelings of competence grew visibly in class interactions, he had temporal concepts in place and could visualise using new strategies in the future. Isaac was able to justify how and why he was improving. This is an example of ipsative self-assessment; Isaac is successfully and mindfully assessing his own progress.

Awareness of Others

Continued mediation for Isaac included a deeper awareness of his class-mates. He could be quite esoteric in his answers. He answered in great depth and with insight but at such a higher order level that he left his peers confused. He had an excellent bank of general and science based knowledge to draw on for his age. He transcended concepts with ease and could confidently demonstrate his thinking strategies. With regard to his self-efficacy I noticed he was reluctant to write, previous failures and a lack of ability in articulating specific detail in his responses had taken their toll. I mediated by asking him to specifically focus on how he was answering and consciously focus on the likely perspective of those the others who were listening. With practice and the resulting awareness of his peers he became more articulate and less egocentric in his perspective.

Through his mediation the others in the class also gained an awareness of how they were communicating. A highlight in the project included an unexpected demonstration by Isaac and a fellow student who confidently collaborated and explained the Liar and the Grandfather paradox to the delight of their class.

Assessment during class time was targeted at the class wide impulsivity in answers. We focused on any inability to define the problem or poor verbal tools in articulating a detailed and precise answer. Curiously, the lack of precision in verbal responses was prevalent in the most academically able boys. Further discussions with their teacher confirmed the same lack of detail in their written work.

The development of self-efficacy in the group was particularly noticeable in the comments and results recorded by Thomas, an 11-year-old European student. He struggled at the start of the programme and considered himself to be the lowest achiever in the class. His self-esteem was low. Interestingly by the end of the project his test and task results were radically improved. He achieved a score of 35 % in the initial Ravens Test and 74 % in his retest.

> Today I learnt how our brain sees things and it was very interesting, also the test was very interesting. My thinking was so fast and I found relationships and used a systematic search.

Thomas understood the need to link relationships visually and use a system in his tasks. His growing confidence was clearly evident. His self-image noticeably changed with the undeniable evidence of his increased successes and results.

Being Logical and Systematic with the Instruments

Pursuing logical evidence was a large part of group work. These students clearly enjoyed learning about their own thinking processes. As part of the 'bridging' process from the Instruments into the NZ Curriculum for the group, their reading teacher introduced a class novel which was themed around ancient Polynesian wayfaring. As a qualified Educational Psychologist she was particularly skilled in the use of Socratic questioning, this was evident during follow up sessions with the class. Impressively the students could connect their answers regarding the novel to the Organisation of Dots Instrument.

Another popular Instrument with this class was the Comparisons Instrument. When using this instrument I particularly enjoyed teaching superordinates: the students were encouraged to think about categorisation and classification at the highest level. They were getting used to comparison as a thinking process and successfully compared two images, Paul Gauguin's 'When Will You Wed?' and Kandinsky's 'Composition IV'. They used their new knowledge of structural analysis to compare both paintings, particularly in terms of the superordinates of colour, shape, line and direction only. This increased their ability to think in the abstract. The task also led to a discussion about the difference between representation and reality.

Mediating Mathematics was easier using the Instruments. We developed terminology in mathematical discussions or when recognising patterns, completing sequences, defining the characteristics of geometric shapes. They improved their ability to describe the direction and labelling of a line accurately. Mediating the Spatial Orientation instrument involved hands on experiences with the use of compasses and maps, etc.

Interestingly throughout the project the class continually asked to do more pages from the Organisation of Dots Instrument. The growth of their self-efficacy through this Instrument was easy to view and as a result they confidently tackled the other tasks. They often commented that they were beginning to enjoy the process of reflecting on their thinking. They were motivated to write. I noted the change in volume and sophistication in each of the students' journals over the time of the project.

Through their written statements for each session I could assess if the students were developing their metacognitive language. For example in the following self-reflection it was evident that Zoe, a 12-year-old Fijian girl, could describe the transference of concepts. She demonstrated that she had a developing understanding of inductive and deductive reasoning. She recognised that she could break something down to its smallest components to build a concept again and could articulate that:

> Today we learnt about Analytic Perception, I think this means when you break a picture apart to bring out the answer. We used jigsaw pieces as an example. Our mediator has taught us the possibilities when you see things, I think those possibilities can be used anywhere, especially in my learning.

I did not share my responses with the students at the time because I did not want to interfere with their growing skills in self-assessment. The students could highlight for themselves most of the areas that needed further mediation. Errors became a source of information and not a source of shame for the students so their dignity remained intact. Organising students into streamed academic 'ability' groups seemed now to be a less effective method of doing assessment in a classroom.

In Conclusion: The Benefits of Feuerstein's Strength-Based and Interactive Assessment Methods

Feuerstein's theories offered a new way of looking at student output in the project and for assessing their propensity. I gained invaluable insight into the students' abilities as a partner rather than as an authority figure in the classroom. Within every interaction the Mediator is simultaneously assessing Feuerstein's Cognitive Functions. These are observed through the students' statements or actions. As a Mediator you are in a state of high interest throughout the process which improves task satisfaction for both parties.

This form of interactive mediation and contextual assessment is echoed in Feuerstein's assessment method, which he termed the Learning Propensity Assessment Device (LPAD) (Feuerstein, Feuerstein, Falik & Rand, 2002). Propensity is defined here as proclivity or inclination towards learning. I was personally fortunate enough to be trained in this form of Dynamic Assessment by Dr. Louis Falik, Senior Scholar at the Feuerstein Institute, distinguished psychologist, confidante and colleague to Reuven Feuerstein. The theory of Dynamic Assessment had a strong influence on my co-constructivist philosophy and approach to this project.

Matthew Poehner, Assistant Professor of World Languages Education and Applied Linguistics at The Pennsylvania State University, has researched the role of Dynamic Assessment in second language development. He explains that Dynamic Assessment is based in the Vygotskian notion of the Zone of Proximal Development (ZPD) and that it offers a framework for co-construction with learners, simultaneously revealing the full range of their abilities and promoting development (Poehner 2008).

Ipsative and Dynamic Assessment are both designed to promote a productive 'strengths-based' approach to learning. During the interactive process of Dynamic Assessment the assessor can see if the student can internalise a strategy and gain the required language to continue the test. The increasing confidence of the student throughout this type of inter-active assessment offers a further growth in self-efficacy. As with ipsative assessment, Dynamic Assessment ensures that dignity and insight are at the core of any assessment process.

During the project it became apparent that Feuerstein's MLE programme created such 'feelings of competency' and self-efficacy in the students that they were eventually taking risks by answering confidently in class. The evidence of student self-efficacy was apparent in their remarks in class and their copious written reflections. The classroom teacher reported that they had a willingness to adopt new thinking strategies in mathematics and writing and this was also described by the students. The students reported a confidence in their improved performance and an emerging sense of control across their curriculum work. In debriefing sessions the students generally concurred that they had a new control over their learning behaviours, especially in tests.

The class dynamic during the tasks was very cohesive and supportive because the focus was not on competitive behaviours or extrinsic reward. As a result the students successfully collaborated, shared their strategies and supported the growth of skills and ideas in each other. From the written reflections it was clear that every student in the class, regardless of level, was aware that he or she was achieving and surpassing their personal best in every session. There is evidence here that ipsative assessment is motivational for all learners and not only for high achievers (Hughes 2014).

Despite varying levels of competence all of the students were engaged in the Instruments and responded immediately to the intrinsic challenges. There was an instant gratification and a desire to increase the level of challenge. They were consistently keen to prove their skills indicating that their self-efficacy had in fact increased. The class confidently used a sophisticated vocabulary well above their expected age level in other areas of their learning.

The project at Royal Oak Intermediate School became a vehicle for improving my skills as a teacher because the process was so interactive. The project confirmed for me that a 'one size fits all' method of assessment is out of step with a modern teaching pedagogy, a pedagogy which promotes individualisation (personalised learning) and differentiation in teaching. I am grateful to the students and the school for their willingness to take a risk and trial something new. It is hoped the students will continue to use the metacognition they have gained as they progress through their school life, and that they will always retain the feelings of self-efficacy they have developed at this young age. I am indebted to them for the lessons they have taught me.

REFERENCES

Bandura, A., (1991). *Self-Regulation of Motivation Through Anticipatory and Self-Reactive Mechanisms*. Stanford University.

Feuerstein, R., Falik, L., & Rand, Y. (2006). The Feuerstein Instrumental enrichment program. In *Revised version of instrumental enrichment: An intervention program for cognitive modifiability 1980*. Jerusalem: ICELP Press.

Feuerstein, R., Feuerstein, R., Falik, L., & Rand, Y. (2002). *The dynamic assessment of cognitive modifiability*. Jerusalem: The ICELP Press.

Feuerstein, R., Rand, Y., Hoffman, M., & Miller, R. (1980). *Instrumental enrichment: An intervention program for cognitive modifiability*. Baltimore, MD: University Park Press.

Gipps, C. (1994). *Beyond testing: Towards a theory of educational assessment*. London: Falmer Press.

Hughes, G. (2014). *Ipsative assessment: Motivation through marking progress*. Basingstoke: Palgrave Macmillan.

Ministry of Education, NZ (a). *Pasifika plan* (years 2013–2017). http://www.education.govt.nz/ministry-of-education/overall-strategies-and-policies/pasifika-education-plan-2013-2017/. Accessed February 2016.

Ministry of Education, NZ (b). *E-Asttle reading test*. http://e-asttle.tki.org.nz/. Accessed February 2016.

Poehner, M. (2008). *Dynamic assessment: A Vygotskian approach to understanding and promoting L2 Development*. Pennsylvania: Springer.

Raven, J. C. (1936). *Mental tests used in genetic studies: The performances of related individuals in tests mainly educative and mainly reproductive*. M.Sc. Thesis, University of London. http://www.pearsonclinical.co.uk/Psychology/AdultCognitionNeuropsychologyandLanguage/AdultGeneralAbilities/Ravens-Progressive-Matrices/Ravens-Progressive-Matrices.aspx. Accessed February 2016.

Kit McIntyre is a Primary School teacher in New Zealand. In her career Kit has taught Art and Art History at Secondary Level, with roles as Head of Department, Dean and National Moderator. In 2005 she received the Royal Society of New Zealand Primary Science Teacher Fellowship, involving 5 invited visits to Thailand. In recent years as Team Leader Kit has specialised in teaching boys, predominantly Polynesian, who have had academic or behavioural delays. In 2014 she worked as a Resource Teacher of Learning and Behaviour. This involved support for students and their teachers in learning differences such as Autism Spectrum Disorder. She is currently pursuing her interest in Feuerstein's Thinking Skills and ipsative assessment in her classroom.

CHAPTER 6

Use of Digital Technology to Capture and Support Student Progress Across a Taught Postgraduate Programme

Gwyneth Hughes, Denise Hawkes, and Tim Neumann

INTRODUCTION

The process of learning is just as important as the measure of outcome of learning. Such a view is widely endorsed in an 'assessment for learning' movement that promotes formative assessment (Black and Wiliam 2009), and has been the cornerstone of educational development philosophy for many decades. Chapter 2 explored such interest in a learning journey or 'distance travelled' by a student. In higher education in the UK, there is growing interest in the idea of 'learning gain' as giving much more information about both learner progress and the quality of teaching than single grades and marks alone (Higher Education Funding Council for England 2015).

The chapter also explored different ways of judging learning gain. Measures of learning gain using examinations and other quantitative assessments are fraught with difficulty and much effort goes into convincing stakeholders of the reliability of marks and grades (Hughes 2014).

G. Hughes (✉) · D. Hawkes · T. Neumann
UCL Institute of Education, UCL, London, UK
e-mail: Gwyneth.hughes@ucl.ac.uk

© The Author(s) 2017   105
G. Hughes (ed.), *Ipsative Assessment and Personal Learning Gain*,
DOI 10.1057/978-1-137-56502-0_6

Feedback on assessments can also provide rich information on individual learning gain instead of, or in addition to, quantitative measures. However, a modular course design tends to discourage feedback that looks to the future (Hughes et al. 2015) and might make it difficult to track learning gain.

One potential solution to capturing the process as well as outcomes of learning is use of digital technology. Recording of marks in digital format is now commonplace, but this chapter focuses on recording feedback. The chapter begins with a discussion of how technology might support an ipsative approach to formative assessment through making feedback more accessible to both assessors and students.

The chapter will then explore a case study of the use of digital technology to review student progress in a taught postgraduate research programme using a tool to generate a feedback history record for each student. Taught postgraduate students at the UCL, Institute of Education, University College, London, submit their coursework online to a Virtual Learning Environment VLE. The current system enables students and staff to view the marks and feedback for each module of a programme, but they do not get a sense of the complete learning journey of the student. The VLE was modified so that an assessment report could be generated which made a student's marks and feedback for all assignments on all modules easy to view in one place. A feedback response form was also provided to help students reflect on what they learnt from feedback. Thus, the programme leader, the teaching team and supervisors would have an overview of the progress of each student during the taught phase of the programme. The intentions were that progress, or lack of progress, would be more visible so that students could make use of past feedback and demonstrate progress in the next assignment and that border line pass/fail cases could be reviewed in detail by a programme leader.

Introduction of a new technology may produce a combination of intended or unintended positive or negative effects that require local monitoring. The feedback recording processes were piloted with a group of staff and students who were interviewed about using the feedback history report and the feedback response process. While some users of the system – including students – could see the potential for feedback and performance monitoring, others raised further technical and pedagogic questions.

Although the issues raised are specific to this case study, there are some more general points that emerge. The chapter will conclude that simply making a new technology available does not cause change: use of technology is a social activity and influenced by values, custom and practice and beliefs about learning (Oliver 2013). A key lesson learnt is that it is easy to underestimate the complexity of responses from different stakeholders when introducing a simple but radical idea.

USE OF DIGITAL TECHNOLOGY TO ENHANCE IPSATIVE FORMATIVE ASSESSMENT

Ipsative Formative Assessment

It is widely recognised that at all levels, learning depends on appropriate formative assessment activity. This means that learners have opportunities to engage with feedback on their work whether from a teacher or from peers or from a self-evaluation (Black and Wiliam 2009; Molloy and Boud 2013). Feedback may be written or verbal or experienced from the learning environment (Laurillard 2012) such as a child touching something that is hot and quickly withdrawing. Irrespective of the source of feedback, there are many forms that feedback can take: it can be corrective, critiquing, praising, interrogating or developmental (Orsmond and Merry 2011; Hughes et al. 2015).

We saw in Chap. 2 that there is wide agreement that feedback should have immediate application and as a consequence feedback is often produced with a short-term developmental and often corrective aim in mind. But such a quick fix may not give learners a sense of a learning journey over time. Hughes (2014) has proposed that feedback can help a learner with an overview of not only where they are now, but also how far they have travelled and what are the appropriate next steps and goals. Focusing on progress rather than outcomes can be motivational for all learners, especially weaker learners, and even those who achieve high marks can be encouraged to raise their game.

It could be argued that grades or marks provide learners and teachers with a measure of learning gain over time and a visible means of marking progress. But to measure learning only as an increase in grades or marks is broad brush approach that omits detail of the obstacles that learners have overcome and the areas in which their skills and knowledge have blossomed. Furthermore, an increase in formally recorded grades or marks may be an unachievable goal for many learners; it may be that standards and expectations rise at the same rate as the learner becomes more proficient in the discipline. Thus, in outcomes-driven assessment any learning gain may be obscured. In schools learning gain may sometimes be explict through identified levels of literacy or mathematics, but in other forms of education a student might continue for long periods with a succession of demoralising or mediocre marks that give little indication of the development and learning that is taking place.

One way to give learners and assessors a much richer picture of the progress they are making is to ensure that feedback includes explicit references to progress – or if necessary lack of progress. This is ipsative feedback – feedback that refers to the learner's previous work or learning gain. Ipsative feedback might, for example, inform a learner about their responses and actions in relation to previous feedback. But, for feedback to be ipsative in this way it is not sufficient to consider a piece of work in isolation, an ipsative approach to formative assessment requires consideration of progress over time and several iterations of learning a particular skill or disciplinary requirement (Hughes 2014). It does not make sense to equate a short-term improvement with what might be a temporary 'blip' in progress: information on progress needs to be repeatedly gathered.

There is a big problem here. While grades and marks are recorded formally and can be made visible to students and assessors, feedback is usually hidden and if it is recorded that is done locally. Students may keep records of past feedback but, unless they are encouraged to assemble a picture of their development over time in for example a portfolio or log book, past feedback is easily 'lost' and if it is looked at once, it may never be referred to again. Teachers may keep personal records of feedback that they have provided for individual learners, but again records are easily displaced or not easily accessed or stored in one place. Teachers and students alike may rely on memory about verbal feedback with all the associated difficulties of accurate recall. Teachers also rarely have access to feedback from other sources such as peers or other colleagues so synthesising evidence of a learner's progress over time would require effort beyond what is normally expected.

The obvious solution to the invisibility and inaccessibility of feedback in this longer term view of learning is to capture and store feedback in a centralised place. The question then becomes one of which technologies might enable a feedback 'history' of each learner to be recorded and accessed.

Use of Digital Technology to Capture Feedback and Make It Accessible

In an age of digital learning, it is not surprising that feedback is becoming digitised. In higher education feedback no longer consists of a few scribbled and often illegible comments on a piece of writing or examination script: it is electronically produced using word-processing software and feedback pro-formas. Peer feedback and self-evaluation can occur in online discussion fora and feedback dialogue may occur in wikis, comments on blog postings, digital portfolios and other media (Rennie and Morrison 2013). Even verbal feedback can be audio-recorded and presented digitally.

But the digitisation of feedback does not necessarily mean that digital feedback is accessible and easily trackable over time to enable ipsative feedback. There remains the problem that feedback may reside in different locations which may or may not be accessible to assessors and learners. Ipsative feedback may still be a challenge in the digital world. What is needed is a technology that pulls together feedback for individual learners from many sources and presents it in an easy to access format. The obvious candidate is the widely used virtual learning environment, but these are not usually set up to capture feedback over time and if they are we know little about how feedback histories are being used, if at all. There are many questions a researcher might ask including:

1. What technologies can support the capture of feedback from different sources over time?
2. Does the capture of feedback from possibly different sources over time provide a useful 'feedback history' of a learner? If so useful for whom?
3. Does the accessibility of 'feedback histories' of individual learners facilitate an ipsative learning and assessment process?

It is worth noting here that capturing and storing feedback does not tell us anything about the quality of feedback and its relevance to overarching learning outcomes and the development of learner attributes. However, we could argue that making feedback by others – peers, teachers and self – more visible for comparative purposes is a vital step in improving feedback practice (Boud and Molloy 2013) and in developing learner understanding of the expectations of assessment (Nicol 2010).

A FEEDBACK HISTORY TOOL – HOW IT WORKS
AND ITS POTENTIAL USE

Our feedback history tool was developed rapidly as a proof of concept with minimal changes to our VLE, which is based on the Moodle platform, and taking advantage of existing functionality as much as possible. Moodle is one of the most widely used VLEs in higher education in the UK (Walker et al. 2013) and the world (Dahlstrom et al. 2014), and new third-party functionality can be added by developing a plugin, which is additional code that communicates with the VLE through standardised mechanisms. This way, the code can be transferred easily to other Moodle installations elsewhere, even though they might be configured differently.

The feedback history tool was developed in collaboration with the University of London Computing Centre (ULCC), who at the time of the pilot were hosting and maintaining our VLE. ULCC had already developed a flexible reporting plugin, to which we added our feedback history report, enabling a rapid release of the report to nominated pilot phase users, which were participating module tutors, programme leaders, and thesis supervisors. Therefore, our report only works with the ULCC reporting plugin, but the report code was later used for the development of the standalone student-facing MyFeedback Moodle plugin (Gramp and Neumann 2015).

Feedback History Report Components

The feedback history report lists the complete submission, grade and feedback history for a single student, as long as the details are stored in the VLE. Figure 6.1 represents a typical feedback history report, with multiple submission items per course, awarded grades according to the assessment item's grading scale, the assessment type, as well as submission and due dates. Submission dates in italics would normally appear red to indicate a missed due date. Underlined text in the figure represents hyperlinks to the containing course, to the assessment item, to the student's original submission file and to the teacher's feedback for the relevant assessment item. Depending on the type of assessment, that is how

Course	Assessment Name	Grade	Assessment Type	Submitted	Due Date	Submission Link	Feedback Link
Module 001	Draft Submission	C	Turnitin	14 Jan 2014 11:08 PM	14 Jan 2014 11:55 PM	JDoe-PrE21Ctry	Feedback
Module 001	Final Submission	–	Moodle Assignment	28 Feb 2014 4:49 PM	25 Feb 2014 11:55 PM	Final-JDoe	Not Graded
Module 003	DRAFT	80	Turnitin	1 May 2013 1:35 PM	26 Apr 2013 5:00 PM	JOHNDOE-mod03-draft	Feedback
Module 003	Final Assignment	A	Moodle Assignment	14 Jul 2013 8:43 AM	17 Jul 2013 5:00 PM	FinalSub-JD	Feedback
Module 006	English Interview	B	Moodle Assignment	4 Dec 2012 3:11 PM	9 Dec 2012 2:50 PM	English-self-assess	Feedback

Fig. 6.1 Feedback history tool

submissions were uploaded technically, the behaviour of the submission and feedback links might differ.

The report can be ordered by each of the columns by clicking on the column title. It therefore provides an immediate overview of the student's overall assessment performance, and teachers can quickly select the relevant items to review colleagues' feedback on previous items, thus enabling them to detect trajectories or to comment on learning gain across submissions.

User Groups

The projected user groups for the report were:

- personal tutors,
- thesis and dissertation supervisors,
- module teachers,
- programme leaders,
- academic administrators,
- external examiners,
- students.

In our pilot, we did not work with personal tutors and students, because the pilot courses did not have personal tutor arrangements and our tool could not be used by students for technical reasons.

The case for personal tutors and thesis/dissertation supervisors was clear: independent access to a review of the overall performance, or specific items, can save time in preparations for student meetings and enable these user groups to pick up on issues that the student might not report or identify, which in turn can improve the quality of the tutoring and the supervision feedback.

Module teachers are a group that needs due consideration. Access to the full assessment and feedback history would enable module teachers to implement a proper ipsative assessment strategy, as the tool would allow them to look back on, refer to and integrate previous feedback given to a student. This, however, assumes a non-anonymous marking policy, because the report would make it easy for module teachers to identify students, which might be problematic in some cases.

Academic administrators highlighted the usefulness of the compiled assessment overview as a comparator to check that data is consistent between the main registry database and the VLE. In the absence of an automatic synchronisation mechanism between these databases, still lacking in UK universities, the report simplifies manual checks.

Proposed Uses of the Tool

The tool enabled programme leaders to keep an overview of the status of submissions across multiple modules, and of the overall performance across their programme, even when a student's module choice included elective modules from other programmes. Without the tool, a programme leader would need to ask relevant programme or module leaders in person for data, and might then receive paper-based information. The feedback history report streamlined this process and thus saved time.

Student use of the feedback history tool was repeatedly requested by module teachers; however, our pilot design was incompatible with this use. However, in a survey, students indicated that access to the report might be useful from a pragmatic perspective, although they seemed to be comfortable with the existing way of accessing their results and feedback. Staff, however, hoped that students would access feedback more or more often if it was compiled on a single feedback history page. Module teachers in particular highlighted that the report would complement a new feedback response form nicely as an additional pedagogical tool, allowing students to easily go back to previous feedback in order to respond more effectively to the feedback reflection form questions. Personal tutors and supervisors might prefer students to use the report in preparation of a tutorial meeting, as they would know better which items were relevant and which were not – thus taking work away from staff. Detail about these potential affordances of the feedback history tool and the related feedback response form is explored in the case study below.

The Case Study: Applying a Feedback History Tool and a Feedback Response Form to a Professional Doctorate Programme

The Programme

The Doctor in Education programme (EdD) is a professional doctorate which has been running at UCL Institute of Education since 1996. The structure of the content on the programme can be separated into two stages: a taught stage, which consists of three courses with an assignment to complete for each that build into a portfolio of practitioner research, and a research phase which consists of two pieces of independent research – the shorter Institution Focused Study (IFS) and then the Thesis. This pilot study was applied only to the taught phase.

The EdD programme recruits around 35 students a year, each of whom have a Master's degree and at least four years professional experience in education. Many of those entering the programme each year are very experienced professionals; most have been out of formal education for some time. The taught phase of the programme is designed to help these experienced professionals to develop an academic research proposal for the research phase which will answer a problem of practice they have identified in their workplace. All EdD students are part-time and their research is usually embedded within the workplace.

The taught phase of the EdD consists of three courses. The first, Foundations of Professionalism (FoP), is designed to introduce the students to doctoral level study and provide insights to professionalism and associated theories in education. In the assignment, the students are asked to reflect on professionalism within their own area of education in light of the theories discussed. Feedback on this assignment is provided at two points. The initial draft submission provides the opportunity for the students to receive formative feedback in relation to the grade criteria and this is followed by feedback on the final piece of work. Possible transferable information in this feedback, with regard to the future courses, is largely about academic styles of writing and how to construct an academic argument.

The second course is Methods of Enquiry One (MoE1). In this course, the students are supported in developing their research focus and research questions. They are introduced to research design and strategy while thinking through the possible ethical implications of their proposed plan. In the assignment the students are asked to develop a proposal for their first piece of research, IFS. Once again they receive formative feedback on their draft and summative feedback on their final piece of work.

The final course is Methods of Enquiry Two (MoE2). In this course, the students are introduced to a wide range of research methods in education and social science. In the assignment the students are asked to undertake a pilot study for their IFS building on their proposal developed for the MoE1 assignment. The students again receive formative and summative feedback. The result of this design for the taught phase is that each assignment should ideally build on the previous one to support the students in their design for their IFS. The formative and summative feedback can be ipsative for each course and the feedback history tool should make it easier for the programme team to make feedback across the taught phase ipsative. A student feedback response form also aimed to encourage ipsative self-assessment.

Once the taught courses are completed, the students finish the taught phase of the programme by pulling together what they have learnt from the taught courses into a portfolio of practitioner research. This process involves looking back at the feedback received from all the formative and summative feedback, as well as the content of the course and assignments, to consider that they have learnt and how this will feed into their work at the research phase.

Historically, the building of the EdD portfolio was a paper based activity, with the student printing off copies of their three assignments and all feedback and adding this to a 2000 word statement. They would then give this to the supervisor to read. The supervisor would then complete the supervisor sign off form and this would be added to the other papers to be bound and submitted. This was then approved by the programme leader and passing the portfolio meant the student was ready for the research phase.

Introducing the Feedback History Tool

The feedback history tool was first introduced to the EdD programme team at a team meeting of seven academic staff, including the programme leader, as a potentially useful way of viewing student assessment data in the VLE. After a short demonstration they were asked how they might find the tool useful. The discussion was recorded with permission. Although the core team members are also supervisors, a further five of the supervisors who were not at the meeting were also introduced to the feedback history report and invited to comment on how they might use it. After being instructed by the programme leader on how to use the feedback history report, supervisors were also invited to further interviews but responses indicated that they had not used the tool so the interviews were not appropriate. Two student focus groups of a total of 18 students were also shown the tool and asked to comment on its value for them and any concerns about their assessors and supervisors using the tool. Students were also asked to comment on the feedback response form.

Programme Leader Experience

The EdD programme leader is tasked with the signing off of all the portfolios of practitioner research. In order to progress to the research stage the student needs to pass the portfolio with at least three C grades, although those obtaining three C grades or BCC at the taught courses (two students in this case study) are interviewed by the programme leader to see if they are suitable for the research phase. The EdD has an exit award (PG Diploma in Practitioner Research) for those who leave at the end of the taught phase and students with lower grade profiles are encouraged to consider this option.

There were two benefits of the feedback history tool for the Programme Leader. Firstly, signing off all the portfolios passes online made the process easier. The task could be completed anywhere where internet access was possible, as the physical portfolios did not need to be carried, and the tool provided a quick way to view the original feedback on the assignments.

The second benefit related to the identification of struggling students in preparation for the interviews. Two students were identified as BCC passes, no CCC passes were in this cohort. For the first case using the feedback history tool it was possible to see that they applied the formative feedback received to turn very weak drafts into passes. In the interview the programme leader was able to ask the student about their experiences in the taught phase and they said they had learnt a lot from the feedback, largely struggling with writing rather than a lack of understanding of the area. In light of the fact the student was able to react to feedback and was allocated to a supervisor who was able to support writing, the student was allowed to continue.

The second student clearly showed progression over the courses. Their first assignment just scraped a pass (C) but the second course was a good C and the third just scraped into the B band. It was clear from the grade profile and the feedback given that the student was improving; this was confirmed by the student in the interview that confidence had grown over the year as the student worked out the level of doctoral study. In light of the fact that the student was on a clear improving track, the student was also allowed to continue.

Overall, experience of using the feedback history tool as a programme leader was positive; it enabled the programme to make a big step towards being paperless and made tracking of student progress through the feedback significantly easier, which provided additional evidence to the student's own view on their progress over the taught phase.

Supervisor and Teaching Team Experience of the Feedback History Tool

The feedback history tool looked to be a useful device for EdD supervisors. All EdD students have a supervisor appointed at the start of their studies, who they are encouraged to meet termly to discuss their evolving research ideas in light of the taught courses. Although the EdD supervisor would have been at the recruitment interview, most have very little contact beyond the termly meetings with their EdD students until the second year when they sign off the portfolio of practice. At this point the supervisor is required to read the 2,000 word reflective statement and look through the existing assignments with feedback in order to write their own short statement on their review of their student's progress.

The supervisors who were shown the feedback history report agreed that it would be useful to have all the feedback in one place. One supervisor explained that it would help to get an overview of a recently transferred student:

> Well for example I have recently taken on an EdD student, I don't know if this would work. . . . I have taken her on quite late in the day and she is doing her thesis now but in the case that that feedback was available to me that would be inordinately helpful for me because I am new to her and her work and her style of writing.

The feedback history tool provided the team with the opportunity to remove the paper from the process and go paperless. Although there are many e-Portfolio programmes which can be used, the feedback history tool provided supervisors with a single place to access all of the submitted work and feedback, making it unnecessary for the student to print it. This was especially helpful for the third of our cohort based outside of the UK. The portfolio could then be completed with the student submitting online a 2000 word reflective statement and their supervisor statement. This substantially reduced the administration costs and time associated with the portfolio and of course reduced costs for the students in terms of the need to print and post the portfolio.

Supervisors were contacted to explain the new process, where the tool could be found and how it would be used to replace the paper-based portfolio. However interviews with supervisors after the portfolio was submitted suggested that many had not noticed the difference and found other ways, including e-mail, to get the portfolio materials they needed to assess.

In the team meeting where the feedback history report was presented to the team a senior staff member suggested that the feedback history report would be useful to enable them to review each other's feedback but the emphasis here was on consistency rather than building on the feedback of others:

> It would be very useful for making our feedback more uniform... the amount you write and the degree of detail because there is always the problem that some students say look I've only got half a side and he's got two and a half. Consistency is better for students.

Such a statement hints at a management use for the tool in monitoring the quality and quantity of staff feedback – a point which re-emerges in the next section on student views.

Student Views of the Feedback History Tool

Students were generally in favour of the feedback history report as it might encourage them to look at past feedback:

> Good idea to revisit old work so you don't make the same mistakes and build on positive feedback.

At doctoral level, students not surprisingly suggested that they already review past feedback and the tool might only make this easier rather than prompt new behaviour.

There was some concern about the feedback of all students being visible to all members of the teaching team:

> Staff may be anxious about putting feedback in writing if is more public.

This again demonstrates awareness of the potential use of feedback histories for quality monitoring of feedback.

Another student was concerned that a marker who could see past grades might be influenced but did not say whether or not this might also apply to past feedback:

> As with juror's not knowing a defendant's past, markers seeing previous grades may be influenced.

While any parallels between trial by jury and educational assessment could be extensively debated, removing the marker's access to past grades might easily dissipate this concern. For feedback history use the benefits of building on past feedback will need to be weighed against the possible influence of past feedback on grading impartiality.

Feedback Response Forms: Encouraging Cumulative Learning from Feedback for a Portfolio Assessment

While during the pilot the students did not have access to the feedback history report, the EdD programme team changed their assignment submission forms in time for the pilot. The purpose of the changes to the assignment forms was to introduce a reflection on the feedback process and support the students in building this into their end of first-year portfolio.

At the draft/initial submission stage the following was added to the assignment submission forms (Fig. 6.2).

At final submission stage the following addition was made (Fig. 6.3).

The aim of the changes was to engage students in a feedback journey: to change a view that feedback was given to justify a grade into a view of feedback as an interactive process in which they had a stake. The final assignment of the year one students was a portfolio of practice which asked them to draw in their learning across the programme and provide a 2000 word reflective statement. The assessment feedback response forms were worded to acknowledge this portfolio to prompt engagement and subsequent use in the reflective statement of the portfolio.

PREPARING FOR THE PORTFOLIO—a key part of the portfolio is to reflect on the feedback you have received on the assignments

Thinking of any feedback on a past essay (or essays), please indicate any feedback that helped you prepare for and write this draft essay:

If you would like feedback on any particular aspects of your draft essay, please make a note of what you would like the feedback to address:

Fig. 6.2 Feedback response form for draft submission

PREPARING FOR THE PORTFOLIO—a key part of the portfolio is to reflect on the feedback you have received on the assignments

Thinking about the feedback on your draft of this essay, please indicate what the key points were and what action you took to respond to this feedback to help you prepare for and write this essay:

What did you do well in this assignment? What could be improved?

If you would like feedback on any particular aspects of your final essay, please make a note of what you would like the feedback to address:

Fig. 6.3   Feedback response form for final submission

Table 6.1 considers the number of times the student referred to their feedback in the 2013 portfolios, paper-based and before the use of the revised assignment form, and in 2014, with the electronic submission of the portfolio and the use of the feedback response form.

On average the students in 2014 were more than twice as likely to mention their feedback as those in 2013 (on average, 2.06 mentions in 2013 compared to 4.80 in 2014). This increase in the average rate of discussion of their feedback is statistically significant at 1 % ($t = 4.0053$, $p = 0.0001$). Much of this difference is driven by a large reduction in the proportion of students not mentioning their feedback at all (from 38.9 % in 2013 to 10 % in 2014). This fall in the proportion of those not discussing their feedback is significantly different at 1 % ($z = 2.6732$, $p = 0.0038$). The introduction of the feedback response process seems to have helped to reduce significantly the number of students ignoring their feedback in their portfolio and to have helped to significantly increase the amount of consideration students gave their feedback. These results suggest that the feedback response form made a difference to the amount of space given in the portfolio to the student's reflections on their feedback; however, it is possible that an increased staff and student discussion about feedback due to the piloting of this form and the feedback history tool also had an effect.

In addition to possibly increasing the frequency of the mention of feedback in the portfolios, the redesign of the feedback forms helped the students to engage with the feedback rather than report it as a reason for a grade. In 2013, most who mentioned their feedback did so to justify lower than expected or desired grades. By 2014, the discussion of feedback was much more related to what they had learned from it. This shift also changed how students felt about

Table 6.1 Frequency of feedback discussed in the EdD Portfolios

No. of references to feedback	2013 students (n = 36)	2014 students (n = 30)
0	14	3
1	3	0
2	3	6
3	8	4
4	3	5
5	4	2
6	0	1
7	0	2
8	0	1
9	1	1
10	0	3
11	0	1
12	0	1
Mean no. of references	2.06	4.80
Standard Deviation	2.13	3.38
Proportion with no mention of feedback	38.9 %	10 %

their feedback, with the 2013 cohort often reporting feedback that had aggrieved them while the 2014 cohort reported the feedback that impacted most on their learning. We might also suggest that student access to a feedback history report might further improve the student engagement with feedback by making the process of responding to past feedback easier.

BENEFITS AND CHALLENGES OF MAKING PROGRESS VISIBLE THROUGH FEEDBACK

Supporting and Enhancing Learning

Capturing feedback and making it easier to access has some potential learning benefits that have been evidenced in this case study. Three enhancements are digital efficiency savings, learning overviews and stimulating feedback dialogue.

First, moving to digital from paper-based provided efficiencies for staff. However, the degree to which technology can make existing processes more efficient will depend on the social context: some users might be resistant to a new technology because they perceive it to be difficult to use or not intuitive, while others may see savings of effort. The application of technology is not just about the affordances of the technology, that is what the technology enables users to do, in this case access past feedback; it is also about the social context of both the design and application (Oliver 2013; Wajcman 2015). In the case study the programme leader was enthusiastic about the feedback history because paperless assessment is faster to administer and efficient administration is part of the role, but the supervisors did not use the new technology and continued with previous practices perhaps because they did not perceive any immediate time saving for them and possibly were deterred by a need for investment in time to find out how to access the system.

Second, getting an overview of student progress can be valuable for helping make decisions about progression for struggling students or to see the assessment history of a newly acquired supervisee. In the case study there was evidence that a teacher can use past learning to help a student make decisions about future learning. This constitutes an ipsative view of feedback and learning where students are helped to build on past mistakes and limitations to develop in appropriate steps *for that learner* (Hughes 2014). So a decision on whether or not an apparently weak student should continue on the programme depends not on performance alone, but the progress they have been making towards expected goals.

Effective feedback helps the student see where they are now and where to go next (Hattie and Timperley 2007). Enabling students to be self-regulating, that is managing their own learning trajectory through responding to feedback, is potentially more powerful than teachers doing all the work (Nicol and Macfarlane-Dick 2006). Prompting to reflect on feedback can also really make a difference to student's engagement and this is why it is widely recommended that feedback should be in the form of a dialogue (Nicol 2010; Orsmond and Merry 2011). The increased references to feedback in the portfolios of these students after the new feedback response form had been introduced does suggest that a systematic process set up to encourage reflection on feedback is useful and provides at the very least an internal dialogue or self-dialogue about feedback, and possibly further dialogue with tutors and peers. It might also be that simply drawing more attention to feedback through the teaching team explaining the new processes to the students might have a positive effect on how seriously students take feedback.

It is perhaps the combining of these two innovations: prompting to reflect on past feedback and making past feedback easy to access that is the most valuable way of taking the findings of the case study forward, particularly for students who may not be as highly motivated to access and reflect on past feedback as these postgraduate students.

Challenges of Introducing Unfamiliar Technology and Making Feedback More 'Public'

Introduction of an unfamiliar technology that is not part of mainstream practice not surprisingly produced a range of responses. This is not simply about differences in technical skills in that younger students – digital natives – are more able and willing to adopt new technologies than their probably older supervisors and tutors. Helsper and Eynon (2010) have suggested that there are many factors that influence digital technology adoption and that while many older people may lead technology-enriched lives, some supposed digital natives have a limited view of using technology for learning. Of particular concern is the inertia that can arise if the technology is not easy to access, or its benefits are not immediately obvious.

Not surprisingly the vision here for adopting technology was largely to support existing practice and maintain the status quo rather than stimulate new practice. The feedback history tool was viewed as making existing processes more efficient. Drawing together material for a portfolio could be easily done digitally and the feedback history report was useful for some in generating an overview of a student's work perhaps to make decisions about progression for struggling students. There was not much evidence of support for the original intention of the tool developers which was to enable students and staff to explicitly identify progress (or lack of progress) drawing on the now more visible past feedback as evidence, but greater awareness of a student's learning journey might emerge more strongly with time.

Nevertheless, a reflective process that encourages students to revisit past feedback and reflect on changes they had made may be more immediately successful at promoting a longer term approach to learning gain. The very simple feedback response form was easy for students to use and may have helped them pay more attention to feedback and how to address it. The evidence suggested that portfolios produced after the introduction of the new assessment and feedback processes contained more discussion of past feedback and it may be a combination of the feedback response form and the 'background noise' about feedback in programme meetings and teaching sessions has resulted in an increased student response to feedback.

In this background noise there may be some concerns about making feedback more 'public'. Both students and teaching staff may have concerns about feedback being available to others when in the past much feedback was only visible to the sender and recipient and maybe a couple of other assessors and examiners. Revisiting historical feedback by a wider team of people could produce staff development opportunities through comparing and discussing different approaches, but feedback samples might also be used for quality monitoring which might be viewed less favourably by academic staff. Similarly, students could see advantages of assessors having a sense of their learning trajectory, but also might be wary that past feedback, or even more so past grades, might influence a marker's ability to judge a piece of work objectively according to current criteria.

FUTURE DIRECTIONS FOR E-ASSESSMENT AND FEEDBACK HISTORY REPORTING

The feedback history tool was developed in the context of an institutional change initiative, which introduced mandatory electronic submission of both assignments and feedback at an institutional level. This was a necessary precondition for leveraging digital technology as an effective facilitator to gain a holistic overview of a student's assessment and feedback journey, which as an idea fed into a nationwide concerted effort in the UK to articulate and provide guidance about the electronic management of the assessment lifecycle, including feedback (Gray et al. 2015). At the same time, the digitisation of the feedback management process contributes additional data about students that can be used to automatically capture and process more details about individual progress and performance with potential predictive analyses.

This field, learning analytics, has emerged as a key element of a wider trend towards 'data-driven learning and assessment', which Johnson et al. (2015, p. 12) identified as a mid-term driver for learning technology adoption in Higher Education for three to five years. But even though Johnson et al. recognise the potential of learning analytics, they warn that the field, while gaining traction, is still evolving and 'solutions are elusive' (p. 26). It is here where developments such as our tool can pave steps towards a better understanding of learning analytics and how they can provide practical and beneficial information to learners, teachers and administrators.

Additional benefits of the feedback history tool can be gained from better understanding of who needs what data in order to improve student feedback and the overall assessment process. The initial lessons learned from the project were fed into a follow-up project by UCL to develop a more flexible and user-friendly assessment and feedback dashboard which would provide different user groups (now including students) with different information according to their requirements. Even in our small scale pilot, we realised that requirements differ according to local preferences, assessment approaches and regulations, so an institution-wide solution needs to take into account different contexts and, for example, allow for adjustments of module teacher permissions between various parts of the institution.

Our feedback history tool assumes that feedback is already digitised and deposited into the VLE. It is also a relatively simplistic listing of data fields that are supposed to contain feedback. Our pilot used the formal submission points using two common VLE assignment activities: Turnitin and Moodle Assignments. The future UCL assessment and feedback dashboard will also list automated feedback from quizzes, but feedback, in particular informal feedback, often appears elsewhere, for example, as messages in free-flowing discussion forum threads, audio feedback or in private messages including email. Our tool does not capture such feedback, and it does not qualify or categorise feedback in any way. To address this and facilitate effective use of digital feedback, our vision is a tagging mechanism within the VLE that would allow a teacher – or student – to flag any item in the VLE as an instance of feedback so that it would be listed in the feedback history report which could later help users find and identify particular aspects of feedback in order to pick up learning gains and other improvements more effectively.

Managing such complexities is a challenge for the future developments of VLEs. Our experiences and new ideas informed a wider discussion supporting the assessment and feedback lifecycle with digital technology in the UK under the leadership of the Joint Information Systems Committee (JISC) (Gray et al. 2015). The IMS Global Learning Consortium picked up this discussion and is working towards technical definitions of assessment and feedback information to facilitate the exchange of relevant assessment information across VLEs and related learning technologies (Kraan 2015).

CONCLUSION: TECHNOLOGY SUPPORTED CHANGE
IN FEEDBACK PRACTICE

It is difficult to draw any firm conclusions from early-stage and small-scale pilots such as this one. However, we have demonstrated the huge potential for using digital technology to support and encourage ipsative assessment processes. The ubiquitous VLE was selected in this case study to capture and present feedback over time and this could be from different sources such as peers and in different formats such as audio if the VLE will support these options. In other contexts different technologies might provide a similar feedback history report for students.

The key question is then not about the technology, but about the value of visible feedback histories. Our case study has suggested that the value might be different for different stakeholders and again this will be context-dependent. In our study academic staff requiring an overview of student progress, such as programme leaders making progression decisions for borderline students, or supervisors taking on new students, were particularly in favour of a feedback history. Students also could benefit from having feedback more accessible, and when combined with a process for enabling students to reflect on feedback – in this case the student feedback response form – there was evidence of enhancement of learning from feedback or at least greater awareness of past feedback. There was some concern from both staff and students about who has access to the feedback history reports and this will be something to be negotiated locally with the likelihood of different outcomes in different contexts. It seems that the increase in digital assessment opens up exciting possible futures of data analytics. Certainly we hope that learners will be beneficiaries as the accessibility of 'feedback histories' of individual learners facilitates an ipsative learning and assessment process.

REFERENCES

Black, P., & Wiliam, D. (2009). Developing the theory of formative assessment. *Educational Assessment, Evaluation and Accountability, 21*, 5–31.

Boud, D., & Molloy, E. (2013). What is the problem with feedback?. In D. Boud & E. Molloy (Eds.), *Feedback in higher and professional education: Understanding it and doing it well* (pp. 1–10). London: Routledge.

Dahlstrom, E., Brooks, D. C., & Bichsel, J. (2014). *The current ecosystem of learning management systems in higher education: Student, faculty, and IT perspectives, research report.* Louisville, CO: ECAR. http://www.educause.edu/ecar. Accessed 13 October 2016.

Gramp, J., & Neumann, T. (2015, September 8–10). Moodle my feedback: Assessment reports for staff and students, *ALT Conference,* Manchester. https://altc.alt.ac.uk/2015/sessions/moodle-my-feedback-assessment-reports-for-staff-and-students-950/. Accessed 13 October 2016.

Gray, L., Ferrell, G., & Sheppard, M. (2015). *Electronic management of assessment, project website.* Bristol: JISC. https://jisc.ac.uk/rd/projects/electronic-management-of-assessment. Accessed 13 October 2016.

Hattie, J., & Timperley, H. (2007). The power of feedback. *Review of Educational Research, 77*(1), 81–112.

Helsper, E., & Eynon, R. (2010). Digital natives: Where is the evidence?. *British Educational Research Journal, 36*(3), 503–520.

Higher Education Funding Council for England (HEFCE). (2015). *Learning and teaching excellence: Learning gain.* http://www.hefce.ac.uk/lt/lg/. Accessed 13 October 2016.

Hughes, G. (2014). *Ipsative assessment: Motivation through marking progress.* Basingstoke: Palgrave Macmillan.

Hughes, G., Smith, H., & Creese, B. (2015). Not seeing the wood for the trees: developing a feedback analysis tool to explore feed forward in modularised programmes. *Assessment & Evaluation in Higher Education, 40*(8), 1079–1094.

Johnson, L., Adams Becker, S., Estrada, V., & Freeman, A. (2015). *NMC horizon report: 2015 higher education edition.* Austin, TX: The New Media Consortium.

Kraan, W. (2015). Vendors start work on assignment interoperability in IMS. *Electronic Management of Assessment Blog.* Bristol: Jisc. http://ema.jiscinvolve.org/wp/2015/08/20/vendors-start-work-on-assignment-interoperability-in-ims. Accessed 13 October 2016.

Laurillard, D. (2012). *Teaching as a design science: Building pedagogical patterns for learning.* London: Routledge.

Molloy, E., & Boud, D. (2013). Changing conceptions of feedback. In D. Boud & E. Molloy (Eds.), *Feedback in higher and professional education: Understanding it and doing it well* (pp. 11–23). London: Routledge.

Nicol, D. (2010). From monologue to dialogue: Improving written feedback processes in mass higher education. *Assessment and Evaluation in Higher Education, 3*(5), 501–517.

Nicol, D., & Macfarlane-Dick, D. (2006). Formative assessment and self-regulated learning: A model and seven principles of good feedback practice. *Studies in Higher Education, 31*(2), 199–218.

Oliver, M. (2013). Learning technology: Theorising the tools we study. *British Journal of Educational Technology, 44*(1), 31–43.

Orsmond, P., & Merry, S. (2011). Feedback alignment: Effective and ineffective links between tutors' and students' understanding of coursework feedback. *Assessment & Evaluation in Higher Education, 36*(2), 125–126.

Rennie, F., & Morrison, T. (2013). *E-learning and social networking handbook.* London: Routledge.

Walker, R., Voce, J., Nicholls, J., Swift, E., Ahmed, J., Horrigan, S. (2013). *2014 survey of technology enhanced learning for higher education in the UK.* Oxford: UCISA.

Wajcman, J. (2015). *Pressed for time: The acceleration of life in digital capitalism.* Chicago: The University of Chicago Press.

Gwyneth Hughes is Reader in Higher Education at UCL, Institute of Education, London, UK. She leads and teachers on Masters programmes in higher education and supervises doctoral students. She is on the editorial board for the journal London Review of Education. She has researched and published widely on learning and teaching in higher education and she specialises in both assessment and e-learning. She is co-author of *Learning Transitions in Higher Education* (Palgrave Macmillan, 2014). Her latest book *Ipsative Assessment: Motivation through marking progress* was published by Palgrave Macmillan also in 2014. She is a Senior Fellow of the Higher Education Academy.

Denise Hawkes is a Senior Lecturer at the UCL Institute of Education, London, UK. She is the Program Leader for the Doctor in Education (EdD) and teaches doctoral student courses in Secondary Data Analysis. Her research is broadly applied social economics and truly multidisciplinary using econometric techniques to topics in education, work and unemployment. She has held research grants with ESRC and National UK Government Departments, and has published in a range of journals including *American Economic Review and Journal of Social Policy.* She is a Fellow of the Higher Education Academy.

Tim Neumann is the Learning Technologies Unit Lead at the UCL Institute of Education. He advises on policies related to the use of technologies in Higher Education, and on blended and online course design, including the development of Massive Open Online Courses (MOOCs). Tim leads postgraduate modules on e-learning as well as educational research. He has held research grants in various e-learning areas, and he consults on technological aspects of educational development projects.

CHAPTER 7

Ipsative Learning: A Personal Approach to a Student's PBL Experience Within an Integrated Engineering Design Cornerstone Module

Emanuela Tilley and Kate Roach

INTRODUCTION

Design is an increasingly important part of the engineering curriculum. Capstone projects have been a part of that experience for decades, but recently cornerstone Problem-Based Learning or Project-Based Learning (PBL/PjBL) elements have become much more common. The reforms of undergraduate curricula within the Faculty of Engineering Science at University College London (UCL) are in line with the trend to increase the experiential elements of engineering

E. Tilley
Integrated Engineering Programme (IEP), Faculty of Engineering Sciences at UCL, London, UK

K. Roach (✉)
UCL Department of Science Technology Engineering and Public Policy, London, UK
e-mail: katherine.roach@ucl.ac.uk

© The Author(s) 2017   129
G. Hughes (ed.), *Ipsative Assessment and Personal Learning Gain*,
DOI 10.1057/978-1-137-56502-0_7

education. The Integrated Engineering Programme (IEP) introduces new interdisciplinary curriculum elements to each of the existing undergraduate degree programmes in the faculty. Its most significant contributions are experiential and authentic learning opportunities that allow students to apply their technical knowledge and develop their professional skills in engineering design modules year on year. Spearheaded by the cornerstone Integrated Engineering Design (IE Design) year 1 module, the programme is moving towards a design-centred learning approach by offering students a grounded learning experience in which knowledge is created through processes of divergent and convergent thinking as well as through independent research, critical analysis, creating and making, testing and decision-making. Design-centred, experiential learning in the constructivist learning environment of PBL/PjBL is, however, often plagued with complexities that can overwhelm learners. Learning in these settings is expected to be largely self-directed where tutors are facilitators of a problem-solving process rather than instructors who impart knowledge. As a result the content that students learn from the process can remain unstructured (Hemker 2001). Indeed PBL/PjBL has been shown to offer only modest benefits in terms of student learning of content, although it brings other benefits to the engineering context, by enhancing the integration of new knowledge, increasing student engagement, critical thinking ability and a number of soft skills (Allen et al. 2011).

This chapter presents evidence on how the inclusion of ipsative learning and assessment can help students deepen their engagement with the process of design and complex problem solving. The ipsative focus on progress, by its very nature aids in structuring the student journey and it may also aid in structuring the content of student learning. Practical guidance on how ipsative assessment was embedded into the cornerstone engineering design module and reflections on how it was received by students are also provided. Our evidence suggests that timely formative assessment and feedback, which focuses on the learner's progress as defined by an ipsative approach, can help students to be more self-reflexive. An ipsative approach helps students gain an understanding of what is required from them, which can positively influence confidence levels and increases their attentiveness to their progress in developing general 'soft' skills and competencies that are not formally assessed, but that support their achievement of the standards set by criteria.

BACKGROUND TO THE IPSATIVE APPROACH

Feedback is critical to improving knowledge and skill acquisition, whilst also providing students with information about themselves as learners (Hughes 2014; Stobart 2008). According to Hattie and Timperley (2007), feedback is one of the most powerful influences on learning and achievement and is a significant factor in motivating learning (Hattie 2009). There is a growing concern in higher education institutions within the UK that the amount of summative assessment is too high creating missed opportunities to enhance a student's learning experience through effective formative assessment and feedback (Hughes 2014). Hughes (2014) points out that although there have been concerns within universities to make moves to include formative assessment, these concerns have not always translated into practice. Providing the most appropriate formative feedback methods – defined as information communicated to the learner that is intended to modify the learner's thinking or behaviour for the purpose of improving learning – is not trivial.

Historical reviews of formative feedback over the past fifty years are characterised by constant debate, conflicting findings and little or no consistent pattern of results (Shute 2006). Shute believes that this could be attributed to the diversity of practice that is deemed fundamental to its approach. Given that researchers in the area believe that formative feedback should be multidimensional, non-evaluative, supportive, timely, specific, credible, infrequent and genuine it is hard to collect data that is comparable across programmes, let alone across disciplines (Schwartz and White 2000; Brophy 1981).

Ipsative assessment is an assessment based on a learner's previous work rather than on performance judged against external criteria and standards. Ipsative learning is perhaps more widely used in early education, rather than in secondary or higher education (i.e. post-secondary education), as the focus on grades is often stressed over personal development. However, one can argue that measuring students' personal progress is as important as measuring their competencies and skill development. One feature that could constrain its use in higher education is modularisation of curricula which makes it difficult for individual grade and feedback information to be shared across a degree programme to encourage the consideration of a learner's personal progression.

Ipsative feedback and assessment can be designed to include all aspects of the 'good' feedback measures summarised by Shute (2006) and its structure should consist of comparative and developmental statements from assessors as well as self-assessment by learner(s). In this framework, its best feature is its motivational effect. It can help tackle de-motivating effects of failure and poor performance and increase learner's resilience. Hughes (2014) argues that ipsative assessment can enhance learner self-esteem, provide incentives to act on feedback by making feedback more useable and enhance both intrinsic and extrinsic motivation. Student reflections of the ipsative feedback and formative assessment process included in the Integrated Engineering Design cornerstone PBL/PjBL module support this notion and are presented below.

The analogy often used to describe the ipsative approach is an achievement of a 'personal best' from athletics. Comparing existing and previous performance is often used in informal and practical learning experiences such as sport. Introducing an ipsative approach to feedback within an academic setting which aims to give credit for how far a learner has advanced since the previous work is an alternative to criteria-based assessment. Positive evaluations are common when ipsative feedback is incorporated into formative assessment; however past studies have suggested that the connection to summative assessment is not fully utilised as criteria are still seen by students as a transparent measure to pass or reach a graded level (Hughes 2014). Confidence in the ipsative approach may be diminished because of the widely held belief that summative assessment alone drives student motivation and behaviour, as it is what students pay most attention to (Shute 2006). Because of the complexities involved in teaching and assessing a 'formal' or academic discipline, criteria are recognised as a practically applicable set of standards or descriptors essential to the learning experience. One drawback of using criteria alongside ipsative feedback may be that students come to expect top marks for achieving a personal best, regardless of how the quality of their work (best or not) matches up to the criteria (Hughes 2014). Yet, there seems to be potential to turn this around and to use ipsative elements to help the students better understand and engage with the set assessment criteria and learning outcomes and see meeting these as goals that they are progressing towards. Accordingly, the simple ipsative question posed to teachers of '*How can we help students experience a personal best?*' may be better suited in higher education, particularly in engineering and design-centred problem-based modules, if it then becomes, '*What parts of the experience of getting a personal best can we give to our students to encourage and motivate them to reach the criteria we set?*'.

In the PBL integrated engineering design setting at UCL we hoped that ipsative feedback might help to deepen student engagement with the process of design and complex problem solving by increasing personal confidence and motivation levels, whilst providing clarity, correction and direction that clearly aligns with the set assessment criteria. Designers and design engineers, as well as those who research the process of design, continually describe design itself as a way of organising complexity or finding clarity in chaos. We wanted to know if the addition of ipsative feedback during the students' own process of pulling organisation from chaos would help students to:

1. believe that they were on a productive journey
2. understand and feel that they were able to attain the standard of outputs that are required of them.

In our design modules we also devised marking criteria in order to assess the students' ability to navigate and engage with the iterative process of engineering design in a PBL environment, particularly at the early stages of research, creativity and communication. Students are required to realise and isolate the problem, understand the needs of all stakeholders, investigate new cultures and technologies and formulate and share ideas, before refining their chosen final solution. Three key practical elements, described in the remainder of this paper, aided the successful application of ipsative feedback in combination with the use of criteria-based grading within a PBL module. The ipsative elements were included specifically for the benefit of student learning. They consisted of:

- Using scheduled class time to give feedback face-to-face, supported by written feedback provided by academics on draft submitted work;
- Connecting formative 'ipsative' feedback to the final summative assessment criteria;
- Spending time on academic training, since the inclusion of formative feedback as part of a dialogue with students is a new experience for many and ipsative feedback is even more novel.

INTEGRATED ENGINEERING DESIGN: UCL ENGINEERING'S CORNERSTONE DESIGN MODULE

The IE Design module is intended to give the students an opportunity to put their learning into practice by working in an interdisciplinary, problem/project-based learning, industry linked and design focused environment. At its core is the deliberate attempt to make use of and explore the creative and stimulating aspects of human-centred design as practiced by 'real' engineers and computer scientists in industry. This is supplemented by embedding the exploration and use of professional skills needed to be successful in the enticing and highly competitive working world (Mitchell et al. 2015).

The basic structure of the first-term IE Design module consists of two five-week 'Challenges', which have the students working in teams of mixed disciplines. The themes for the ill-defined problems, which form the basis of the two Challenges, are linked to such global challenges as sustainability and health. The learning objectives of the second Challenge build from those of the first. The first Challenge puts into practice the pedagogy of problem-based learning, whilst the second has a higher level of specification that aligns well with the principles of project-based learning (Savin Badin and Howell 2004). The technical focus and level of difficulty also increases from the first to the second as the students in their first five weeks are bright, inquisitive, enthusiastic, high-achieving and well versed in Science Technology Engineering and Mathematics (STEM) subjects, but have little technical knowledge of their chosen engineering discipline. Upon completion of the full IE Design module, an initial sense of autonomy among the students is expected as they take responsibility for their own learning through their individual and team-based experiences.

Both Challenges are presented to the teams of students with a human-centred design approach to problem solving, pioneered by IDEO (2014) an American innovation and design firm, in order for them to take into consideration stakeholder and user needs. Students are given some experience and understanding of what it is like when they are accountable to actual stakeholders beyond the classroom. External community groups and cultural and industry partners as 'holders' of the Challenges that are presented to the students help achieve this. Students are requested to identify and define the requirements, constraints and design parameters of their project, whilst engaging in research-based activities and self-study through enquiry-based learning. They are taught to explore the iterative processes of design and engineering thinking whilst applying mathematics and engineering analysis to the development and creation of an integrated engineering solution. There is a focus in the first Challenge on the use of creativity to generate concepts, exercise critical thinking, implement a methodology to compare ideas and use engineering judgment to choose a final solution. By contrast, the second Challenge affords the student an opportunity to demonstrate knowledge and understanding of the equipment, materials and processes employed in the design, production and testing of integrated engineering systems, including specialised test and measurement equipment relevant to their chosen engineering discipline.

The assessment of student work varied between the two Challenges. Portfolios, a design solution video, team and client meetings, team and individual presentations, technical prototype performance testing and reflective writing comprised the body of work completed by the students for (formative and summative) assessment. In some instances these were designed to add an element of fun whilst others resemble authentic deliverables and experiences typically associated with the engineering profession. The summative assessment associated with the first Challenge was primarily based on the creation and collation of a digital portfolio throughout the five weeks and included collaborative teamwork as well as individual aspects from each team member. A schedule of weekly mile- stones for the submission of draft work was given to the students from the module's onset. These strategically aligned with the planned ipsative feed- back and formative assessment meetings between the academic leaders and student design teams.

Formative Assessment and Ipsative Feedback Within Scheduled 'Design Review Meetings'

At two timely milestones within the first five-week Challenge, meetings were scheduled between each student team and their academic leaders. The meet- ings took place during timetabled workshops, in which academic leaders would move around from team to team within the two-hour timeslot, sitting and conversing with the students. Students were given guidance notes ahead of the meetings in order to understand how they should prepare and what draft portfolio work needed to be submitted online in advance. The meetings themselves were set out in a working-life setting, and were designed to mirror those in which engineers are called upon by directors and/or clients to report details of their project work as well as update on progress. Students were asked to prepare and deliver short presentations summarising their work at the start of the meeting and then the academic would follow up with an appraisal of progress made and ask any questions. The academic assessors' feedback was centred on the learner's progress whilst serving to provide the two main functions of formative feedback, direction and facilitation (Black and William 1998). It was also intended to provide learners with the two key types of information, verification and elaboration, as reported by Kulhavy and

Stock (1989). There is, however, an expectation set up with the students that they are to lead the meeting and that they should make the most of the meeting with the academic to clarify any misunderstandings or uncertainties they were encountering.

The ipsative feedback and assessment consisted of comparative and conditional or developmental statements verbally presented by both the assessor and by student self-assessment. Both the students and academics entered the design review meetings having assessed the submitted draft work. Scoring of draft work utilised relevant criteria taken from the final summative assessment rubric. A short conversation at the end of the meeting involved dialogue that helped students understand how their own 'perceived' level of achievement aligned with that of the academic assessor. The full formative assessment session ended with students discussing the academic feedback amongst their teammates, often with a teaching assistant present, before completing a piece of individual reflective writing prompted by questions. This process commonly resulted in closing the gap between student and academic perceptions of quality of draft work and an increased understanding of the assessment criteria on the part of the students, particularly at the second meeting.

In order to prepare the students for their summative assessments, the full assessment process during the five-week Challenge is clearly described step-by-step below and supported by Fig. 7.1:

- The students submit their draft portfolio (Assessment 1)
- The academic leaders meet with the students in their working space, during Design Review Meeting 1 (formative assessment)
- The students prepare and deliver a short informal presentation at the beginning of the meeting
- The academic leader provides the students with verbal comments and questions for improvement (feed forward) and the students self-assess their own work using the set criteria rubric associated with final summative assessment (self-assessment)
- A conversation occurs about the students perception compared to the lead's perception regarding the quality of the submission and the students then submit a reflective piece about the process (reflection)
- The students submit their second draft submission, Assessment 2 (based on the feed forward they received), followed by the second Design Review Meeting with their academic leader (formative assessment)

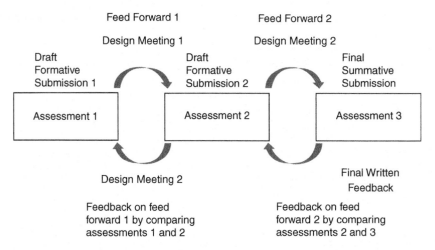

Fig. 7.1 Schematic of the process of feedback and assessment (adapted from Hughes 2014)

- In the second meeting the students get verbal feedback on how they have developed compared to their previous assessment (ipsative feedback). They also receive comments and questions on the second assessment that helps them prepare for their final submission, Assessment 3 (feed forward).
- The students self-assess their own work, a second time, using the criteria rubric associated with final summative assessment (self-assessment)
- A final conversation occurs about the students latest perception compared to the lead's perception regarding the quality of the second draft submission and the students then submit reflective writing about the process (reflection)
- The students submit their final submission, Assessment 3 (based on the feed forward they received) and academic leader provides final written feedback with final mark based on set criteria (summative assessment and ipsative feedback).

Feed forward, ipsative feedback and formative assessment are fed into the final summative assessment, which is undertaken by academic leader.

Typical examples of ipsative feedback provided to the students during the five-week Challenge by an academic leader include:

> There is a vast improvement in the quality of your team's research on the scaling and sizing of off shore wind farms due to the increased detail you've provided regarding the mechanical and electrical systems involved. Suggest that more can be done to simplify the technical language.
>
> The presentation of your ideas has been enhanced by the addition of your sketches. I am, and your external audience will be, able to better understand the intricacies of the connections between the mechanical components. Further improvements can be made with clearer labelling of components and captioning of images.

REFLECTIONS AND THE STUDENT EXPERIENCE OF DESIGN REVIEW MEETINGS

The following are a set of reflections completed by a student after the first and second meetings, when asked to write about the outcomes of the meeting as well as the ipsative feedback and assessment provided by the academic.

First Meeting student reflection:

> The marks that I and my academic leader gave my team under each of the items in the Design Review Meeting 1 Assessment Rubric are different. For instance, we gave ourselves quite high mark for stakeholders, and problem & brief definition, but we only got 2s for both criteria. I was surprised by the differences as I thought our team was doing a good job. I realized our team was falling behind based on the criteria in those categories of the assessment. In order to get high marks, we must improve a lot to get back on track. Our academic leader thought we have done a very great job on the presentation during the meeting. But for some reason, some of the content of the presentation is missing in the team portfolio. So, we have to figure out what we can do to make it better based on how we prepared for the meeting. When I self-evaluated it, I realized it is a bit unorganised and rather long in content. To improve the quality of it, I should cut down the content and make it more precise.

Second Meeting student reflection:

> The marks that each of us gave to ourselves, are quite similar to the ones given by our academic leader. This means we have a better understanding of what quality and kind of work will end up getting us a good mark on the project, compared to our first Design Review Meeting.

The last sentence of this student's reflection after the first meeting provides evidence that an ipsative PBL environment can empower students to make self-reflexive judgements in order to improve his/her own quality of work on this project. S/he has been able to pinpoint specific tasks that s/he or the team need to improve on, such as making a greater effort with the team portfolio, being more organised, cutting down content and being more precise. In the reflection for the second meeting, the focus is on the progress that this student has made in understanding what the required output standards are. This, in itself, is a highly desirable piece of learning to have undergone during the first five weeks of an undergraduate career. Arguably these reflections taken together demonstrate this student's increasing understanding of how to achieve good results in this kind of project work, and of the effort and depth required to attain a higher quality of research.

Discussions with students in focus groups afterwards support what is implied in the set of individual reflections provided, which is that student confidence levels can be negatively affected at the first meeting, but the ipsative feedback appears to increase student motivation to improve the quality of their outputs. After the second meeting, comments reflecting a sense of achievement were common in the student reflections: progress is acknowledged and their self-assessments are much more closely matched to that of the academic. Having two of these meetings gives academics an opportunity to provide an ipsative learning experience to their students on two occasions.

For example, after the second meeting, another student reflected on how the focus of the feedback was on improving the individual skill sets of students that are critical to successful engineering design and improvement in the quality of their team project.

The following are the lessons I learned from our meeting with our academic leader:

- To not give information we cannot back up with facts and correct statistics.
- We need to do more research into the stakeholders (people affected by this project e.g. mining companies) of this project and how are they affected.
- We need to understand what sustainability is properly; however we were told that we did a great job summarising the initial research provided.

- Our arguments need to be more technical and very detailed.
- We need to find out answers to some very detailed questions like, 'How much do these people earn?' and 'How much energy is used in schools, by females, males and children?'
- If we don't know something we should not assume but be honest and say that 'we do not know etc... and we need to find out'.

LESSONS LEARNED

Ipsative feedback and assessment can address the argument often raised in discussions regarding the effectiveness of feedback that 'feedback is only useful if the task is repeated'. The student reflections provided gives an early indication of potential conceptual and skill-based links that should be emphasised and supported across programmes in modularised curricula through feed forward and acknowledgement of progress made since past performances. Monitoring progress is very difficult to implement practically; however the Engineering faculty at UCL are committed to developing new administrative and online systems to support a connected curriculum that enables the collation of feedback and grades for each student to be kept as a personal record and shared with their personal tutors.

Ipsative feedback can add to what is missing in many PBL/authentic learning assessment methods. A group of academics from Aston University in Birmingham, UK led recent curriculum reforms that introduced CDIO, an international engineering education framework stressing engineering fundamentals set in the context of Conceiving, Designing, Implementing and Operating real-world systems and products (Andrews et al. 2011) across the first-year undergraduate curriculum in the department of Mechanical Engineering and Design. They have highlighted that even widely practised methods of PBL still struggle to provide adequate assessment and feedback, particularly in the provision of individual feedback.

The content of the student reflections lends support to the notion that in PBL, facilitation helps to build confidence and spark motivation in students by letting them know that they are on a productive path. Both reflections cited above show that the students aim to improve the quality of their work, a feature that in itself takes confidence to reflect on and acknowledge, and motivation to achieve. Our sense that students increase their confidence from this process of monitoring progress arises from the fact that they are apparently clear about what they have to do after the first meeting and then they are able to confirm their learning from the first meeting in the second. The ipsative feedback has been an orienting experience for these students, allowing them to improve the quality of their research and go into added depth with their ideas and concepts.

Moreover, academics expect the students to formulate opinions, gather evidence to provide a supporting technical argument and make decisions on matters that perhaps they would have ignored, if not challenged to do so. These meetings have highlighted the importance of having the students experience some degree of failure with the potential to re-orientate and attempt to do better next time. In other words, as long as there is potential for acknowledged progress, that is clearly facilitated by judicious feed forward and feedback, then students are able to understand that such difficult experiences can be beneficial to their learning and future achievements. Adding an element of ipsative feedback provided by an academic facilitator can help students make such personal realisations more readily, and this ultimately contributes to their ability to make self-reflexive judgements and decisions critical to their progress in learning and coursework.

STUDENT REFLECTIONS ON PROGRESS

The ipsative feedback given by academic leaders was designed to enhance student confidence and motivation and to enable them to better achieve the criteria upon which they would also be assessed. As mentioned previously, the students were asked to complete a set of three individual reflections: one after their first team design review meeting, another after their second meeting and the third after completing the design project.

The reflections were guided by questions, none of which explicitly called for students to describe their progress so far, although some questions asked them to reflect on what they had learned and one question specifically asked about whether things had changed in their teams between first and second meetings. The following questions were asked as part of the first two reflection assignments:

- Were there any differences in the marks that you and your academic leader gave your team under each of the items in the Design Review Meeting Assessment Rubric?
- Were you surprised by the differences?

- What feedback did you get from your academic leader that you and your team can use to improve your project and your myPortfolio coursework pages?
- How are things going in your team? (Reflection 2 only: Have things changed from your first reflection submission?) Please describe using a personal experience to convey how well or how poorly things are within the team.
- How is your team project coming along?

The final reflection included the following question, which was aimed at understanding the individual student experience of the iterative nature of the engineering design process:

- Describe your experience of the design process. Highlight the stages of cycle that you explored and provide a description of your experiences of every stage. Explain what you've learned about the design process, identify the lessons you've learned and those that you think you need more time to explore and learn about.

In one cohort consisting of 48 students, 31 (64 %) included an ipsative element in one or more of their reflections. They did this in one of two ways. Some specifically referred to progress, improvements or getting better, whilst others described a narrative shift from a state of not understanding or of not being able, to a more competent state of understanding or skill.

Narrative shifts from incompetent to more competent include:

... the first stage when only four people were doing work was absolutely terrible. This stage was full of angry, irritated, and confused individuals, which was extremely detrimental to the overall synergy of the group. In the latter stage, when all the members were making big contributions to the project, people were well communicated, happy and overall pleased with the work that was produced.

... Start from 'not knowing anything' to 'having a little understanding and concept what the challenge is about' to 'start to listen and give opinion' to 'having meeting and brainstorming' to 'found mistake and make change' to 'rushing to do all the research and team pages to meet the deadline' and 'done all the video and all team pages'. It is just like a mother going through pregnancy, tiring but happy, and finally the baby born.

Specific references to progress and/or improvement include:

> Things have changed since the submission of the first individual reflection. Our team is getting better and better in terms of communication and commitment.
> We are very happy with our progress so far, the research that we have collated has been most interesting, whilst enabling us to design our specification accordingly.

Despite the fact that students were not primed to focus specifically on their progress per se, many of them have naturally done so. It is perhaps possible that the ipsative feedback, which they received from the academics in their team meetings, encouraged them to think in the context of their own progress. It is notable that the majority of ipsative reflections are clustered in the second reflection (see Table 7.1), which was due for submission shortly after the second team meeting, approximately three quarters through the five-week project, when they received feedback on their progress since the first meeting.

Prompting questions for reflections two and three (see below) provided the best opportunity for students to focus on the improvements they made during the course of their first Challenge. Reflection three tended to call forth more specific statements about the content of the Challenges and specifics of the design process that students had learned. These were focused more on measuring a progression in their knowledge of the content and their understanding of processes, as in 'how to do something', than they were on the state of their skills or competencies, such as communication or organisation. The state of development of their skills might be referred to as competencies and competencies were not subject

Table 7.1 Spread of students referring to progress in relation to outputs versus progress in relation to skills

	Progress in competencies	Progress on outputs	Total
Reflection 1	1	4	5
Reflection 2	15	4	19
Reflection 3	8	5	13
Total	24	13	

to any criteria-based marking. The state of their understanding of knowledge, content or process might usefully be referred to as output-related progression, in the sense that knowledge of content or process that they referred to was specific to achieving the standards set by the criteria used to mark outputs (e.g. a portfolio, design idea, presentations, etc.)

Questions that were most likely to prompt 'ipsative statements' in reflections two and three were as follows:

Reflection 2: How are things going in your team? Have things changed from your first reflection submission?

Reflection 3: Explain what you've learned about the design process, identify the lessons you've learned and those that you think you need more time to explore and learn about.

Among the students who focussed on progress, some statements were output-related, whilst others purely referred to their own state of skill, competency or understanding.

Examples of output linked ipsative reflections:

> The project is making great progress and my team and I are working very well on new ideas that could help influence the success of our design.
>
> We are adding to our original idea every time we have something intriguing but we are also focused in our making gradual progress.

Examples of competency-linked ipsative reflections:

> Lately, our team's progress has been very good! The delegation of works has been made more efficient and fair, and everyone is now involved in the meeting and discussion.
>
> And while working on this project we have improved and developed skills that we had before and learnt some new (ones) as well.

This distinction is significant because one of the key differences between criteria-referenced assessment and ipsative assessment is that the former focuses on outputs alone whereas the latter focuses on the state of the learner or student and the difference in their state between now and before. Table 7.1 shows the spread of output-linked statements as opposed competency-based statements. Competency-based statements are related to the state of the student themselves, whereas output-based statements linked progress to their drive to achieve a good grade on their outputs.

In this set of reflections, roughly two-thirds of students have focussed on their own or their team's abilities and have not linked their improved skills to any specific output. It is worth making note that the competencies that the students have reflected on were not assessed and no marks were allocated for competencies. It is clear, however, that the students have understood that effective team working is an essential skill that they need to develop in order to meet the standards required of them. This is a major breakthrough for the IE Design module since there is a drive in engineering education as a whole to produce undergraduates who are 'work ready' by the time they graduate. One of the significant criteria for 'work readiness' for 21st century engineers is teamwork along with other soft skills (Finelli et al. 2011; Royal Academy of Engineering 2007).

There is a legitimate concern that in any assessment system that combines criteria-based assessment, with ipsative feedback and formative assessment such as this one, the whole program of assessment is at risk of being overshadowed by the criteria-referenced grading. This doesn't appear to have been the case for these students especially when it came to reflections on teamwork skills. Team-working skills per se were not assessed by reference to criteria yet the majority of reflections were in fact about teams. 24 of the 31 (77 %) students who reflected on their progress did so in relation to team-working skills although they were not asked to think about teamwork in Reflection 3. So these students have submitted ipsative reflections, despite the fact that they were not specifically directed to talk about progress and of those that did this, most of them have referred to the competencies involved in team-working skills, which were not subject to any criteria-referencing system.

These student reflections suggest an exciting opportunity for the future of Problem-Based Learning in the assessment of competencies, such as team-working skills, which engineering programs are increasingly designed to teach.

CHALLENGES TO PROVIDING IPSATIVE FEEDBACK AND FORMATIVE ASSESSMENT

The experience of providing face-to-face formative assessment and feedback sessions as part of the scheduled review meetings has highlighted some issues surrounding the practical implementation of ipsative feedback. Both students and academics need to be fully committed to the set (formative and summative) assessment schedule. The students need to see the benefit in submitting draft work for the academics to give feedback on and the academics need to be comfortable with giving feedback on progress, not just criteria-based content, in live meetings with students through dialogue. For the students, it is essential that the ipsative feedback and formative assessment clearly link to the summative assessment. For the academics, this requires the provision of training and practice opportunities as well as a clearly devised system to reduce the administrative load associated with providing written feedback and draft marking. Further operational support is needed within departments and/or faculties and across degree programmes to provide opportunities to collate, connect and share with personal tutors, individual student grades and feedback between modules and degree years to promote feed forward opportunities and acknowledge progress made on past performances.

CONCLUSIONS

This chapter has described how cornerstone engineering design modules form the basis for future problem/project-based modules and how conceptual tasks can be repeated and skill sets developed. Such modules provide students with an opportunity to understand and realise very early on in their engineering education that there are plenty of opportunities to benefit from the feedback and lessons learned. A significant conclusion to report is the capacity for ipsative feedback to increase the effectiveness of formative feedback to orientate the students within their own journey not only to give students a good understanding of the standards that are expected of them particularly in criteria-based engineering design modules, but also to give students an understanding of their own progress in skills-based competency as well as output-linked knowledge. The ipsative approach supports the student-centred teaching and learning methods of PBL/PjBL pedagogy whilst valuing learner progress. We believe that student self-reflections written after each of the two design review meetings support common themes of increased confidence and motivation levels, shown by the way in which students have demonstrated a clear of understanding of what they need to improve upon as well as the project aims and assessment criteria. There is a suggestion that implies that an ipsative PBL environment empowers students to be self-reflexive even in generalised skills and competencies, which are important for their general development, but are not assessed in the criteria-based system. This appears to be a pleasing side effect of the ipsative process, which will go some way to producing graduates who are work-ready.

REFERENCES

Allen, D. E., Donham, R. S., & Bernhardt, S. A. (2011). Problem-based learning. *New Directions for Teaching and Learning, 128*, 21–29.

Andrews, J., Clark, R., Thompson, G., & Evans, C. (2011). Reviewing and evaluation CDIO (Conceive, Design, Implement & Operate): An empirical approach to engineering education curriculum development. In *Problem Based Learning Annual Conference*, Nottingham.

Black, P., & William, D. (1998). Assessment and classroom learning. *Assessment in Education: Principles, Policy & Practice, 5*(1), 7–74.

Brophy, J. E. (1981). Teacher praise: a functional analysis. *Review of Educational Research, 51*(1), 5–32.

Finelli, C., Bergom, I., & Mesa, V. (2011) *Student teams in the engineering classroom and beyond: Setting up students for success.* Centre for Research on Learning and Teaching University of Michigan. http://www.crlt.umich.edu/sites/default/files/resource_files/CRLT_no29.pdf Accessed 21 December 2015.

Hattie, J. (2009). *Visible learning. A synthesis of over 800 meta-analyses relating to achievement.* London: Routledge.

Hattie, J., & Timperley, H. (2007). The power of feedback. *Review of Educational Research, 77*, 81–112.

Hemker, H. C. (2001). Critical perceptions on problem-based learning. *European Review, 9*, 269–274.

Hughes, G. (2014). *Ipsative assessment: motivation through marking progress.* Basingstoke: Palgrave Macmillan.

IDEO. (2014). *Human-centred design toolkit.* 2nd edition. Seattle: Bill & Melinda Gates Foundation. http://d1r3w4d5z5a88i.cloudfront.net/assets/toolkit/IDEO.org_HCD_ToolKit_English-5fef26ba5fa5761a3b021057d1d4a851.pdf Accessed 8 January 2016.

Kulhavy, R. W., & Stock, W. (1989). Feedback in written instruction: the place of response certitude. *Educational Psychology Review, 1*(4), 279–308.

Mitchell, J. E., Bains, S., Nyamapfene, A., & Tilley, E. (2015). *Work in progress: Multi-disciplinary curriculum review of engineering education. UCL's integrated engineering programme. IEEE EDUCON 2015 Conference.* Estonia: IEEE.

Royal Academic of Engineering (2007). *Educating engineers for the 21st century.* London: Royal Academic of Engineering.

Savin Badin, M., & Howell, M. C. (2004). *Foundations of problem-based learning, the society for research into higher education.* Maidenhead: Open University Press, McGraw-Hill Education.

Schwartz, F., & White, K. (2000). Making sense of it all: giving and getting online course feedback. In K. W. White & B. H. Weight (Eds.), *The online teaching guide: A handbook of attitudes, strategies, and techniques for the virtual classroom* (pp. 57–72). Boston: Allyn and Bacon.

Shute, V. J. (2006). *Assessments for learning: Great idea, but do they work?* Paper presented at the annual meeting of the American Educational Research Association, San Francisco, CA.

Stobart, G. (2008). *Testing times: The uses and abuses of assessment.* Abingdon: Routledge.

Emanuela Tilley is the Director of the Integrated Engineering Programme (IEP) in the Faculty of Engineering Sciences at UCL, London, UK. She led on the development of experimental, research and enquiry-based learning across multi-disciplinary first-year cohort of engineering students at UCL. Educated in mechanical and civil structural engineering, she has worked as a consulting engineer, leading multi-disciplinary engineering teams in the design and testing of the world's most unique tall towers and structures. Her current research focus is on effective assessment and feedback methods that improve student resilience for real-world engineering practice such as design iteration and teamwork. Emanuela is a Fellow of the HEA and a Principal Teaching Fellow within the Faculty.

Dr Kate Roach is a senior teaching fellow within the UCL department of Science Technology Engineering and Public Policy, London, UK. She manages a large-scale experiential engineering-policy design challenge for undergraduates along with a minor in Engineering and Public Policy at Bachelors level. She has studied the ways in which scientific thought is assimilated into popular culture and continues to have an interest in the interface between science, engineering and cultures. She has developed an interest fostering creativity within the undergraduate engineering cohorts at UCL. To do this she works with methods and techniques used by the creative arts educators to teach engineers. This is also an active research interest for her.

CHAPTER 8

Assessing Liminality: The Use of Ipsative Formative Assessment During a Postgraduate Taught Induction Programme to Support the Development of Criticality

Julie Rattray

INTRODUCTION

Since the publication of Meyer and Land's first papers in 2003 (Meyer and Land 2003a, 2003b) a substantive body of work has emerged exploring aspects of the Threshold Concepts Framework from a range of different perspectives (Flanagan 2016). This work has considered, for example, the nature of disciplinary and professional thresholds as well as those pedagogical approaches that might support their mastery (ibid). Within this body of research, however, elements of the Threshold Concepts Framework remain elusive or problematic. The movement of learners through the so-called liminal space from the first encounter with the threshold to mastery and subsequent ontological shift is relatively uncharted (Land et al. 2014). Similarly it has proven difficult to identify satisfactory approaches to the

J. Rattray
School of Education, Durham University, Durham, UK
e-mail: julie.rattray@durham.ac.uk

© The Author(s) 2017
G. Hughes (ed.), *Ipsative Assessment and Personal Learning Gain*,
DOI 10.1057/978-1-137-56502-0_8

149

assessment of threshold concepts – it may be possible to identify individuals who have moved beyond the mastery of a particular threshold and progressed within their chosen discipline or profession, but it is more challenging to identify those who have only a developing or partial understanding of the threshold (Davies and Mangan 2008). We know that as the threshold is encountered learners must enter, and pass through, the liminal space (Meyer and Land 2005) or liminal tunnel (Land et al. 2014; Vivian 2012) if the threshold is to be mastered and the learner is to be transformed. Determining what stage of understanding the learner is at or precisely where they are in the liminal tunnel is not easy, and as yet satisfactory attempts to assess this movement are not forthcoming.

The above characterisation of liminality as a tunnel, rather than simply a space, as in the original Meyer and Land (2003a, 2005) work, represents an increasing acceptance that the liminal experience is both cognitive and emotional. It is an experience that is associated with both intellectual and affective, or emotional, transformations that take the learner into a dark and often foreboding place (Cousin 2006; Land et al. 2014; Vivian 2012). The tunnel metaphor was first introduced by Vivian (2012), taking a semiotic approach to liminality, and has utility as a way of thinking about liminality in a number of ways. First, it encourages us to think of liminality in terms of a journey, with the tunnel something to be passed through en route to our destination in this case the mastery of a threshold concept. It captures the temporal nature of liminality implying as it does that passage through the tunnel may take time and effort, as the threshold is encountered, explored and mastered. Finally, tunnels are frequently dark places that are only illuminated as we move through them and this again would seem to fit with the experiences of threshold transformations as we understand them. Meyer and Land (2005) argue that one of the important defining features of a threshold concept is its troublesomeness, which creates in the learner a state of uncertainty which is only resolved as the learner works to master the threshold. As they do this, according to Meyer and Land (2005), aspects of the concept will come in and out of focus much as the tunnel walls are illuminated briefly as we pass through it.

This chapter draws on a case study from a postgraduate taught induction programme designed for education students to support the suggestion that forms of formative ipsative assessment can serve as a useful pedagogical tool to facilitate students' development of the threshold concept of criticality and as a potential means of assessing progress through the liminal tunnel.

What Is a Threshold?

Meyer and Land (2003b) define a threshold concept as 'akin to a portal opening up a new and previously inaccessible way of thinking about something' (p. 3). Threshold concepts are not simply aspects of content that need to be learned but rather they refer to those concepts within a discipline or profession that change the way we think, practise and talk within that discipline or profession. In short, they represent points of transformation (Meyer and Land 2003a, 2003b, 2005). They are typically associated with those aspects of knowledge that are the most troublesome (Perkins 1999) and foster discursive and ontological transformations in learners that cause them to view their discipline or profession in a subjectively different way (Meyer and Land 2005). The threshold concepts of a discipline also serve to create a set of boundaries for the discipline, framing in a way the particular body of disciplinary knowledge or ways of practising associated with that discipline. They might be thought of as creating the boundaries of a discipline or learning community (Davies 2006). Communities in this sense are identifiable as being framed by the fundamental principles or concepts, the thresholds, of the subject that hold it together and which establish a common or shared perception of that subject which is both tacit and implicit (Davies 2006).

As well as being potentially troublesome and transformative Meyer and Land (2003a, 2003b, 2005) suggest that the mastery of threshold concepts may also be integrative in that it brings together other aspects of the discipline in new and hitherto unconsidered ways. Learners actively bring together previously unrelated disciplinary knowledge in a reconstituted and irreversible way as their disciplinary outlook shifts. The learner is unable to return to the prior state of knowing, before the threshold was mastered – the portal operates in a uni-directional way. However, it is worth noting that if the threshold is not mastered the learner will return to their original state of knowledge on the brink of a threshold never truly breached.

Work utilising the Threshold Concepts Framework has identified that an understanding of heat transference in physics (Meyer and Land 2003a) or opportunity cost in economics (Meyer and Shanahan 2003; Shanahan and Meyer 2006) arguably irreversibly changes the ways that a learner will engage with physics or economics. Once these troublesome concepts are mastered, they necessitate that the learner will approach problems in economics or physics differently in the future. Work within the domain of biology, with its numerous and at times seemingly disparate sub-domains, that is, zoology, genetics or botany, suggests that the discipline as a whole is bounded and often integrated by a shared understanding of concepts such as complexity, scale and change. These serve to distinguish biology as a discipline from physics or chemistry where these concepts have a different meaning or significance (Taylor 2006). Research in the area of threshold concepts also tells us that doctoral supervisors and students agree that coming to understand the purpose and function of a conceptual framework which frames and guides their research represents a key moment of transformation in the life of a doctoral candidate (Trafford 2008).

As a threshold is understood or mastered, not only does it necessitate a new way of thinking about the discipline but it also fosters a potentially new way of talking about the discipline (Meyer and Land 2005; Cousin 2006). The majority of disciplines and professions have an associated discourse which acts as a code or signifier for that discipline or profession. The use of disciplinary discourse can serve as a means of identifying those individuals who might be considered to be part of that disciplinary group or community and those who are outsiders (Davies 2006; Meyer and Land 2005). It is important to note that use of the discourse does not in itself indicate that the threshold has been mastered and that the learner understands the concept. Many learners use the discourse of a discipline, sometimes in a mode of mimicry, or community before they master the thresholds associated with that discipline or community (Cousin 2006). Mastery of a threshold thus refers not simply to the use of disciplinary discourse but rather reflects a true shift in understanding of the threshold concept or concepts associated with that discipline. In this chapter the use of the terms threshold mastery, or mastery of the threshold, refer to the idea that the learner has an understanding of the concept being learned; it does not reflect any qualitative or quantitative judgement about a requisite level of understanding. Within the area of threshold concepts we tend to talk about thresholds being mastered or not rather than seeing understanding of the concept as operating on a sliding scale. Thus, whilst the learner traverses the liminal tunnel they may develop a partial understanding of the threshold concept, it is not until they emerge from the tunnel transformed that we would identify them as having mastered the threshold.

CRITICAL THINKING AS A THRESHOLD CONCEPT

The ability to engage critically with existent research literature and evidence represents a significant key to successful Masters study, with grades often being associated with evidence, or lack thereof, of critical engagement with the material at hand. Students who fail to engage critically with their Masters study or who fail to develop critical reasoning frequently get 'stuck' and find themselves unable to progress their studies beyond an ability to reproduce or report what they are learning (Giancarlo and Facione 2001). In short, they do not develop the capacity to think critically. Drawing on the epistemological model of critical thinking as proposed by Baxter-Magolda (2009), encompassing four levels of knowing, Chen and Rattray (in press) argue that critical thinking is a threshold concept. Baxter-Magolda (2009) argues that as their critical thinking develops learners progress from a point of absolute knowing to transitional knowing to independent knowing and finally to contextual knowing as they construct their own meaning (Baxter-Magolda 2009; Boes et al. 2010). Critical thinking and the associated idea of criticality is, to this end, potentially troublesome, integrative and transformative, empowering learners with a new way of thinking, approaching and talking about the nature of evidence, warrant and reasoned argument (Chen and Rattray in press). Mastery of the threshold concept of critical thinking brings about changes in the way that learners engage with the academic argument and evidence with which they are presented, and the associated ontological shift changes their academic practices (Meyer and Land 2005; Perkins 2008).

Within the discipline or field of education, like other areas of the social sciences such as sociology, political science or even psychology, the learner who has not mastered the critical thinking threshold is likely to approach their work in a descriptive way, reporting arguments from the research literature in a linear and non-integrated fashion. They will typically fail to see the links between central constructs within their disciplinary context and be able to recite theory rather than explain it. Learners who do not think critically about their disciplinary area frequently seem to be unaware that the same problem or issue can be discussed or explored from a range of different perspectives that are equally valid yet distinctive in nature. Such learners might, for example, ask questions aimed at eliciting a definitive answer – 'which is the right theoretical explanation of how people learn?', whereas the learner who has mastered the threshold concept of critical thinking will realise that within the discipline or field of education this is not a reasonable question. They would understand that the different theories of learning that have been proposed simply reflect different ways of explaining the learning process. They will equally be aware that the merits or otherwise of any individual theory will depend on a number of issues, not least of which is the quality of argument and evidence used to support it.

In addition, learners who have mastered the critical thinking threshold in education would understand the interconnectedness of theory, policy and practice, understanding that each is informed by the other. So, for example, they are able to understand the inter-relationship between ways of thinking about disability, medical or social models, educational policies relating to educational inclusion and special educational needs, and classroom practices designed to support the learning of individuals with special educational needs. Critical thinking in this way acts as a threshold capability (Baillie et al. 2013) that allows learners to integrate other disciplinary thresholds such as the link between theory and practice (Chen and Rattray in press).

Assessing the Threshold?

As already mentioned threshold transformations are frequently accompanied by a change in disciplinary discourse. The discursive aspect of the threshold is interesting as many learners actually start to use the new discourse associated with the threshold before they come to have a full mastery of it. Meyer and Land (2003a, 2003b, 2005) to this as 'mimicry', arguing that learners frequently mimic or reproduce the discourse of the threshold using specific terms or discursive forms of language associated with the threshold but with no apparent understanding of the concept that sits behind this discourse. This mimicking behaviour is one reason why the assessment of movement through the liminal tunnel has proven to be so problematic. We are not simply able to rely on the learners' use of specialist language as an indication of their level of transformation (Davies and Mangan 2008).

Davies and Mangan (2008) argue that assessment of threshold transformations is fraught with difficulties, not least because of the potential for discursive mimicry. They argue that the need not simply to identify knowledge acquisition, but to be able to identify a qualitative difference in ways of thinking and practising makes threshold transformations particularly difficult to assess. Threshold transformations involve three different kinds of conceptual change. Students first acquire, at least, a rudimentary understanding of some basic concepts within their discipline. These may not be fully understood, and indeed Davies and Mangan (2008) argue that they cannot be until integrative disciplinary thresholds have been mastered. Two further conceptual developments are then needed. The first of these relates to mastery of more complex, or superordinate, knowledge-based disciplinary thresholds and the second relates to conceptual changes in disciplinary practices (Davies and Mangan 2008). One of these conceptual developments is not enough to bring about a full threshold transformation. There needs to be both a change in knowledge and an associated change in ways of practising if we are to witness an ontological shift. Thus, the integrative and bounded nature of threshold concepts mean that they bring together other, more basic level concepts within the discipline as they serve their transformatory function (Davies and Mangan 2008). The speed of transformation is not uniform and it can take learners varying amounts of time to master a threshold, and yet most assessment practices in higher education frequently assume a more-or-less uniform pattern of learning with students moving from naivety to expertise in a linear way during their period of study (Alexander et al. 1995).

Thus, many traditional approaches to assessment in higher education, relying as they do on students' knowledge of their discipline at fixed time-points during their study, are insufficient to capture the fluid nature of threshold transformations. Current approaches allow us to identify students with no real understanding of the discipline and those who have already mastered some of the important thresholds associated with their disciplines, but what we are less well able to capture are those students who are moving towards mastery but who have not accomplished it yet. We need to find an approach to the assessment of threshold concepts that permits us to uncover what is going on when students are passing through the liminal tunnel en route to full mastery and subsequent transformation. In addition, we need an approach which acknowledges the non-uniformity with which these changes might occur.

IPSATIVE ASSESSMENT AND THRESHOLD TRANSFORMATIONS

One way of achieving this might be to apply the principles of ipsative assessment to the assessment of threshold transformations (Hughes 2011, 2014; Hughes et al. 2014). Ipsative assessment offers a move away from normative or criterion-referenced assessment to a more individualised approach to the assessment of learning and understanding (Hughes 2011, 2014). It encourages learners to reflect on their own progress and accomplishments and identify, through the interpretation of appropriate feedback and self-reflection, what they need to do to continue to develop their learning (Hughes et al. 2014). The dialogical and developmental nature of ipsative assessment would recommend it as having potential utility in relation to the assessment of a learner's developing mastery of a threshold concept. The need, in this approach, for students both to self-assess and to respond to the feedback of others and to focus on their own learning journey, rather than a specific grade or score, pushes them to think about what it is they are trying to master, and how they are trying to master it, rather than simply comparing their performance against that of others (Hughes 2011, 2014). In the case of the development of threshold understandings this is particularly important as the speed of passage through the liminal tunnel is so varied that to try to assess this with a single fixed point assessment can be problematic – we need a way to capture the journey and establish that movement is actually taking place. Ipsative assessment may allow us to do this more effectively than other forms of assessment as it necessitates that learners focus on the process of learning, not simply the product (Hughes et al. 2014). In terms of the mastery of a threshold this is important as it will support the shifts in ways of thinking and practising that are central to threshold mastery.

Ipsative assessment may serve to support the development of Baxter-Magolda's (2009) four stages of knowing, which give rise to critical thinking. As such the learner who embarks on the journey of mastery of critical thinking may pass through Baxter-Magolda's four developmental stages as they move through the liminal tunnel. Thus, on entering the tunnel the learner may demonstrate what Baxter-Magolda terms 'absolute knowing', where ideas are treated as absolutes and arguments repeated but not analysed. Through the use of carefully constructed formative assessment tasks that encourage learners to think about how they are engaging with the material to be learned and their treatment of information, they may then move from this form of knowing to transitional knowing characterised by a growing acceptance that knowledge is less certain than it was previously believed to be. A continued engagement in learning activities that focus on the very nature of knowledge and evidence transitional views of knowledge in turn may develop into independent knowing where the learner accepts that knowledge is uncertain and is able to articulate their own views and subjective arguments based on available evidence. Finally as the learner continues to develop their engagement with the discipline and the nature of argument, the learner who masters the threshold of critical thinking will emerge from the liminal tunnel demonstrating what Baxter-Magolda (2009) has termed 'contextual knowing'. At this point they are able not simply to formulate and support their own arguments but to locate these arguments within the wider disciplinary context and understand that any argument must be judged according to a set of contextually-relevant criteria and the context itself. Such a transformative journey, even when well-structured and supported, will not be the same for all learners and it may take some learners longer than others. Such a transformation, when successful, will then influence how the learner engages with other aspects of disciplinary knowledge as they come to see it in its disciplinary contexts, for example, the treatment of Marxist or postmodern theory is no longer something simply to be critiqued as abstract theory but something to be critiqued and evaluated within an educational context.

As already indicated, the pace of movement through the liminal tunnel will vary with some learners taking longer than others to achieve mastery of the threshold. Likewise not all learners will follow the same path through the tunnel. For some, the journey will be smooth and the shift from one form of knowing to another, whilst challenging, will represent a logical and manageable shift in thinking (Meyer and Land 2003a, 2005). Other learners however, will experience a different kind of journey, one that is more troublesome, with progress being made through a series of stops and starts and even backwards steps. These learners may experience what Meyer and Land call 'oscillation' as they inhabit a place on the edge of understanding, with the path ahead being illuminated briefly before it is lost again in the darkness of the tunnel. For these learners it is not uncommon to experience a kind of back and forth movement on the brink of transition which is then lost. The new idea or knowledge comes briefly into focus before it disappears from view. Ipsative formative assessment tasks may help the learner hold the new concept in focus whilst it is explored and understandings are reached.

Whilst the case study of practice that will be presented in the remainder of this chapter does not attempt to address all of these issues, it represents an attempt to use the principles of ipsative assessment to start to explore the potential for us to understand in more detail the liminal journey. It reflects an attempt to see how one pedagogical approach might help to foster mastery of the threshold concept of critical thinking as a starting point to developing meaningful forms of assessment within the Threshold Concepts Framework.

THE POSTGRADUATE INDUCTION PROGRAMME

The Issues of Transition

Transitions to postgraduate study can be difficult for many students as they are required not simply to engage with increasingly complex ideas in relation to their academic studies but to demonstrate more sophisticated levels of academic practice (Rattray and Smith 2015). Many students struggle to make this transition smoothly and this can often be as a consequence of not having the requisite academic practices that will help them succeed at Masters level (Rattray and Smith 2015). Some of these ways of practising are skill-based and can be taught in very direct ways, for example, how to use an appropriate referencing style, or how to present data, but others require a different, less didactic, pedagogical approach to support their development.

As already mentioned, the ability of students to engage critically with their Masters level study of education improves their ability to do well on their programme as it opens up more sophisticated treatment of knowledge and ways of dealing with the claims and evidence they are introduced to. Students who take a critical approach to their studies typically see the relationships and interrelationships between the different ideas they are presented with and can construct arguments that are derived from a critical appraisal of theories and research within their disciplinary contexts. Those who do not take such an approach typically are able to reproduce what they are told or what they read, but will describe rather than analyse arguments, produce assignments that are reproductions of lecture notes and readings but which do not develop ideas beyond those that they were originally presented with. Whilst this can, if done well, be sufficient to obtain a passing grade at Masters level, it will not gain them a merit or distinction level grade.

Being concerned that we supported the development of those academic practices that we might think of as skills, and those that are more akin to competencies, a new induction programme was developed for Education Masters students which took a more holistic approach to academic practice as a foundation for supporting students to make the transition to Masters level study (Rattray and Smith 2015).

The Programme

Using threshold concepts as a framework for curricular design, the induction programme for Education Masters students at a research-intensive higher education institution in the UK was re-designed. The resulting induction programme integrates elements of ipsative formative assessment (Hughes 2014) with Nicol's (2011) idea of peer review and feedback to support students movement through the difficult liminal phase where notions of criticality frequently oscillate as students work to reach a point of understanding and subsequent transformation.

The full induction programme lasts for two terms and is a non-compulsory, non-credit bearing addition to the suite of Masters level education programmes offered by the institution. It runs in parallel to the credit-bearing Masters programmes. During the academic year that the programme was introduced, 46 students participated in the initial two-week induction programme, but only 16 students completed the full series of induction activities. Some students of course enrol on Masters programmes having already mastered the critical thinking threshold and demonstrate a contextual understanding of knowledge right from the start. These students are not the focus of this chapter and will therefore not feature in subsequent discussions.

This chapter will not present a full description of the programme, but focuses on those elements that were specifically designed to support the development of critical thinking and criticality (see Fig. 8.1). A series of workshops and assessment tasks were designed with the aim of facilitating students' understanding of the meaning of critical thinking in relation to education. These activities start by encouraging students to explore their own understandings of criticality, something that is essential if we are to explore its development as a threshold concept. We need to establish if students already have a view of critical thinking that is aligned to that which is espoused by academic colleagues in the design delivery and assessment of Masters level work. If students are to develop their academic practices and make sense of feedback on their written work and expectations of them in seminars and other learning situations, they need to develop an understanding of the meaning of critical thinking that is being applied by those teaching and assessing them. This is important, as a key element of the standard assessment criteria for any Masters programme is the ability to demonstrate critical engagement with the research literature. Anecdotal evidence from student discussion forums tells us that the comment they least understand on their written feedback is 'you did not show evidence of

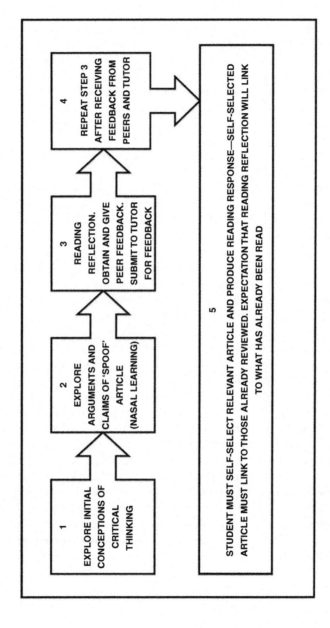

Fig. 8.1   Induction activities designed to develop critical thinking

critical engagement with the arguments' or 'you failed to develop a critical line of argument in this work'. Thus the induction programme takes as its starting point how students themselves view criticality and then presents them with the definition as applied on their programme of study:

> The ability to make informed, evaluative judgments based on evidence as well as values and to see the interconnectedness of ideas.

At the start of this process many of the Masters students have a limited understanding of criticality, as demonstrated by the initial written definitions of critical thinking by our students:

> It means we should look at both sides of an issue, not only focus on the evidence that supports my argument but also take those opposite ideas into consideration as well.
> Learning how to construct an argument and balancing your thinking in order to come to a conclusion.
> It may mean not accepting all and everything. If one hears or reads anything he/she must think about it before accepting it or believing it.

These three quotes suggest that whilst students view critical thinking as something to do with argument and evidence they do not fully seem to be integrating the idea of evaluation and judgement. The final student perhaps shows more understanding of this. As we might expect, these students have moved beyond Baxter-Magolda's (2009) first stage of knowing in that they see critical thinking as reflecting a need to construct arguments that are derived from evidence, suggesting that they do not see knowledge as absolute but rather as something subjective. Some students saw critical thinking as being about judgements, but even then the view was fairly narrow. They seem to be demonstrating what Baxter-Magolda would call a transitional view of knowledge that reflects their understanding of the need for evidence but does not really extend to a full acknowledgement that knowledge is uncertain and must be viewed within a contextual framework. For example criticality is:

> Being able to read texts objectively and find ways to challenge or support the ideas and theories outlined. (Masters Student)

Following this initial activity where students were asked to provide their working definitions of critical thinking, they were presented with ours.

Students then participate in the induction programme proper which includes tasks designed to develop an understanding of critical thinking that is aligned to that which is applied to their work by assessors. Each task or activity is cumulative in that it builds on the previous activity in some way to support a potential shift in thinking. The tasks are designed to be as non-threatening as they can be in an attempt to reduce the negative emotional experience that can be associated with liminality (Rattray and Smith 2015).

The programme starts with a discussion of a spoof article from 'the Onion' website (www.theonion.com) outlining the arguments for the existence of 'olfactory' or 'nasal' learners as an extension of the visual/auditory/kinaesthetic (VAK) learning styles approach to learning (Barbe and Milone 1981). Many of the students enrolled on Masters in education programmes are familiar with the learning styles idea and vocabulary, if not the research base that sits behind them. It is not uncommon to find that initial responses to the article are not based on evaluations of the evidence but whether or not the learner has undergone a learning styles assessment at some point in their educational history. Those who have and feel that this benefited them typically are more willing to accept the arguments in the article than those who have not, or than those who did, but felt that it did not help them.

What we see in doing this activity is that the article often polarises students into taking a position in support of, or against, the ideas. They see them as representing a view of learning styles that is favourable (or right) or unfavourable (or wrong), which would suggest that for many students initial responses to ideas are being treated in terms of absolute knowledge. This would seem to be at odds with their definitions of critical thinking which appeared to reflect a transitional and in a small number of cases, independent view of knowledge (Baxter-Magolda 2009). One possible explanation for this may be that in their written definitions, students use the language of critical thinking but are simply demonstrating what Meyer and Land (2003a, 2003b) referred to as 'mimicry' of the discourse. They will already be familiar with the discourse surrounding critical thinking and criticality from their undergraduate study experiences and are using this language to represent their own definitions.

Having asked students for their initial responses to the article, we used small-group and in-class discussions to encourage students to go beyond their initial responses to the article to the construction of justifications for their responses that were based on a more detailed consideration of the arguments presented and supported in the piece. The choice of a spoof article here is important – proposing what might at first seem ridiculous but which cannot simply be dismissed. Presenting evidence to support its claims forces students to think about the merits of an argument and how claims, even preposterous ones, might be supported. Thus it pushes students away from an absolute view of knowledge to (initially) a transitional one as students are encouraged not simply to dismiss what might seem like a preposterous idea but to consider the potential support for the claims made, and if these can be substantiated. The article is also non-threatening as it does not rely on specialist knowledge in order to understand or decode the ideas it contains.

Students are then asked to read another article and write a response. The response should include an appraisal of the arguments and evidence in the article and the extent to which the students feel the authors support their claims. Again, articles are specially selected so as to minimise the need for extensive specialist knowledge, reflecting the fact that the students are only just starting their study of education. Instructions as to how to go about writing a reading reflection, including some suggested sentence starters and sub-headings are given to support engagement with the task. This task is intended to support students' development of an independent and eventually contextual approach to the nature of knowledge and support their eventual mastery of the critical thinking threshold.

The purposes of this task are twofold: it encourages students to start writing early which is beneficial for their ongoing academic development, and it encourages self-reflection and assessment at a very early stage in their Masters experience. The utilisation of peer review, tutor feedback, and a requirement that the student provides a written response to this feedback, encourages self-reflection and assessment, a cornerstone of ipsative assessment (Hughes 2014).

Students are asked to provide peer feedback to another member of the cohort and to ask a peer to reciprocate this. They then reflect on that feedback and submit it to us for comment. In doing this we are trying to encourage students to self-assess their progress as they respond to the peer feedback, thinking about what this tells them about where they are and how they might develop their work. The comment from academic tutors builds on both the peer review and students' own self-reflection and should encourage students to reflect further. This cycle is then repeated with a second article and students are again encouraged to obtain and provide peer review and self-assessment. This process encourages students to evaluate their own work in relation to their developing understanding of criticality. The need not simply to read feedback but to provide a response to the feedback given encourages reflection and self-assessment which helps students to think about their learning in a qualitatively different way (Hughes 2014).

The Reading Reflection Task

The students' initial attempts at completing the reading reflections task demonstrated a transitional, and sometimes independent, treatment of knowledge. They tended to provide summaries of the articles with the majority of appraisal or comment on the arguments and claims being linked to very generic and non-contextual critiques of the article. Thus students might comment on the sample size saying it was too small, but might not take into account the qualitative nature of the research being described. They would comment in their reflections about their enjoyment of the article and its readability, but did not typically locate their reflections within the broader educational context. This is perhaps reasonable given that many of the students were new to the academic study of education.

> I liked reading this article because it made sense. (Masters student)
>   The article was easy to follow and the arguments were clear. (Masters student)
>   The study only had ten participants and this makes it hard to see how the work applies in other situations – the sample should be bigger in order to support the claims. (Masters student reading reflection 1)

These statements reflect a sense that the students were not sure what to write about in the reflective part of the task, something that was further substantiated by their comments on the work of others and in response to the peer feedback they received:

> I think you gave a good summary of the paper and I also enjoyed it. You could maybe write a little more about the methods as that is important. (Peer feedback on reading reflection 1)

The response to this feedback was the following:

> Yes I should have written more about the method, I will do this next time.

It was a symptom of the students' early reflections that they appeared reluctant or uncomfortable when commenting on the work of others, and so early comments tended to be of the kind shown above with little that would encourage students to reflect on their learning. Whilst peers did not comment on the treatment of evidence by their peers in their initial reading reflections, academic tutors did:

> You provide a good summary of the article which captures the research question and methods used well. You summarise the findings and why they might be important. However, you do not discuss the strengths of the claims made in the paper and whether or not the authors fully address their research questions. (Tutor feedback on reading reflection 1)

Feedback such as this reminds the student that they need to consider the evidence for the claims made in the paper but does not provide any suggestions as to how the student might go about doing this. It does not support the idea of contextual knowing, where the claims might be evaluated within the particular disciplinary context. This kind of feedback is typical of that given in higher education, but is not in line with the principles of ipsative assessment.

Feedback given by another tutor however, which is more detailed and specific, does encourage a more sophisticated treatment of the materials.

In response to a generic comment about the sample size being too small the tutor writes as follows:

> It's interesting that you critique the sample, given that the authors have made it clear that this is widening participation work, and their focus is on direct entry from FE, not school-leavers (and, with maturity and HNC/D quals, these are people who may not have been successful at school at all). We know attrition to be higher amongst this group, so finding out a bit more about what the obstacles are gives us a good starting point for providing teaching and/or support for successive generations of learners with these particular characteristics.

Whilst the tutor does not say how the student can learn to make a more sophisticated or nuanced comment about the sample, they do contextualise comments about the sample within the research context being described and this serves to demonstrate to the student that they need a more sophisticated and contextualised treatment of the sample, that is, contextualised knowing.

Evidence from students' reading reflections and interviews with students indicated that initially they found the reading reflections task challenging but the more experience they had of it the more they were able to engage with the process:

> Giving feedback to someone else was scary at first and I did not want to share my work. But reading what someone else had done made me think about my work differently.
>
> I did not know what to write at first in the part about responding to the feedback... it was hard... but then I thought it makes me think about how to improve and that I had been telling things but not really... thinking about if what they (the authors) were saying and if it was ok or you know supported.

These quotations from two student interviews reflect a general sense from the students that having to share their work was initially an uncomfortable experience for them as it was not part of their general academic practices. Furthermore, being asked to engage more actively with the feedback they were getting, and to self-assess by responding to the feedback and then thinking about what to do (and what it told them about their learning) was challenging. Students often read feedback and then dismiss it, but being required to respond in a written way to their feedback appears to have focused their minds on their learning.

> I had to think more about my work going back and thinking – do I agree with these comments and if I did what could I do next?

As students continued to do reading reflections (see Fig. 8.1) they became more comfortable with the processes of giving peer feedback and responding to comments on their own work, but it became evident that more support is needed to develop this element of the programme. Students would identify in the work of others where they felt arguments were not fully supported but found it difficult to then apply this kind of assessment to their own work. It appeared they could see the limitations of others' work more easily than their own:

> When I read someone else's stuff I could see where they had not really justified their argument but then I would sometimes find it hard to see that in my own work – so I would think that I had made my argument and

supported it with evidence and then I would get feedback to say that I had not really justified my claim and I was, you know, a little surprised. But then, when I read it again and thought about their comments, I could see it and that was frustrating. (Masters student interview after reading reflection 3)

Students also suggested that working in this way did help them develop their understanding of criticality:

At the start I thought criticality was about making arguments... and you know well yes it is but it is more – you need to justify your arguments and think about the strength of the claim... you can't just say something is good because lots of people say so you need to know why.

I have started thinking about what I read in a different way now. I try to think about the links between the chapter I am reading and what I have read before to try to build up a bigger picture of what I am learning about. I even try to link one module to another but not sure I always do that well. Still get confused when tutors talk about the same things but in different ways. (Masters student interview)

Through engagement with the reading reflection and peer review process, the students who participated fully with the different activities seemed to share the views expressed above that the process of peer – assessment, in combination with peer review, encouraged them to think not just about what they were learning but also how they were learning. So both the product and the process became important. This is a key aim of ipsative assessment practices which are designed to encourage students to really think about learning as a more holistic activity. In addition, the written record of feedback given and responses to it can perhaps allow us to address Davis and Mangan's (2008) argument that in order to fully assess threshold transformations we need to find a way to identify both changes in thinking and changes in the ways of practising associated with those changes in thinking.

What is missing from this case study is real documentation of the students' self-reflections on their feedback and the feedback dialogue. Tutors and students reported finding this aspect of the process difficult:

I did not always know what to write in response to my feedback. Not sure what I should be commenting on at times – sometimes it was about what I had read and others it was about what to do with what I had read. I think being able to do this better would have helped me get at what my feedback meant... but hmm it was hard sometimes. I wanted to ask questions in the feedback bit but was not quite sure how to ask them. (Masters student interview about the process of commenting on feedback)

As self-assessment is an important aspect of the ipsative assessment process, it is important to try to develop this element of the induction programme so that we can get at how students move from independent to contextual ways of knowing. We need to find ways to support tutors' use of feedback that does not simply comment on the products of learning but helps to emphasise the process. This will help to shift the students to a contextual treatment of knowledge which sees them being able to embed their discussions of educational theory and research within a broader context. The ability to do this constitutes evidence of mastery of the critical thinking threshold.

CONCLUSIONS

This chapter presents only a very preliminary exploration of the potential for ipsative assessment to be used as a pedagogical tool to support learners' and tutors' understanding of where they (the learners) are in the liminal tunnel as they move from the first encounter with a threshold concept to a transformed understanding of that concept. It suggests that ipsative self-assessment does not only serve as a vehicle to support students' movement through the liminal space, as they explore their understandings of what they are learning and how, it also tells us about the strategies that they might use to help them move their thinking along. In addition, the dialogue that is established between tutor peer reviewer and learner can serve not only as a source of insight for the tutor about what makes these concepts so troublesome, but also show what pedagogical approaches might help to support threshold transformations.

Whilst the induction programme described in this chapter draws on the principles of ipsative assessment, it has to be acknowledged that the extent to which the principles of ipsative assessment were employed consistently and wholly across the programme must be questioned. For the tutors involved in the programme, ipsative assessment represents a new way of thinking about assessment and the students who participated in the programme were not accustomed to providing or receiving peer comments on their and others' work. Thus the ipsative aspects of the programme need to be thought through more extensively in terms of how students' engagement with the process can be better supported, and how tutors can be supported to give the most beneficial forms of feedback. Attention to these elements of the delivery of the programme will ensure that we can better understand the potential contribution that this approach to assessment might make to student learning and our understanding of liminality. We need to find better ways to encourage and support the self-reflective elements of the process and facilitate a more bi-directional dialogue between student and tutor.

It is acknowledged that what is in this chapter is mostly a theoretical idea about what might be possible. The description of the programme, and the limited data, give only a glimpse into the potential benefits of ipsative assessment as a means of helping us identify where learners are in their liminal journeys. It is hoped, however, that it will serve as a starting point for future teaching, learning and research activities which will help to elucidate in more depth the ideas outlined herein.

References

Alexander, P. A., Jetton, T., & Kulikowich, J. M. (1995). Interrelationship of knowledge, interest, and recall: Assessing a model of domain learning. *Journal of Educational Psychology, 87*(4), 559–575.

Baillie, C., Bowden, J. A., & Meyer, J. H. F. (2013). Threshold capabilities: Threshold concepts and knowledge capability linked through variation theory. *Higher Education, 65*(2), 227–246.

Barbe, W. B., & Milone, M. N. (1981). What we know about modality strengths. *Educational Leadership, 38*(5), 378–380.

Baxter-Magolda, M. B. (2009). The activity of meaning making: A holistic perspective on college student development. *Journal of College Student Development, 50*(6), 621–639.

Boes, L. M., Baxter-Magolda, M. B., & Buckley, J. A. (2010). Foundational assumptions and constructive-developmental theory: Self-authorship narratives. In M. B. Baxter-Magolda, P. S. Meszaros, & E. G. Creamer (Eds.), *Development and assessment of self-authorship: Exploring the concept across cultures* (pp. 3–23). Sterling, VA: Stylus Publishing.

Chen, D., & Rattray, J. (in press). Transforming thinking through problem-based learning in the news media literacy class: Critical thinking as a threshold concept towards threshold capabilities. In R. Land., J. Rattray & R. Matthews (Eds.), *Practice and evidence of the scholarship of teaching and learning in higher education. Special edition: Threshold concepts.*

Cousin, G. (2006). Threshold concepts, troublesome knowledge and emotional capital. In J. H. F. Meyer, & R. Land (Eds.), *Overcoming barriers to student understanding: Threshold concepts and troublesome knowledge* (pp. 134–147). London and New York: Routledge.

Davies, P. (2006). Threshold concepts: How can we recognize them?. In J. H. F. Meyer, & R. Land (Eds.), *Overcoming barriers to student understanding: Threshold concepts and troublesome knowledge* (pp. 70–84). London and New York: Routledge.

Davies, P., & Mangan, J. (2008). Embedding threshold concepts: From theory to pedagogical principles to learning activities. In R. Land, J. H. F. Meyer, & J. Smith (Eds.), *Threshold concepts within the disciplines* (pp. 37–50). Rotterdam and Taipei: Sense Publishers.

Flanagan, M. T. (2016). *Threshold concepts: Undergraduate teaching, postgraduate training and professional development. A short introduction and bibliography.* http://www.ee.ucl.ac.uk/~mflanaga/thresholds.html. Accessed 25 January 2016.

Giancarlo, C. A., & Facione, P. A. (2001). A look across four years at the disposition toward critical thinking amongst undergraduate students. *The Journal of General Education, 50*(1), 29–55.

Hughes, G. (2011). Aiming for personal best: A case for introducing ipsative assessment in higher education. *Studies in Higher Education, 36*(3), 353–367.

Hughes, G. (2014). *Ipsative assessment. Motivation through marking progress.* Basingstoke: Palgrave Macmillan.

Hughes, G., Wood, E., & Kitagawa, K. (2014). Use of self-referential (ipsative) feedback to motivate and guide distance learners. *Open Learning, 29*(1), 33–43.

Land, R., Rattray, J., & Vivian, P. (2014). Learning in the liminal space: A semiotic approach to threshold concepts. *Higher Education, 67*, 199–217.

Meyer, J. H. F., & Land, R. (2003a). Threshold concepts and troublesome knowledge: Linkages to ways of thinking and practising. In C. Rust (Ed.), *Improving student learning – Theory and practice ten years on* (pp. 412–424). Oxford: OCSLD.

Meyer, J. H. F., & Land, R. (2003b). *Threshold concepts and troublesome knowledge: linkages to ways of thinking and practising within the discipline* ETL Project Occasional Report 4. Edinburgh. http://www.etl.tla.ed.ac.uk/docs/ETLreport4.pdf. Accessed 25 January 2016.

Meyer, J. H. F., & Land, R. (2005). Threshold concepts and troublesome knowledge (2): epistemological considerations and a conceptual framework for teaching and learning. *Higher Education, 49*(3), 373–388.

Meyer, J. H. F., & Shanahan, M. (2003). *The troublesome nature of a threshold concept in economics.* Padova, Italy. Paper presented at the Conference of the European Association for Research on Learning and Instruction (EARLI), August, 26–30.

Nicol, D. (2011). *Developing students' ability to construct feedback, QAA Scotland, Enhancement Themes.* http://www.enhancementthemes.ac.uk/resources/pub lications/graduate-for-the-21st-century. Accessed 25 January 2016.

The Onion. (2000). Parents of nasal learners demand odor-based curriculum. *The Onion, 36*(9). http://www.theonion.com/article/parents-of-nasal-learners-demand-odor-based-curric-396. Accessed 14 October 2015.

Perkins, D. (1999). The many faces of constructivism. *Educational Leadership, 57*(3), 6–11.

Perkins, D. (2008). Beyond understanding. In R. Land, J. H. F. Meyer, & J. Smith (Eds.), *Threshold concepts within the disciplines* (pp. 3–20). Rotterdam: Sense.

Rattray, J., & Smith, J. (2015). Principles for reviewing the taught postgraduate induction curricula. In P. Kneale (Ed.), *Masters level teaching, learning and assessment: Issues in design and delivery* (Vol. 61–63). London: Palgrave.

Shanahan, M., & Meyer, J. H. F. (2006). The troublesome nature of a threshold concept in economics. In J. H. F. Meyer & R. Land (Eds.), *Overcoming barriers to student understanding: Threshold concepts and troublesome knowledge* (pp. 100–114). London and New York: Routledge.

Taylor, C. E. (2006). Threshold concepts in biology: Do they fit the definition?. In J. H. F. Meyer, & R. Land (Eds.), *Overcoming barriers to student understanding: Threshold concepts and troublesome knowledge* (pp. 87–99). London and New York: Routledge.

Trafford, V. (2008). Conceptual frameworks as a threshold concept. In R. Land., J. H. F. Meyer, & J. Smith (Eds.), *Threshold concepts within the disciplines* (pp. 273–288). Rotterdam: Sense Publishers.

Vivian, P. (2012). *A new symbol based writing system for use in illustrating basic dynamics.* Unpublished Ph.D. thesis, Coventry University.

Wenger, E., McDermott, R., & Snyder, W. M. (2002). *Cultivating communities of practice.* Boston, MA: Harvard Business Press.

Julie Rattray is director of postgraduate taught programmes and a lecturer in Education and Psychology in the School of Education at Durham University, UK. Her research interests include, the affective dimensions of learning with a particular focus on liminality and threshold concepts. Julie teaches on a range of undergraduate and postgraduate modules that take a psychological approach to teaching and learning. In addition she contributes to the Postgraduate Certificate in Academic practice. Julie has recently become a Senior fellow of the Higher Education Academy.

CHAPTER 9

Use of Learning Gain Measurements to Compare Teacher-Centric and Student-Centric Feedback in Higher Education

Hui-Teng Hoo and Gwyneth Hughes

INTRODUCTION

This chapter explores the measurement of a cohort's average learning gain in a comparative study of two approaches to feedback. We compare the relative influence of the agents of assessment and feedback – teacher and student – on developing intercultural conflict resolution skills in higher education through monitoring personal learning gain or loss across five assessments. The teacher-centric and student-centric formative feedback models of Molloy and Boud (2013) are discussed and adapted to create the theoretical models of teacher-centric and student-centric assessment

H.-T. Hoo (✉)
Nanyang Business School, Nanyang Technological University, Singapore
e-mail: HTHoo@ntu.edu.sg

G. Hughes
UCL Institute of Education, UCL, London, UK
e-mail: Gwyneth.hughes@ucl.ac.uk

© The Author(s) 2017   173
G. Hughes (ed.), *Ipsative Assessment and Personal Learning Gain*,
DOI 10.1057/978-1-137-56502-0_9

and feedback. As well as presenting the results of the study, the use of learning gain data is also scrutinised to understand both the strengths and weaknesses of using learning gain cohort data to make pedagogic choices. The theoretical models were tested using test score data collected from two cohorts of 47 and 44 students by applying the two different feedback models and at multiple time points over thirteen weeks of an undergraduate course in Singapore. The following key questions formed the basis of the study:

1. Between teacher-centric and student-centric assessment and feedback, which is more effective in increasing students' capability to resolve intercultural conflict?
2. How far does any increase in capability as a result of either teacher-centric or student-centric assessment and feedback persist beyond short-term testing?

Findings from the research indicated that with both teacher-centric and student-centric feedback, students' intercultural conflict resolution skills improved over time and small differences in the learning gains from the assessments were not significant. However, although a conclusion might be that both methods have equal merit, comparison of test results does not give a full picture.

The chapter explores two further issues that arose from the learning gain data. First, although the data indicate that there is little difference in learning outcome, this does not mean that the two methods are equally valuable. The overall recommendation is that student-centric assessment is preferable because it has added benefits that the teacher-centric assessment cannot offer. Student-centric assessment lays the foundation for sustainable assessment and feedback practices (Sadler 1998; Boud 2000; Tan 2007; Molloy and Boud 2013), and particularly for large classes, helps learners develop self-referential and self-regulatory skills (Hughes 2014), and builds capability of making judgements about subsequent work of self and others in employment and other life-learning contexts (Molloy and Boud 2013).

Second, we might assume that learning gains persist after a course has ended, but students are unlikely to be reassessed after a period of time has elapsed to check that their learning has a permanency. In this study there was the opportunity to re-test student performance three weeks after their final assessment to estimate the longevity of any learning gains. The results unexpectedly and alarmingly indicated that the learning gain fell away almost completely with time once the feedback processes had ended. Use of learning gain measurement in this way thus has significant implications for evaluation teaching effectiveness beyond short-term teaching for the test.

The chapter concludes with a discussion of the challenges in using cohort learning gain data particularly in the reliability of the results of five different assessments. We suggest that learning gain data may need to be supplemented with other data if it is to be of value in enhancing feedback practice.

Understanding Assessment and Feedback

> Feedback is one of the more instructionally powerful and least understood features in instructional design. (Cohen 1985, p. 33)

Indeed, feedback is 'least understood' because there exists conflicting research findings with no regular pattern of interpretations. The variation may be partly due to a corpus of research that continues to present multiple definitions of feedback. We draw on the literature to present feedback as an integral part of learning, with the 'information provided by an agent...regarding aspects of one's performance or understanding' (Hattie and Timperley 2007, p. 81). This information functions to bridge the gap between task goal and task performance (Ramaprasad 1983; Sadler 1989; Randall and Zundel 2012). Beyond task, the contexts of feedback include processing of the task, self-regulation and self as a person (Hattie and Timperley 2007). Closing the gap requires a medium to communicate established criteria to judge goals and performances and helps to reduce uncertainty and cognitive load related to inappropriate task strategies, procedural errors or misconceptions (Ilgen et al. 1979; Hoska 1993; Mason and Bruning 2001; Mory 2004; Narciss and Huth 2004).

To summarise the key concepts and to apply the ideas in the literature to the study, we developed an acronym for what are the essential components of assessment and feedback, M.E.A.T.

- M stands for modality of assessment and feedback which can be ipsative (self-referenced), criterion-referenced or norm-referenced
- E is the environmental milieu or context in which assessment and feedback are provided and received

- A is for agent of assessment and feedback in regard to who provides the assessment and feedback
- T stands for typology of assessment which can be summative and/or formative.

MODALITY OF ASSESSMENT AND FEEDBACK ('M' IN MEAT)

The general modes of assessment instruments which produce feedback are in norm-referenced and criterion-referenced forms (Linn and Gronlund 2000). *Norm-referenced assessment* provides a measure of performance that is interpretable in terms of an individual's relative standing in a known group. This mode of assessment and feedback has fallen out of favour in higher education and has largely been replaced by criterion-referenced assessment.

Unlike norm-referenced assessments, *criterion-referenced assessment* is designed to measure performance that is interpretable in terms of a clearly defined set of criteria and standards of achievement before the assessment takes place. There is typically no restriction in the percentage of people falling within categories of below, meeting or above the standard. Standards and criteria are often used interchangeably causing some confusion (Hughes 2011). Criteria are specific to the observable traits in a piece of work that a student produces. Standards are the levels of achievement for each criterion and these levels can be compared if the same, or equivalent, performances are repeated.

The work of authors Hughes (2011, 2014), Scott et al. (2013), Hughes et al. (2014) and Hughes et al. (2015) revived the term ipsative assessment which is unfamiliar to many education practitioners. *Ipsative assessment* is defined as assessment that 'compares existing performance with previous performance' (Hughes 2011, p. 353, 2014). Hughes (2011, 2014) refers to a qualitative comparison of students' previous performance to further performance in a succession of related activities as ipsative formative feedback. This comparison can also be quantitative as in two or more comparative measurements which indicate a learning gain (or loss) and can be used to capture a personal best score. It is this approach to comparison that we take in the study using series of teacher-marked tests, although students may also have engaged with ipsative feedback.

ENVIRONMENTAL MILIEU OR CONTEXT OF ASSESSMENT AND FEEDBACK ('E' IN MEAT)

The environmental milieu or context is important because assessment and feedback do not happen in a vacuum. The learning context needs to be taken into consideration to include the type of assessment and how feedback is provided.

The context of this study is the development of intercultural conflict resolution skills in a higher education course via multimedia (high-fidelity) intercultural simulation (Rockstuhl et al. 2015). Students are required to perceive and interpret the situations marked by cultural differences between people representing a dyad of nationalities. The video scenarios were developed by Ang et al. (2014) along with intercultural experts following best-practice recommendations for script identification (Weekley et al. 2006) and video-development (Walker et al. 2008). Students who demonstrate intercultural conflict resolution skills produce appropriate and creative ways to resolve the intercultural conflicts which in most cases are win-win resolutions, advantageous to both sides. Feedback is provided using criteria-referenced rubrics with win-win resolutions as the optimal outcome.

AGENTS OF ASSESSMENT AND FEEDBACK ('A' IN MEAT)

Agents of feedback can be teachers or students (through self and/or peer review). Peer assessment is a process during which students deliberate the quality of a peer's work or performance, evaluate the extent to which it reflects targeted goals or criteria and provide suggestions for improvement (Topping 1998). Student self-assessment is often used synonymously with self-evaluation, self-monitoring, self-reflection, self-rating, self-marking, self-scoring and self-grading (Andrade and Valtcheva 2009; Brown and Harris 2013; Falchikov and Boud 1989; Valle and Andrade 2014).

In the study, teacher and student as agents of feedback are compared using the model developed below.

TYPOLOGY OF ASSESSMENT ('T' IN MEAT)

While assessment drives learning because it makes the student accountable to self and/or to others, assessment followed by feedback accelerates the process of learning when understood by students to bridge the gap between the current status and desired status (Sadler 1989). Assessment and feedback take summative and formative forms.

Summative assessment, often referred to as assessment of learning, is evaluative and is used to assess how much learning has taken place at the end of the instructional unit. A model of information giving and receiving and then testing is challenged in higher education literature, but often acceded to in practice because it is effort- and time-efficient in the short run. The potential to use assessment in its formative form is under-utilised or over-shadowed by summative criteria-referenced grades in higher education (Gibbs 2006; Hughes 2011; Scott et al. 2013) because of the rapid expansion of class sizes which is often unmatched by increases in teaching faculty. Nevertheless, information from summative assessment can also be used formatively when students or teachers use the information to guide effort in subsequent modules or courses. As Perrenoud (1991, p. 80) recounts, 'any assessment that helps a pupil to learn and develop is formative'.

Formative assessment, often regarded as assessment for learning (Black et al. 2004; Boyle and Fisher 2007), is designed to provide effective feedback to teachers and students about the gap between present performance and the desired standards of performance so as to improve and accelerate learning (Sadler 1998). In contrast to summative assessment which is more product-oriented and focuses on assessment of a final product, formative assessment aims to improve learning while it is happening in order to maximise success rather than merely determine success or failure only after the event. Ideally, formative assessment is a cumulative process that is extended over time, and not a one-off act. Models of feedback processes are useful for guiding a longer-term approach and Molloy and Boud (2013) outline different models for teacher and students as agents.

MODELS OF TEACHER-CENTRIC AND STUDENT-CENTRIC FEEDBACK

Teacher-centric formative assessment and feedback takes place when teachers hold the responsibility to design and administer tasks for their students so that students have an opportunity to demonstrate changes in their performance and/or behaviour.

Molloy and Boud (2013) demonstrated in their model 'Mark 1 Feedback' an iterative task design which suggests teachers transmit information to students, with the underpinning assumption that the transmitted information is understood, useful and turned into action.

Student-centric formative assessment and feedback, by contrast, reflects increasing attention on assessment and feedback practices that can develop and sustain students' self-assessment ability beyond its immediate programme of study (Tan 2007, p. 115). The literature argues that higher education students have a capacity to make evaluative judgements both about their own work and that of others, independently of teachers (Nicol and Macfarlane-Dick 2006; Boud 2007; Hattie and Timperley 2007; Sadler 2010). Students are seen as 'active constructors of feedback information' (Nicol 2010, p. 503) for both self and peers.

Self-assessment is the 'involvement of students in identifying standards and/or criteria to apply to their work and making judgments about the extent to which they have met these criteria and standards' (Boud 1991, p. 5), and is assumed to be volitional on the part of the student. The concept is linked with the concept of self-regulation and internal feedback (Butler and Winne 1995; Nicol and Macfarlane-Dick 2006) where a learner monitors and regulates learning and performance.

Peer assessment is defined as students grading the work or performance of their peers using criteria and standards (Falchikov 2007). Falchikov and Goldfinch (2000) found from their meta-analysis of 48 quantitative peer assessment studies comparing peer and teacher marks that peer assessments resemble more closely teacher assessments when judgements are based on well-defined and understood criteria. These criteria of quality help students build 'guild knowledge' (Sadler 1989) and allow them to differentiate between levels of performance for their work and that of others, and by so doing gain a sense of what it means to produce quality performance.

These strategies for effective learning, self- and peer assessment and feedback are applicable in the second feedback framework that Molloy and Boud (2013) created. The framework, known as Mark 2 Feedback or student-centric formative feedback, embraces both self and peer feedback, situating learners as agents in the assessment and feedback process. Mark 2 Feedback proposes that students are oriented to the standards of work and purpose of feedback before an activity is carried out. After the activity, student judges his or her own work. Students then participate actively in soliciting feedback from peers and they compare self and peer judgements so as to plan for improvement in future performance. Although teachers may still provide some feedback on assessed tasks, with students taking the foreground in assessing self and others the effect of teacher as transmitter of feedback is reduced.

The effectiveness of the Mark 2 feedback framework has yet to be tested empirically (Molloy and Boud 2013) and there are few experimental (or quasi experimental) studies on peer assessment (Van Zundert et al. 2010). One method of testing the models is to use learning gain measurements that can demonstrate the impact of a student-centric feedback process compared with other methods.

THE STUDY: COMPARING STUDENT AND TEACHER FEEDBACK USING LEARNING GAIN DATA

Theoretical Models

The Mark 1 and Mark 2 feedback models from Molloy and Boud (2013) were adapted to anchor the theoretical models of teacher-centric and student-centric assessment and feedback in intercultural conflict resolution (Fig. 9.1). In the teacher-centric formative feedback model, the process starts with the teacher providing the rubric of criteria and standards of work and the purpose of feedback so that students can appreciate their strengths and weaknesses from information provided to them on one intercultural conflict video case before they embark onto the next video case. This initiation stage is not present in Molloy and Boud's Mark 1 feedback model.

In Fig. 9.1, there is an intentional illustration of a black box of 'information to student' to illustrate the point that even though the teacher can provide feedback, it is not known whether students will understand and reflect on the information provided so as to better subsequent work.

The student-centric process also starts with the teacher explaining the criteria and standards of work, and the purpose of feedback before students embark on the first activity. With the completion of the first activity, a student judges his/her work based on criterion-referenced rubrics. He/she asks for specific feedback from a peer who will assess the work. The student will then compare the judgements of his/her work based on peer feedback so as to plan for subsequent improved work.

The development of self-assessment skills requires 'appropriate scaffolding with the teacher working with the student as part of co-regulation' (Evans 2013, p. 88). The student-centric assessment and feedback model is scaffolded by a self-assessment and peer-assessment system, with underlying cognitive, constructivist and social constructivist theories of learning. Students use previous learning as a foundation upon which to modify,

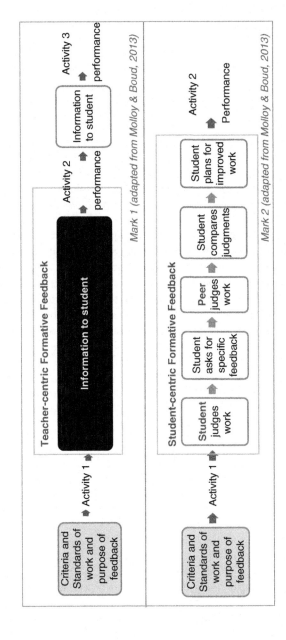

Fig. 9.1 Theoretical models of feedback

build and generate new knowledge. Knowledge is constructed by self and co-constructed between students through student interactivity.

Methodology: Using Cohort Learning Gain Data

To compare the two pedagogies for increasing students' capability to resolve intercultural conflict, the theoretical models were tested in two quasi-experimental groups. Non-random sampling was adopted, using students in the undergraduate course as convenient samples. Cohort 1 contained a sample of 47 students in one semester where the teacher-centric model was used and cohort 2 consisted of 44 students in another semester with the student-centric assessment and feedback model. In an analysis of the student characteristics, mean differences between four variables – gender, age, ability and number of languages spoken – and their levels of significances showed that both studies had equivalent groups (Cohen et al. 2007).

In the semester course, all students completed teacher-assessments on intercultural situational judgement. Students were exposed to five video vignettes over a period of eleven weeks. Students were required to create the most appropriate and creative actions to resolve intercultural conflicts after they viewed a short two to three-minute video vignette depicting a challenging intercultural interaction. A rubric which consisted of the meta-framework of conflict resolution strategies was provided for rating. Data were collected at five time points in total but only the first four tests used the feedback model and the final test was held after a further three weeks had elapsed with no feedback from the previous test. Their task was to write down their resolution to an open-ended question on the intercultural conflict situation. The tasks were teacher assessed by a single assessor on a 0–5 scale. The assessor remarked a 10 % sample of assessments several months after the initial assessment and estimated that the reliability of the marking was high.

The aim of including the fifth assessment without feedback was to find out if any increased capability as a result of the teacher-centric assessment and feedback or student-centric assessment and feedback would persist beyond the four time points.

Analysis

Data analysis was performed using SPSS (Statistical Package for the Social Sciences). The data were analysed as repeated measurements in time, four time points then for all five points, using General Linear

Model (GLM). The GLM output shows the trend of performance across the assessments.

LEARNING GAIN FINDINGS FOR THE FOUR ASSESSMENTS WITH FEEDBACK

The results are tabulated in Table 9.1 and illustrated graphically in Fig. 9.2.

In both groups, assessment scores improved between the second and fourth administrations. Students' intercultural situational judgement performance increased over time for both the teacher-centric and student-centric assessment and feedback groups. The results support the potential of both the teacher-centric and student-centric assessment and feedback models in helping students improve their task performance over time.

The fall in student performances – in both teacher-centric and student-centric assessment and feedback between Assessment 1 and Assessment 2 – seems anomalous as we might expect an increase in scores not a decrease. The dip in performance in the second assessment could be attributed to its difficulty. Based on feedback gathered from other instructors, Assessment 2 was deemed more difficult than most assessments. Also, data collected from previous semesters suggested that most students obtained a lower score for this assessment. Variation in difficulty of assessments is a potential problem with measurement of learning gain which we will return to later.

Between Assessment 3 and Assessment 4, the group with teacher-centric assessment and feedback performed slightly better than the group with student-centric assessment and feedback. In the fourth intercultural situational

Table 9.1 Comparative means of teacher-centric and student-centric formative feedback

Assessment	Teacher-centric Formative Feedback (N = 47)		Student-centric Formative Feedback (N = 44)		Test of Significance of Difference	
	M	SD	M	SD	Δ	P
1	2.87	1.01	2.81	1.36	0.06	0.83
2	2.21	1.19	2.59	1.14	–0.38	0.13
3	2.95	0.77	2.59	1.29	0.36	0.10
4	4.19	0.79	3.81	0.81	0.38	0.03*

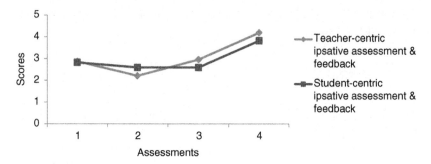

Fig. 9.2 Comparative mean of student scores for the two cohorts

judgement test, the mean score of students with teacher-centric assessment and feedback was 0.38 higher than the mean score of students with student-centric assessment and feedback and this was significant (p = 0.03<0.05).

The Positive Effects of Feedback

The results support the extensive literature on the positive effects of feedback on learning. The use of peer collaboration over feedback enabled students to develop greater levels of competence as seen from their performance. Similarly, the teacher-centric assessment and feedback is helpful in guiding students' performance, through teacher's guidance and/or students' reflection on their learning and teacher's feedback so as to build and expand knowledge.

Formative tasks provide teachers and students with information about performance and enable them to adjust teaching and learning in ways that promote achievement. The results suggest that Molloy and Boud's (2013) models of Mark 1 and Mark 2 feedback are both useful in guiding the course structure and design, facilitating student learning and evaluating the assessment and feedback process.

TEACHER-CENTRIC FEEDBACK AND STUDENT-CENTRIC FEEDBACK: LITTLE DIFFERENCE IN OUTCOMES

Based on four assessments over a short time span of seven weeks, the teacher-centric assessment and feedback has helped students perform possibly slightly better in intercultural conflict resolution than the student-centric assessment and feedback. The mean difference in performance between the teacher-centric and student-centric formative feedback ranges between 0.06 and 0.38, out of the maximum 5 points attainable in the rubric. This translates to between 1.2 % and 7.6 %. There are a couple of factors that could be at play here.

First, as Sadler (1998) suggests, teachers possessed intellectual and experiential resources required for giving feedback to self and others. These resources are accumulated through practical experience and a body of conceptual knowledge. The teacher has superiority in subject matter, and in this case the teacher possessed a repertoire of resolutions based on her experiences of evaluating students' resolutions which helped in assessing creative tasks or what Sadler (1998) refers as non-convergent learning. Furthermore, students' knowledge of the subject matter is by definition partial. Hence, it may take students a longer time to build the capability to be as effective as the teacher in providing feedback to enhance performance.

Second, Ashford and Cummings (1983) suggest that a public assessment method can be less effective than a private one because of potential face loss through negative inferences about ability. If students perceive that peer assessment and feedback is threatening, they are less likely to be open with their peers on the corrective aspect of feedback. This is especially relevant in the Asian environment which is characterised by high-context and facework behaviours (Masumoto et al. 2000). A high-context communication or message is one in which most of the information is either internalised in the person with very little said in the explicit part of the message (Hall 1976). This is particularly common when the other party is not within the in-group, and/or when negative information is relayed. Thus setting a trusting, non-threatening and cohesive learning environment is crucial to encourage collaborative assessment and feedback so that overt and explicit information can be passed on to peers.

Selecting Which Feedback Method to Employ

The decision to use either pedagogy for engaging students depends on the learning outcomes set by teachers. If the learning outcome is solely to improve the intercultural conflict resolution skills, it seems we could recommend teacher-centric assessment and feedback from the learning gain data. However, the decision could also be influenced by time and resources. If very similar outcomes can be obtained with peer feedback then there are time savings for the teacher. These may, however, be offset by the time taken in advising and training students for peer feedback. Until students gain sufficient prowess to self-regulate, teachers must scaffold and work closely with students to co-regulate their learning before they self-regulate. For example, teachers may need to set aside more class time for students to engage in self and peer feedback, as compared with directive telling of 'correct' answers. Teachers can use this extra time to move around the class to ensure students are participative in the peer discussion; observe students' ability to articulate the resolutions and identify the criteria to rate the resolutions; pick up some good and counter-productive resolutions which could then be shared in class.

Another possible benefit is that peer learning may have a more lasting and wider impact because the students have been more actively involved. In the study an additional assessment was used to test if there is significant difference in the assessment scores beyond the short-term assessment outcome and we will explore this point further.

DOES LEARNING GAIN EXTEND BEYOND THE TESTING PERIOD?

The results of the fifth assessment showed that the performance of both groups decreased. Although the teacher-centric assessment and feedback group again performed slightly higher than that of the student-centric assessment and feedback, the difference of mean scores at 0.15 is not significant, p = 0.38>0.05.

In the fifth assessment, we can see from Fig. 9.3 that students' performance decreased for both groups. The performance of the student-centric group and the teacher-centric group follow a similar trajectory.

The reason for the decrease in performance in the fifth assessment, which was conducted three weeks after the fourth assessment, could be attributed to the (lack of) recent practice with the assessment items and/or lack of recent feedback. Students may have a tendency to do well with practice in the short term, but performance may decrease in the long term as they forget the material they have learnt. Here learning gain data is particularly valuable for estimating the persistence of learning after a teaching period has ended and may show up some worrying trends in learning loss over time. Another explanation could be that assessment 5 was more difficult than the others but this was not judged to be the case in

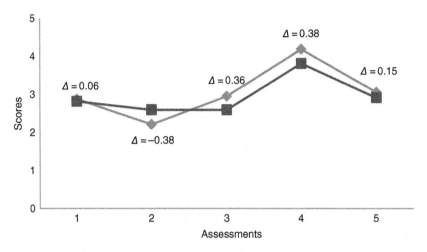

Fig. 9.3 Teacher-centric and student-centric assessment and feedback outcomes (all 5 assessments)

contrast with the case of assessment 2 which was evidently more difficult. In this case study the reason for the apparent lack of persistence of the learning gain over time is certainly worth further exploration.

WIDER BENEFITS OF STUDENT-CENTRIC FEEDBACK

Though the teacher-led assessment and feedback with criteria and standards is beneficial to students' performance, it is also arguable that this pedagogy is equivalent to teaching to the test. There should be other pertinent lifelong skills that a teacher should consider. These include sustainable assessment and feedback so that students develop regulatory skills and build capability to make judgements of subsequent work of self and others aligned with social constructivist learning theory (Vygotsky 1978). Opportunities to practise these skills abound in structured student-centric formative feedback (Andrade and Du 2007; Evans 2013; Falchikov 2007).

Self-referential and regulatory skills are essential skills for the workplace (Carless 2006; Andrade and Du 2007; Boud and Falchikov 2007; Falchikov 2007; Hattie and Timperley 2007; Nicol 2010; Evans 2013). Learning outcomes potentially go beyond the knowledge and skills of the subject to include developing and sustaining students' self-assessment ability beyond this course (Sadler 1998; Tan 2007; Molloy and Boud 2013); building capability of making judgements about subsequent work of self and others (Boud 2000); and providing the opportunity for collaborative forms of assessment such as peer learning so that students build 'guild knowledge' (Sadler 1989).

These aforementioned skills and attitudes are enduring learning benefits, reflective of the comprehensive nature of education system, which are transferable across learning environments and can equip students for the future workplace. However, when assessments are tightly defined as in this study the more generic and potentially transferable skills are not measured so there is no way of knowing if the students here benefited in other ways from student-centric feedback, all we can say is that they were not significantly disadvantaged. It would need a much larger study with more qualitative as well as quantitative data to identify any longer-term generic learning gains.

Thus, teachers who are experimenting with student-centric assessment and feedback should not be discouraged by lack of immediate learning gains. They should persist with more tries and gather a broad range of learning gain data before making a decision on whether they ought to switch assessment and feedback methods.

LIMITATIONS OF USING LEARNING GAIN DATA AND FUTURE RESEARCH

Despite the strength of the theoretical models and longitudinal design, this study has limitations that provide avenues for future research.

First, there is the limitation of the learning gain data because some assessments may be harder than others. Chapter 2 argued that it is difficult to obtain reliable learning gain data. This study has demonstrated that where different tests are compared it must be assumed that the tests are equivalent in difficulty. Anomalous results may be attributed to the limitations of this assumption. In this study variation in difficulty of questions was recognised as very likely influencing the results, but making such judgements is not straightforward. Future studies could include a set of ordered benchmark tests. These tests could be rolled out to a group of undergraduate students, with similar demographics, in one sitting. This would provide the average score of each test and help determine the difficulty levels of each test.

Second, the comparative effectiveness of innovations in assessment and feedback is drawn solely from averaged cohort assessment scores. An average gain in each cohort does not take into account students who showed little or no improvement amongst others who achieved marked improvement. Future research could look into the trajectory of scores for each student and identify why students had little improvement over time with a specific feedback type whilst others progressed over time. This would pave a way for further research on ipsative feedback that is changing the focus of feedback towards improvement regardless of achievement (Hughes 2014) so as to motivate learners.

Third, the studies were designed and taught by one teacher but variation in the assessor is common. Even with careful marking schemes reliability between assessors cannot be certain. A single assessor might provide better reliability, but an assessor can become tired or distracted. Double checking marking is a remedy and in this study the marking did appear to be consistent, but this is time consuming and may not be practical. To ascertain the generalisability of the results, future research could attempt to replicate the design in similar contexts of conflict resolutions, such as in negotiation and cross-cultural classes, and/or across other subject matters, with different assessors and possibly test effects of student characteristics on performance via the two feedback types.

Fourth, the assumption that students transfer the knowledge, skills and attitudes they learnt from one situation to another is untenable if educators cannot judge whether or not the transfer takes place. Transfer of learning in higher education encompasses transfer of learning of knowledge and skills within a course, from one course to another, from one discipline to another, between school and home, and from school to workplace (National Research Council 2000). The raison d'être of higher education is that it provides a foundation on which a lifetime of learning in work and other social settings can be built (Boud and Falchikov 2007). Thus, longer-term rigorous data could be explored in future research on what happens over time if students had the chance to transfer their learning of intercultural conflict resolution, self-regulation and capability of making judgements to subsequent work on self and others. Such data would need a method of tracking individual students over long periods of time and a range of contexts and would be difficult to acquire.

Learning gain data can show up some interesting trends as this study shows, but numerical data may need to be combined with qualitative data to be widely applied in judgements and choices about pedagogies and student learning. The study has demonstrated that further information on personal learning gain such as from student self-evaluations is required before decisions are made on the effectiveness of different pedagogies.

CONCLUSION

The study aimed to compare the effectiveness of teacher-centric and student-centric formative assessment and feedback. The MEAT acronym provided the key elements of assessment and feedback – *modality* of feedback such as ipsative-referenced, criterion-referenced or norm-referenced; *environmental milieu* or context in which feedback is provided and received, *agent* of feedback centres on who provides the feedback, and *typology* includes summative and formative assessments.

Two models of assessment and feedback, teacher-centric and student-centric, were tested at multiple time points and across two samples. The comparative and longitudinal findings of the two types of assessment and feedback point to similar effectiveness of both practices for building students' skills in intercultural conflict resolution. However, the study also suggested that there are both learning gains and losses over time. Feedback, both teacher-centric and student-centric, had a temporary effect and learning gain did not persist in the longer term, between assessment four and five after some time (three weeks), which is a worrying phenomenon both for assessment of intercultural conflict resolution and possibly for other disciplines.

The teacher-centric assessment and feedback produced marginally higher scores than student-centric assessment and feedback in the short term, but the difference between the scores is not significant in four out of five assessments and the trajectory of scores in both groups overlap considerably.

Thus, from the learning gain data alone it would appear that either model could be selected, but this data gives us a very limited picture and supplementary information is needed before decision is made, such as about the efficiency of each model. Student-centric assessment and feedback may produce other personal learning gains which might make its pedagogy worth pursuing as this environment emphasises self-comparison of progress which is well suited for building a sense of self efficacy (Bandura 1993) that promotes academic achievement. The model also lays the foundation for sustainable assessment and feedback practices in which students develop self-referential attitudes and regulatory skills to distinguish what is quality performance, enact it and then monitor their progress over time by comparing previous performance with current performance. In addition, student-centric assessment and feedback gives students opportunities to practise twenty-first century work-related skills in communicating ideas orally. Peer discussion increases students' opportunity to talk with one another, discuss their ideas for resolutions thereby increasing their reasoning skills to put forth their ideas logically and convincingly. Thus, student-centric assessment and feedback in intercultural conflict resolution may also have wider application in other disciplines, apart from cross-cultural classes.

Finally, the trends may be moving towards 'big data' collection, but this study has indicated that even if the reliability issues are addressed, which is not an easy task, cohort learning gain data alone is insufficient of itself for pedagogic research purposes. The study thus supports the assertion in Chap. 2 that learning data at scale needs to be combined with other personal learning gain data to be of value in comparing different teaching methods.

References

Andrade, H., & Du, Y. (2007). Student responses to criteria-referenced self-assessment. *Assessment & Evaluation in Higher Education, 32*(2), 159–181.

Andrade, H., & Valtcheva, A. (2009). Promoting learning and achievement through self-assessment. *Theory into Practice, 28*(1), 12–19.

Ang, S., Rockstuhl, T., & Ng, K. Y. (2014). *Performance-based cultural intelligence (CQ): Development and validation of an intercultural situational judgment test (iSJT).* Nanyang Technological University: Center for Leadership and Cultural Intelligence.

Ashford, S. J., & Cummings, L. L. (1983). Feedback as an individual resource: Personal strategies of creating information. *Organisational Behavior and Human Performance, 32*, 370–398.

Bandura, A. (1993). Perceived self-efficacy in cognitive development and functioning. *Educational Psychologist, 28*(2), 117–148.

Bangert-Drowns, R. L., Kulik, C. L. C., Kulik, J. A., & Morgan, M. (1991). The instructional effect of feedback in test-like events. *Review of Educational Research, 61*(2), 213–238.

Black, P., Harrison, C., Lee, C., Marshall, B., & Wiliam, D. (2004). Working inside the black box: assessment for learning in the classroom. *Phi Delta Kappan, 86*(1), 8–21.

Boud, D. (1991). *HERDSA Green guide no 5. Implementing student self- assessment.* 2nd edition. Campbelltown: The Higher Education Research and Development Society of Australasia, HERDSA.

Boud, D. (2000). Sustainable assessment: Rethinking assessment for learning society. *Studies in Continuing Education, 22*(2), 151–167.

Boud, D. (2007). Reframing assessment as if learning were important. In D. Boud & N. Falchikov (Eds.), *Rethinking assessment for higher education: Learning for the longer term* (pp. 25–46). London: Routledge.

Boud, D. (2013). *Enhancing learning through self-assessment.* London: Routledge.

Boud, D., & Falchikov, N. (2007). Developing assessment for informing judgement. In D. Boud & N. Falchikov (Eds.), *Rethinking assessment in higher education: Learning for the longer term* (pp. 181–197). London: Routledge.

Boyle, J., & Fisher, S. (2007). *Educational testing: A competence-based approach.* Oxford: Blackwell Publishing.

Brown, G. T. L., & Harris, L. R. (2013). Student self-assessment. In J. H. McMillan (Ed.), *The SAGE handbook of research on classroom assessment* (pp. 367–393). Thousand Oaks, CA: Sage.

Butler, D. L., & Winne, P. H. (1995). Feedback and self-regulated learning: A theoretical synthesis. *Review of Educational Research, 65*(3), 245–281.

Carless, D. (2006). Differing perceptions in the feedback process. *Studies in Higher Education, 31*(2), 219–233.

Cohen, V. B. (1985). A re-examination of feedback in computer-based instruction: Implications for instructional design. *Educational Technology, 25*(1), 33–37.

Cohen, L., Manion, L., & Morrison, K. (2007). *Research methods in education [Electronic resource].* Hoboken, NJ: Taylor & Francis.

Dochy, F., Segers, M., & Sujismans, D. (1999). The use of self-, peer and co-assessment in higher education: A review. *Studies in Higher Education, 24*(3), 331–350.

Evans, C. (2013). Making sense of assessment feedback in higher education. *Review of Educational Research, 83*(1), 70–120.

Falchikov, N. (2007). The place of peers in learning and assessment. In D. Boud & N. Falchikov (Eds.), *Rethinking assessment in higher education: Learning for the longer term* (pp. 128–143). London: Routledge.

Falchikov, N., & Boud, D. (1989). Student self-assessment in higher education: A meta-analysis. *Review of Educational Research, 59*(4), 395–430.

Falchikov, N., & Goldfinch, J. (2000). Student peer assessment in higher education: A meta-analysis comparing peer and teacher marks. *Review of Educational Research, 70*(3), 287–322.

Gibbs, G. (2006). Why assessment is changing. In C. Bryan & K. Clegg (Eds.), *Innovative assessment in higher education* (p. 11). Abingdon: Routledge.

Hall, E. T. (1976). *Beyond culture.* New York: Doubleday.

Hattie, J., & Timperley, H. (2007). The power of feedback. *Review of Educational Research, 77*(1), 81–112.

Hoska, D. M. (1993). Motivating learners through CBI feedback: Developing a positive learner perspective. In J. V. Dempsey & G. C. Sales (Eds.), *Interactive instruction and feedback* (pp. 105–132). Englewood Cliffs, NJ: Educational Technology Publications.

Hughes, G. (2011). Towards a personal best: A case for introducing ipsative assessment in higher education. *Studies in Higher Education, 36*(3), 353–367.

Hughes, G. (2014). *Ipsative assessment – Motivation through marking progress.* London: Palgrave Macmillan.

Hughes, G., Wood, E., & Kitagawa, K. (2014). Use of self-referential (ipsative) feedback to motivate and guide distance learners. *Open Learning: The Journal of Open Distance and e-Learning, 29*(1), 31–44.

Hughes, G., Smith, H., & Creese, B. (2015). Not seeing the wood for the trees: Developing a feedback analysis tool to explore feed forward in modularised programmes. *Assessment & Evaluation in Higher Education, 40*(8), 1079–1094.

Ilgen, D. R., Fisher, C. D., & Taylor, M. S. (1979). Consequences of individual feedback on behavior in organizations. *Journal of Applied Psychology, 64*(4), 349.

Kulhavy, R. W. (1977). Feedback in written instruction. *Review of Educational Research, 2*, 211–232.

Kulhavy, R. W., & Wager, W. (1993). Feedback in programmed instruction: Historical context and implications for practice, interactive. In J. Dempsey & G. Ales (Eds.), *Interactive instruction and Feedback*, (pp. 3–20). Englewood Cliffs, NJ: Educational Technology Publications.

Linn, R. L., & Gronlund, N. E. (2000). *Measurement and assessment in teaching.* 8th edition. Upper Saddle River, NJ: Prentice Hall.

Mason, B. J., & Bruning, R. (2001) *Providing feedback in computer-based instruction: What the research tells us: What the research tells us.* Lincoln: Center for Instructional Innovation, University of Nebraska. http://dwb.unl.edu/Edit/MB/MasonBruning.html. Accessed 7 April 2014.

Masumoto, T., Oetzel, J. G., Takai, J., Ting-Toomey, S., & Yokochi, Y. (2000). A typology of facework behaviors in conflicts with best friends and relative strangers. *Communication Quarterly, 4*(48), 397–419.

Molloy, E., & Boud, D. (2013). Changing conceptions of feedback. In D. Boud & N. Falchikov (Eds.), *Feedback in higher and professional education – Understanding it and doing it well* (pp. 11–33). New York: Routledge.

Mory, E. H. (2004). Feedback research revisited. *Handbook of Research on Educational Communications and Technology, 2*, 745–783.

Narciss, S., & Huth, K. (2004). How to design informative tutoring feedback for multimedia learning. In H. M. Niegemann, D. Leutner, & R. Brunken (Eds.), *Instructional Design for Multimedia Learning*, (pp. 181–195). Munster, NY: Waxmann.

National Research Council. (2000). *How people learn: Brain, mind, experience, and school: Expanded edition.* Washington, DC: The National Academies Press.

Nicol, D. (2010). From monologue to dialogue: improving written feedback processes in mass higher education. *Assessment and Evaluation in Higher Education, 35*(5), 501–517.

Nicol, J. D., & Macfarlane-Dick, D. (2006). Formative assessment and self-regulated learning: A model and seven principles of good feedback practice. *Studies in Higher Education, 31*(2), 199–218.

Perrenoud, P. (1991). Towards a pragmatic approach to formative evaluation. In P. Weston (Ed.), *Assessment of pupils' achievement: Motivation and school success* (pp. 79–101). Amsterdam: Swets and Zeitlinger.

Ramaprasad, A. (1983). On the definition of feedback. *Behavioral Science, 28,* 4–13.

Randall, L., & Zundel, P. (2012). Students' perceptions of the effectiveness of assessment feedback as a learning tool in an introductory problem-solving course. *The Canadian Journal for the Scholarship of Teaching and Learning, 3*(1), 3.

Rockstuhl, T., Ang, S., Ng, K. Y., Lievens, F., & Van Dyne, L. (2015). Putting judging situations into situational judgment tests: Evidence from intercultural multimedia SJT. *Journal of Applied Psychology, 100,* 464–480.

Sadler, D. R. (1989). Formative assessment and the design of instructional systems. *Instructional Science, 18*(2), 119–144.

Sadler, D. R. (1998). Formative assessment: revisiting the territory. *Assessment in Education: Principles, Policy and Practice, 5*(1), 77–85.

Sadler, D. R. (2010). Beyond feedback: developing student capability in complex appraisal. *Assessment & Evaluation in Higher Education, 35*(50), 535–550.

Scott, D., Hughes, G., Evans, C., Burke, P. J., Walter, C., & Watson, D. (2013). *Learning transition in higher education.* UK: Palgrave MacMillan.

Tan, K. (2007). Conceptions of self-assessment. In D. Boud & N. Falchikov (Eds.), *Rethinking assessment in higher education: earning for the longer term* (pp. 114–127). London: Routledge.

Topping, K. (1998). Peer assessment between students in colleges and universities. *Review of Educational Research, 68*(3), 249–276.

Valle, C., & Andrade, H. (2014). Student self-assessment. In R. Gunstone (Ed.), *Encyclopedia of science education,* (pp. 1–4). Heidelberg: Springer.

Van Zundert, M., Sluijsmans, D., & Van Merriënboer, J. (2010). Effective peer assessment processes: Research findings and future directions. *Learning and Instruction, 20*(4), 270–279.

Vygotsky, L. (1978). *Mind in society. The development of higher psychological processes.* Cambridge, MA: Harvard University Press.

Walker, D., Cucina, J., & Kannan, S. (2008, April). *Lights, camera, action! How to develop a video-based test.* Presented at the 23rd Annual Conference of the Society for Industrial and Organizational Psychology, San Francisco.

Weekley, J. A., Ployhart, R. E., & Holtz, B. C. (2006). On the development of situational judgment tests: issues in item development, scaling, and scoring.

In J. A. Weekley & R. E. Ployhart (Eds.), *Situational judgment tests: Theory, measurement, and practice* (pp. 157–182). Mahwah, NJ: Erlbaum.

Hui-Teng Hoo is a Lecturer and Director of Accreditation at the Nanyang Business School, Nanyang Technological University, Singapore. She teaches the University Liberal Studies course, "Cultural Intelligence: How to be an Explorer of the World" to local and exchange students from more than ten nations each semester. Her academic background includes a Master of Business Administration, a Bachelor of Arts, and professional teaching qualification, Postgraduate Diploma in Education (Secondary). She is currently working on her Doctorate in Education at the Institute of Education, University College London (UK) and National Institute of Education, Nanyang Technological University.

Gwyneth Hughes is Reader in Higher Education at UCL, Institute of Education, London, UK. She leads and teaches on Masters programmes in higher education and supervises doctoral students. She is on the editorial board for the journal London Review of Education. She has researched and published widely on learning and teaching in higher education and she specialises in both assessment and e-learning. She is co-author of *Learning Transitions in Higher Education* (Palgrave Macmillan, 2014). Her latest book *Ipsative Assessment: Motivation through marking progress* was published by Palgrave Macmillan also in 2014. She is a Senior Fellow of the Higher Education Academy.

CHAPTER 10

The Effect of Video Feedback on the Self-Assessment of a Music Performance by Pre-university Level Classical Guitar Students

Mathieu Boucher, Francis Dubé, and Andrea Creech

INTRODUCTION

Learning a musical instrument requires a vast amount of practice that the musician mostly regulates by him or herself. A musician must therefore learn how to effectively *self-regulate* his/her practice in the absence of a teacher's feedback. Self-regulation of learning involves various cognitive processes, including a continuous cycle of planning, self-evaluation and adaptation (Zimmerman 1998b) that can occur, for example, between each repetition during a musician's practice. A crucial component of self-regulated learning in music is the ability to adapt performance according

M. Boucher (✉) · F. Dubé
Instrumental Pedagogy, Music Faculty in Université Laval, Québec, Canada
e-mail: mathieu.boucher.1@ulaval.ca; Francis.Dube@mus.ulaval.ca

A. Creech
UCL Institute of Education, London, UK
e-mail: andrea.creech@mus.ulaval.ca

© The Author(s) 2017   197
G. Hughes (ed.), *Ipsative Assessment and Personal Learning Gain*,
DOI 10.1057/978-1-137-56502-0_10

to feedback obtained while performing (Mcpherson and Zimmerman 2002). In a complementary way, ipsative assessment involves comparing the performance of a skill with a previous one (Hughes 2011). Hughes highlights the potential for 'explicit ipsative feedback' (see Chapter 1 of this volume) to underpin purposeful diagnosis of performance progress. In this vein, McPherson and Zimmerman (2002) theorised that video feedback could help musicians assess which sections of the pieces they needed to work on and how much they had improved since their last recording. Amongst developing musicians, this process of self-regulation supported by video feedback may be interpreted as a form of ipsative feedback, providing information that informs ipsative self-assessment – conceptualised here as the act of comparing performances. Many studies addressed the pedagogical use of video feedback in athletic and sports disciplines, but a comparably small number of studies has focused on its use by performing artists such as musicians.

This chapter will explore the possible links between ipsative feedback and self-regulation of music practice, drawing upon studies concerning the use of video feedback in athletic and musical learning. The chapter will also present the results from a study that explored the effect of repetitive use of video feedback on the self-evaluation of college-level classical guitarists (n = 16) engaged in learning a new piece of music.

IPSATIVE ASSESSMENT

Ipsative assessment (Hughes 2011) is accomplished by comparing an existing performance with a previous performance. It informs the learner with regards to how she or he has progressed since the previous assessment, and how effectively she or he responded to previous feedback. This sort of assessment represents an important educational shift by focusing on the process rather than the product. In academic learning, marking and grading are for the most part linked to criteria that are fixed and generalised; thus they fail to highlight any potential improvement that might have occurred since the previous assessment (Hughes 2011). In such a regime, incremental progress is hindered and goals are essentially left to the learner to establish for her or himself with little or no explicit guidance. Moreover, the feedback provided through traditional grading is useful only if the assessed task is repeated in the short term.

Hughes (2011) considers music learning as a valid example of ipsative assessment. Learning a musical instrument requires many hours of practice in which a musician progressively masters different skills through repetition. The repetitive aspect of individual music practice could indeed be associated with the incremental aspect of ipsative assessment, but this assessment must be monitored by the musician alone in the absence of his/her teacher's feedback. It has been argued that music teachers should consequently encourage the development of efficient self-evaluation skills to ensure that their students sustain improvement between lessons (McPherson and Renwick 2011).

CHARACTERISTICS OF MUSIC TEACHING AND LEARNING

Studies have shown that the 'traditional' directive instrumental teaching approach may fail to develop the self-evaluation skills required for effective practising, although music practice could be considered inherently ipsative. Historically, this predominant directive teaching approach has been described as a *master–apprentice* approach, where the master is usually considered a model and the dominating mode of student learning is imitation (Jørgensen 2000). Researchers who investigated this teaching approach found that it is dominated by talk from the teacher with a clear lack of specific goals (Karlsson and Juslin 2008), that it limits the possibility for the students to assume responsibility for their own learning and musical development (Gaunt 2008), and that it obviously emphasises learning products over learning processes by neglecting the students' preparation for practice (Jørgensen 2000). The ipsative assessment process, as an important part of individual music practice, requires musicians to self-evaluate effectively in the absence of their teacher's feedback or of the teacher's preoccupation with the practice activity. The skills associated with the monitoring of individual music practice have been studied under the paradigm of self-regulated learning (McPherson and Renwick 2011; McPherson and Zimmerman 2002).

SELF-REGULATION OF MUSIC PRACTICE

Jørgensen (2004) considers music practising as a self-teaching activity because instrumental students in higher music education are doing most of their instrumental learning away from their teachers. Self-regulated learning is a related concept in educational psychology and refers to 'the processes whereby learners personally activate and sustain cognitions, affects, and behaviours that are systematically oriented towards the attainment of personal goals' (Zimmerman and Schunk 2011, p. 1). Researchers describe self-regulation as cyclical because feedback obtained from prior performance helps a learner to adjust the following performance (McPherson and Zimmerman 2002). The cyclical aspect of self-regulation in music practice can be linked to the incremental aspect of ipsative assessment (Hughes 2011) because a musician should compare every execution undertaken during practice to the previous one to sustain improvement. The next section will discuss how the acquisition of the self-regulation skills needed for this process to function effectively represents a challenge.

THE ACQUISITION OF SELF-REGULATION SKILLS

Studies have focused on the systematic observation of individual practice in order to explore the self-regulation of practice with musicians of different levels of advancement. McPherson and Renwick (2001) videotaped the practice sessions of seven young instrumentalists across 3 years and found no evidence of deliberate practice strategies being used. Amongst the reported observations, the students spent most of their practice time playing straight through pieces without stopping to fix errors. Their inability to correct pitch and/or rhythmic errors suggests that they were not able to process the aural feedback provided by their instrument. The authors concluded that young musicians seem unable to work on their own with an effective and structured method, regardless of their motivation to learn their instrument. On the other hand, Bartolome (2009) interviewed three highly successful 9-year-old beginning recorder students who, while never directly instructed in self-regulation, were exhibiting self-regulated practice behaviours and attaining higher levels of performance achievement than their peers. A prevalent theme was their capacity to identify errors in performance. Nielsen (1999) observed examples of highly skilled self-regulation processes (Zimmerman 1998b) in the practice behaviour and verbalisations of two advanced organ students. However, Jørgensen (1998) reported that only 21% of the conservatory students who participated in his study declared that they were self-evaluating after practice and setting new objectives for subsequent practice sessions.

The results of these studies suggest that the acquisition of self-regulation skills requires time, but also that it would not be a direct consequence of the acquisition of technical and musical skills. Investigating methods for enhancing a musician's self-regulation skills during individual practice could prove useful for students who are not naturally efficient autonomous learners.

THE IMPORTANCE OF FEEDBACK
IN THE SELF-REGULATION PROCESS

A learner's ability to adapt his or her performance on the basis of feedback obtained while performing is central to the process of self-regulation (Zimmerman 2000). *Task-intrinsic* and *augmented* feedback are two types of feedback available during the execution of a motor task (Magill 2001). Task-intrinsic feedback is 'the sensory-perceptual information available to the person as a natural part of performing the skill' (Magill 2001, p. 86). For example, a cellist can hear the sounds she or he produces and see and feel the movement of his or her bowing arm while playing; what is perceived can then be self-assessed. Augmented feedback is 'the performance-related information a person receives *in addition to* task-intrinsic feedback' (Magill 2001, p. 86), but it might not be accessible since it is provided by an external source such as comments from a teacher or a peer. Because student musicians usually receive augmented feedback from their teacher only during the weekly lessons, developing a more acute awareness of the task-intrinsic feedback during individual practice could lead to greater improvement between lessons.

In self-regulated learning, effective task-intrinsic feedback is the consequence of careful self-monitoring, which involves 'observing and tracking one's own performance and outcomes' (Zimmerman 1998a, p. 78). Self-monitoring is critical in all types of self-regulated learning to identify information required for the evaluation of a performance (Butler and Winne 1995). Winne (1995) argues that self-monitoring the execution of a task could be detrimental to the learning effort when it hinders the mental charge already required for the execution itself. Self-monitoring an execution thus represents a challenge for a learner. Zimmerman (1995) suggests that the self-monitoring and the execution of a performance could be separated by videotaping the execution and watching it afterwards to allow the learner to fully concentrate on each task.

VIDEO FEEDBACK

Many studies addressed the pedagogical use of video feedback in athletic and sports disciplines, but a comparably small number of studies have focused on its use by musicians. Emmen et al. (1985) and Van Wieringen et al. (1989) found no advantages of video-assisted instruction over video modelling or verbal feedback in the learning of tennis service, but Rikli and Smith (1980) found an advantage of video-assisted instruction for the first phase of the arm movement. This phase was the only one outside the player's sight during execution, thus implying that video feedback could help a learner evaluate certain aspects of a motor task that she or he cannot be aware of during execution. Guadagnoli et al. (2002) found no advantage of video instruction in practising the golf swing in a 48-hour delayed retention test, but found the advantages in a 2-week delayed retention test. The authors suggest that the positive effect of video analysis may take some time to reveal itself. Selder and Del Rolan (1979) reported a similar effect in a study which compared the performances of a group of young gymnasts who used video feedback with a self-evaluation checklist in individual practice (n = 8) with the performances of another group who received traditional verbal feedback from a coach (n = 8). The authors found no differences between the groups after 4 weeks, but found that the video feedback group had improved significantly more on four out of eight aspects of the performances after 6 weeks. This supports the previously mentioned findings that video feedback could help a learner assess specific parts of a performance, and that its benefits could take time to develop.

A study on how video feedback could affect a learner's reflective process found an interesting orientation to research. Hebert et al. (1998) studied the verbalisations of six advanced tennis players using a think-aloud technique while watching videos of their own performances of a single type of tennis hit. The authors identified four stages of thought process: (1) getting used to seeing themselves, (2) detecting errors, (3) making connections and identifying tendencies and, finally (4) correcting errors and reaching closure. This indicates that video feedback could enhance a learner's reflective processes in ways that might not be observable within performance tests and external judging, as was the case in the aforementioned studies. Interpreted through the ipsative feedback and assessment lens, we could conceive that stages 3 and 4 require a comparison of the performances in order to identify tendencies between them and finally reaching a point of closure at which no further improvement are possible.

Video feedback could help a learner assess certain aspects of a motor task more efficiently, but this positive effect could take time to develop. Exploring the effect of video feedback on a learner's reflective process could reveal benefits that reach beyond immediate performance results. The results regarding the use of video feedback in an athletic context could be related to the motor aspect of a music performance; but a music performance involves many additional aspects, like interpretation, sound or expression, that could also benefit from video feedback.

Little empirical research has focused on the use of video feedback in the preparation of a musical performance. McPherson and Zimmerman (2002, p. 342) stated, however, that:

> Self-recording, rarely used by musicians, is an effective way to monitor one's progress. For example, musicians who tape-record and then analyse repertoire were able to use this information as a means of assessing which sections of the pieces they need to work on most and how much they have improved since their last recording.

Daniel (2001) surveyed thirty five university-level musicians at the end of a one-year performance class in which they used video feedback. After one year of using the video feedback, 86% recognised its usefulness. Forty-nine per cent of the participants declared they were able to identify lacks and mistakes in their playing more easily with video feedback, but no mentions were made in the study concerning how video feedback affected the participants' self-evaluation skills or how they used the information in subsequent performances.

Masaki et al. (2011) developed a measure survey designed to compare musical performances on eight different aspects. Twenty-two university-level piano students were filmed during a rehearsal and a public performance of a piece and were asked to compare both performances before and after watching the videos using the measure survey. The authors compared the results with an expert assessment of the same videos. The statistical results showed that the participants' assessments before and after watching the videos of the performances differ substantially, and that it was the participants' assessment of the video that was closer to the external expert's assessment. These results suggest that video feedback, when used by an advanced musician supported by an observation grid, could prove useful in evaluating and comparing one's own performances via an observer's point of view. In this case, the self-evaluations were guided by an observation grid in which eight evaluated aspects were established a priori, but no mention was made regarding the separate results for each item of the grid. This could have allowed researchers to analyse if video feedback facilitated the assessment of specific aspects of the performances. Furthermore, the experimental design of the study specifically required for the participants to compare their performances, but more information would be needed on whether video feedback could help musicians engage in some form of ipsative assessment when they are not asked to.

PURPOSE OF THE STUDY

The purpose of the study reported here was to evaluate the impact of using video feedback as a self-evaluation tool for pre-university classical guitarists. In this chapter, we focus on the guitarists' ipsative self-assessment following a series of rehearsal performances within the experimentation process. We examine the nature of the guitarists' self-assessment of their performances by highlighting explicit references to direct comparisons between performances, and by examining whether specific aspects of a performance were mentioned more often in the ipsative comments. In doing so, we explore the aspects of the self-assessment practices that, as Hughes emphasises in Chapter 1 of this volume, 'have a purpose for directly enhancing learning from the learner perspective'.

We first examined how these musicians' discussion regarding their own progress was influenced by the use of video feedback by comparing the self-evaluation comments after performance of a group of college-level guitarists who used video feedback with those of a group who did not use video feedback. Second, we compared the self-evaluation comments after performing and after watching a video of that performance amongst the participants in the video feedback group. The implications of this study could allow a better understanding of the potential benefits of video feedback on the development of ipsative self-assessment skills for intermediate/advanced music students.

THE STUDY

The Sample

The study took place in a CÉGEP in the province of Québec, Canada. A CÉGEP (Collège d'enseignement général et professionnel[1]) is an institution offering various specialised curricula, including music performance, that students must attend before entering university. All classical guitar students enrolled in a 2-year music program were offered the opportunity to participate. Thirteen males and three females volunteered and completed a consent form and questionnaire regarding their age, instrumental level in the program, years of experience in individual lessons, most recent grade obtained in an instrumental evaluation and frequency of using video or audio feedback. Only the students who used video/audio recording less than twice a month were accepted in order to verify how video feedback could affect the self-regulation skills of musicians who were not using it regularly. All volunteers respected this criterion.

Participants (n = 16) were randomly assigned to either a control (n = 8) or an experimental group (n = 8). To ensure an even distribution, participants were first balanced for their instrumental level in the institution's program and then paired according to the grade they obtained on the last performance exam in the program. A member of each pair was randomly assigned to the control or the experimental group using a random allocation software (http://mahmoodsaghaei.tripod.com/Softwares/randalloc.html). Table 10.1 presents the descriptive and frequency statistical data for each group.

The Music

All participants were asked to learn the same piece of music, a waltz by French composer Thierry Tisserand. The piece comprises seventy eight bars in the key of E minor with an ABA form. It involves a wide variety of guitar techniques, such as harmonics, arpeggios, slurs or *barrés*. The guitar teachers from the institution validated the choice of the piece as being appropriate for the students' level. The chosen piece had not yet been commercially released, thus ensuring that no participant had heard the piece before; and the music sheet was altered to hide the title and the name of the composer. Participants were also asked not to discuss the music with their teacher or peers during the experimentation.

Table 10.1 Characteristics of participants

	All participants (n = 16)		Control group (n = 8)		Experimental group (n = 8)	
	Mean	*SD*	*Mean*	*SD*	*Mean*	*SD*
Experience in individual lessons	7.1	3.6	7.2	3.9	7.1	3.6
Grade they obtained on their last performance exam	82.8%	8.2	85.9%	3.6	79.6%	10.4

PROCEDURE

Participants (n = 16) practised the piece during ten recorded practice sessions that lasted 20 minutes each. Twelve to eighteen days were needed to complete all ten sessions. In the first practice session, participants received a personal copy of the score that they could annotate, but were required to give it back after each session to ensure that practising the piece happened only within the research protocol. There was no obligation to learn the entire piece by the end of the study, to avoid affecting the participants' practice behaviour.

On four occasions during the experimentation – after practice sessions 3, 5, 7 and 9 – the participants were filmed while playing the piece or any part they were able to perform without stopping, as if they were performing the piece in a concert. Immediately after each performance, the participants were asked to identify which aspects or issues in their playing they would like to improve in the next practice sessions, but they were not specifically asked to compare their performances. These filmed performances followed by self-assessments will from now on be referred to as the post-performance assessments.

Before the following practice, participants from the experimental group watched the video of their performance on a laptop computer equipped with speakers. In previous studies, viewing was guided by a coach (Emmen et al. 1985; Guadagnoli et al. 2002; Rikli and Smith 1980; Van Wieringen et al. 1989) or an observation grid (Masaki et al. 2011; Selder and Del Rolan 1979), thus failing to isolate what the learners could assess by themselves when watching their own performances. Therefore, because of the implicit lack of knowledge on the effects of video feedback in the field of music performance, the viewings in this study were free and unguided. After each of the four viewings, participants from the experimental group had to identify once again which aspects or issues in their playing they would like to improve in the next practice sessions. This will from now on be referred to as the post-video assessment.

The control group began practising right away on the practice session following the recordings and had the opportunity to watch the videos of their performances only after completing the experimentation process.

CODING SCHEME

The self-evaluative comments from the post-performance assessments and the post-video assessments were transcribed and a content analysis was performed to search for recurrent themes (L'Écuyer 1990; Saldaña 2009).

This approach involved a thorough reading of all the data prior to beginning the coding, followed by a coding of the comments into meaningful units representing an aspect of the performance discussed by the participants.

We first analysed the comments from the post-performance assessments 2, 3 and 4 to verify if the participants were discussing the various aspects of their playing from an ipsative standpoint. We considered a comment as being ipsative if the participant was comparing the present performance with a previous one when discussing a particular aspect of his or her playing. For example:

1. 'The phrasing is better. The first time, I remember that the phrasing was really rough, there wasn't any in fact, I think I was able to add more of it'.
2. 'The parts that I found the most difficult, I improved them, they are more solid'.
3. 'For the phrasing, it's not good! I thought I had done it better this time but it is still boring to hear'.
4. 'I went much further now than I did last time'.

Because all participants were French speaking, the examples presented in this text were freely translated from French into English by the first author.

Second, we analysed the ipsative comments made by the participants in the post-performance assessments 2, 3 and 4, and the corresponding post-video assessments with a coding scheme that was already developed for another part of this research focusing on the aspects of playing assessed by the participants in their self-evaluation. To develop this coding scheme, the first author and a fellow researcher/guitarist independently coded the comments by one participant from each group to look for emerging themes. Similarities and differences were discussed afterwards to establish a preliminary categorisation that the first author used to code the complete data. During this coding process, new categories and definitions emerged and were again discussed with the same fellow researcher and the second author until agreement was reached for the definitions of each category. The researcher then revised the previous coding in accordance with the modifications made on the coding scheme.

The final coding scheme comprised five broad categories that encompassed different themes addressed by the participants in their self-evaluation comments. Table 10.2 presents the coding scheme with definitions for each category and comments by the participants that exemplify them.

Table 10.2   Coding scheme: Definition and examples for each category

Themes	Definition	Examples
General evaluation of the performance	General appreciation of the performance or the learning of the piece, with no further details.	'Generally, I think it went pretty well'. 'This was the worst of my three performances'.
Instrumental execution	Comments about general or specific technical aspect of the piece, precision of the playing or hand position.	'Technically, it was not perfect, but it was quite good'. 'Some notes are still not clean; the left hand fingering is not clean, you know. I'm "buzzing" a few notes'. 'Regarding the slurs, I realise that they are weak too. We don't hear them enough; whether the slurs are ascending or descending, there is always a little sound that I don't like...'.
Interpretation	Comments about expressivity, fluidity, sound or dynamics and phrasing.	'Soon, I'll need to add more life to the piece'. 'If I consider the style of the piece, it's too mechanical. I don't think it flowed'. '[I need to] find a warmer sound'. 'The ends of the phrases, the *ritardando* and all this, I don't hold them enough, it's too brutal'.
Performance flow	Comments about the state of mind during the performance, the sequence of the sections or phrases or the performance tempo.	'The performance lacked concentration. In some parts, I was inattentive and then I was "coming back"'. 'I finished the piece, so I'm able to play it entirely without any major problems. I don't need to stop any more'.
Learning stages	Comments about the amount of music played, the familiarisation with the score, the assimilation of the piece of particular sections of the piece that requires work.	'The good thing about the first performance is that I was able to play the whole first page'. 'Regarding the interpretation, I'm not there yet because there was a lot of sight-reading to do today'. 'The next step will be to work on page 2; there is the last line that is not acceptable'.

BETWEEN-GROUP COMPARISON OF POST-PERFORMANCE ASSESSMENTS

The first objective of the study was to verify if the participants who used video feedback would demonstrate ipsative feedback in their subsequent post-performance assessments, and whether this would differ from those who did not have the support of video feedback. To attain this objective, we compared the number of ipsative comments that the experimental group (n = 8) made in the post-performance assessments 2, 3 and 4 with those of a control group that had not used video feedback (n = 8). We can observe in Table 10.3 that the participants in the experimental group gave more ipsative comments after all performances than the control group did.

We also compared the number of ipsative comments made by the participants in each group for the categories presented in Table 10.2. We sought to verify if the participants in each group discussed different aspects of playing in their ipsative comments after performing. In Table 10.4, we can observe

Table 10.3   Between group comparison of the number of ipsative comments in post-performance assessments 2, 3 and 4

Total number of comments	Control group (n = 8) (no video feedback)	Experimental group (n = 8) (used video feedback)
Post-performance 2	1	11
Post-performance 3	4	4
Post-performance 4	3	11
Total (and % of all post-performance comments)	8 (7.4%, SD = 10.55)	26 (21.47%, SD = 17.54)

Table 10.4   Between group comparison of the aspects mentioned in all the ipsative comments in the post-performance assessments 2 + 3 + 4

	Control group (n = 8) (no video feedback)	Experimental group (n = 8) (used video feedback)
General evaluation of the performance	2	5
Interpretation	3	7
Instrumental execution	0	3
Learning stages	3	6
Performance flow	0	5

that the participants in the control group made no ipsative comments about aspects related to *instrumental execution* and *performance flow* after their performances. We can also see that the experimental group made more ipsative comments in all categories. Therefore, their ipsative self-assessment encompassed every aspects of a performance that emerged from the analysis of the comments.

COMPARISON OF POST-VIDEO AND POST-PERFORMANCE ASSESSMENTS FOR THE EXPERIMENTAL GROUP

The second objective of this study was to verify if the participants who used video feedback would discuss the various aspects of their performance from an ipsative standpoint after performing and after watching a video of the same performance. To attain this objective, we compared the number of ipsative comments in the post-performance assessments 2, 3 and 4 with those of the corresponding post-video assessments. The data presented in Table 10.5 indicate that participants who used video feedback made more ipsative comments in the post-performance assessments 2 and 4 than they did in the corresponding post-video assessments. We can also observe an opposite difference between post-video and post-performance 3.

We compared the number of ipsative comments made by the participants of the experimental group for each category of the coding scheme presented in Table 10.2. In doing so, we verified if the participants who used video feedback discussed different aspects of playing in their ipsative comments after performing and after watching the recorded performance. In Table 10.6, we can observe that the participants in the experimental group made more ipsative comments about *interpretation, instrumental*

Table 10.5 Comparison of post-video and post-performance assessments for the total number of ipsative comments

Total number of comments	Post-video assessment	Post-performance assessment
Performance 2	4	11
Performance 3	6	4
Performance 4	2	11
Total (and % of all comments)	12 (11.32%, SD = 14.10)	26 (21.47%, SD = 17.54)

Table 10.6   Post-performance and post-video comparison of the number of comments for each aspect of a performance (Table 10.2) mentioned in the ipsative comments by the experimental group ($n = 8$)

	Post-video assessments (2 + 3 + 4)	Post-performance assessments (2 + 3 + 4)
General evaluation of the performance	5	5
Interpretation	2	7
Instrumental execution	0	3
Learning stages	4	6
Performance flow	1	5

Table 10.7   Comparison of post-video and post-performance assessments for the total number of ipsative comments mentioned by the participants depending on their latest attributed instrumental grade

Total number of comments	Post-video assessment (2 + 3 + 4)	Post-performance assessment (2 + 3 + 4)
High performers ($n = 4$)	11	20
Low performers ($n = 4$)	1	6 ($n = 2$)
Total	12	26

execution, learning stages and *performance flow* after the performances than they did after the videos.

Participants had completed a demographics questionnaire at the beginning of the experimentation, at which time we had asked them what was the grade they had obtained on their most recent instrumental evaluation. We compared the number of ipsative comments made by the participants in the experimental group in both feedback situations, according to this grade. A mean performance grade of 71.5% (SD = 8.81) was found amongst the 'low performers' – comprising the four participants who had obtained the lowest grades on their last evaluation. This contrasted with a mean grade of 87.5% (SD = 2.89) amongst the 'high performers' – comprising the four participants who had obtained the highest grades. In Table 10.7, we can observe that the high performers in the experimental group made more ipsative comments in both feedback situations than the low performers did.

Discussion

The purpose of this study was to evaluate the impact of using video feedback as a self-evaluation tool for pre-university classical guitarists. We explored the nature of the comments made by the participants in different self-evaluation conditions to identify ipsative comments where participants compared their performances. The first objective of the study was to verify if the participants who used video feedback would demonstrate ipsative feedback in their evaluation of subsequent performances, and whether this would differ from those who did not have the support of video feedback. The second objective of this study was to verify if the participants who used video feedback would assess their performances from an ipsative standpoint after performing and after watching a video of that same performance.

Results for the first objective suggest that participants in the experimental group made many more ipsative feedback comments after performances 2 and 4 than found amongst the control group. The fact that participants in the experimental group made more ipsative comments after these performances than their peers in the control group suggests that video feedback may have helped the students to compare the results of their performances.

Exploration of the second objective again emphasised this finding because participants in the experimental group made more ipsative feedback comments in their self-evaluation after performing than after watching this performance on video. It is noteworthy that the effect of video feedback on ipsative self-assessment appears to have had more impact on the assessments made following performance, as compared with assessment of the video recordings themselves. We could speculate that video feedback, because it allows the learner to fully concentrate on the assessment task as well as allowing a performance to be heard twice, would help create a more vivid memory of the previous performance when assessing the following performances without video feedback. This could be related to studies in which video feedback was found to benefit the learner after a certain period had elapsed (Guadagnoli et al. 2002; Selder and Del Rolan 1979), or where its users claimed it was helpful despite the absence of immediate performance results (Rikli and Smith 1980).

Video feedback is logically considered to be an effective tool for comparing performances, but the participants in the experimental group (using video feedback) made more ipsative comments after performances than after video feedback. This could imply that musicians, when not asked to specifically compare performances, would assess their performances from a more analytical than ipsative perspective while using video feedback, but that this process would elicit ipsative assessment afterwards. This adds to the results by Masaki et al. (2011), where video feedback helped pianists compare performances from a more objective standpoint. It also adds to McPherson and Zimmerman's claim that video feedback could help musicians assess 'how much they have improved since the last recording' (2002, p. 342). Thus, video feedback would help musicians compare their performances both when using it (Masaki et al. 2011) as well as in subsequent self-evaluations without its support. In addition, the high performers in the experimental group made many more ipsative comments, as compared with comments made amongst the low performers. Because the participants in this study were not specifically asked to compare their performances, it appears that the higher performing musicians were more naturally inclined to engage in some form of ipsative assessment.

Concerning the aspects mentioned in the ipsative comments in each feedback situation, the participants in the experimental group made more ipsative comments about *interpretation, instrumental execution, learning stages* and *performance flow* in the post-performance assessments than they did in the post-video assessments. Also, participants in the control group made no mention at all of aspects related to *instrumental execution* and *performance flow* in their post-performance assessments. The participants in the experimental group seemed to have been able to compare their performances from a broader point of view in their post-performance assessments. Daniel (2001) found that musicians were able to identify mistakes in their performances more easily using video feedback without specifying which type of mistakes were identified by the participants. To support their participants' comparison of two performances using video feedback, Masaki et al. (2011) used an evaluation grid comprising eight aspects that were not addressed individually in the results. In our study, we found that, when not guided by an evaluation grid or being specifically asked to compare performances, musicians who used video feedback would encompass various aspects of their playing in their following self-assessments of performances.

A further interesting category of comments emerged from the coding. Participants in the experimental group were sometimes comparing feedback conditions (post-performance and post-video) after watching the videos, as demonstrated by comments such as 'The video helped me realise which part of the piece needed my attention' or 'I thought I had put more emotion when I played, but after the video, I realise that it is still lacking'. Such comments suggest that the participant may have been comparing two perceptions of the same performance and could therefore reconsider or reframe his or her self-evaluation process. The process could also bring to the participants a possible added value to their perception of complementary feedback from their teacher or peers.

LIMITATIONS AND FUTURE RESEARCH

We acknowledge that owing to the small number of participants in this study, corresponding to an exploratory design, there are limitations with regards the generalisability of our findings. Other studies could focus solely on the self-evaluation of performances or videos and consequently involve more participants, with different instruments and of different levels of advancement.

The aim of this research was to explore the effect of video feedback on the self-evaluation of student musicians, therefore the self-assessment was purposely unguided towards ipsative feedback. Future research could test whether guided self-assessment would prompt more ipsative feedback, or ipsative feedback of a different nature, but our experimental design allowed us to verify if the participants intentionally engaged in ipsative assessment when not directed to.

This study focused on the comments in which participants were comparing performances. The participants in this study only watched the most recent performance when self-assessing. Providing the possibility to watch the most recent as well as a series of previous performances could have elicited even more comments of a comparative nature by removing the need for the participants to remember the first performance and helping them to concentrate their attention on the comparison process itself.

Our content analysis focused on the self-evaluative comments in which the participants were comparing their performances on various aspects of their playing. However, the participants' self-evaluations also included non-ipsative comments that were qualitatively different: comments could be either positive/negative reactions, comparisons of post-performance and post-video feedback perception, or simply formulated as a goal rather than a critique. Comments also varied in length or level of precision. It would be interesting to include these non-ipsative comments in a deeper analysis of how the participants formulated their comments to explore how video feedback could affect the nature of the musicians' self-evaluation.

In this experimentation, we used a regular camera with a laptop and speakers. This technology simplified the process and represents the type of technology that could be used by musicians or teachers. The recordings in this study were viewed by the participants on the following day; accordingly the transfer of the file from the camera to the laptop was made overnight. However, with advances in technology, during a practice session or a lesson, the transfer of the video file could easily and quickly be made while attending to other topics. Moreover, in future research or practical applications of the ideas presented here, smartphones and tablets could allow the recording and the immediate viewing of a video, although with a possibly lower quality of sound or image.

Notwithstanding the limitations noted here, we would argue that our findings point to the strong potential for the use of video feedback to enhance teaching and learning practice within musical contexts, and we suggest that these findings highlight the scope for further research in this area.

Conclusion

Hughes (2011) considers that music learning is a valid example of ipsative assessment. Arguably, a musician should indeed compare every execution undertaken during practice to the previous one, in order to sustain improvement. In this chapter, we associated the repetitive aspect of individual music practice with the incremental aspect of ipsative assessment and the cyclical aspect of self-regulated learning. Ipsative assessment and self-regulated learning in individual practice require efficient task-intrinsic feedback, but the concurrent efforts required by the self-monitoring of the execution and the execution itself can hinder the efficacy of the process (Winne 1995; Zimmerman 1995).

Video feedback has been presented as a means to separate the self-monitoring and the execution of a performance to fully concentrate on each task (Zimmerman 1995). McPherson and Zimmerman (2002) theorised that video feedback could help musicians assess which sections of the pieces they need to work on and how much they have improved since their last recording. Video feedback is a logical way to record a performance in order to compare it with a previous or an upcoming one. In addition, we found that it would also encourage musicians to compare their performances in subsequent self-evaluation without its support, possibly by allowing them to obtain more information on the first performance and to create a more precise memory of it. Further research could address the micro-structure of practice and verify if musicians who use video feedback would make more ipsative assessment comments between each execution while practising.

This study revealed that, in the absence of specific instructions to compare performances, the higher performing musicians seemed to be more naturally inclined to engage in some form of ipsative assessment. Therefore, designing activities in which lower performing musicians purposely compare the videos of a recent performance with a previous one could develop their ability to self-assess from an ipsative standpoint. During a lesson, the teacher could also point aspects of the performances that remained unmentioned by the student, but that might have improved between the recordings. The stop/play/fwd/rwd functions can allow the teacher to provide feedback at specific points of a performance immediately after they happen, instead of relying on the recall of the students when feedback from the teacher is provided post-performance. Further research could focus on how a teacher could implement a collaborative ipsative assessment with their students using video feedback as a teaching aid.

For a musician, video feedback allows a form of augmented feedback that is as close as can be to task-intrinsic feedback (Magill 2001). Moreover, taking notes during viewings, self-evaluating performances from an external point of view and comparing performances could prove useful to counterbalance a traditional teaching approach that can be too teacher-centred (Gaunt 2008; Jørgensen 2000; Karlsson and Juslin 2008). We conclude that the use of video feedback as a pedagogical tool offers strong potential to promote self-regulation and ipsative self-assessment, both of which have been associated with effective instrumental learning and teaching.

NOTE

1. College of general and professional education.

REFERENCES

Bartolome, S.J. (2009). Naturally emerging self-regulated practice behaviors among highly successful beginning recorder students. *Research Studies in Music Education*, 31(1), 37–51.

Butler, D.L., & Winne, P.H. (1995). Feedback and self-regulated learning: A theoretical synthesis. *Review of Educational Research, 65*(3), 245–281.

Daniel, R. (2001). Self-assessment in performance. *British Journal of Music Education, 18*(03), 215–226.

Emmen, H., Wesseling, L., Bootsma, R., Whiting, H., & Van Wieringen, P. (1985). The effect of video-modelling and video-feedback on the learning of the tennis service by novices. *Journal of Sports Sciences, 3*(2), 127.

Gaunt, H. (2008). One-to-one tuition in a conservatoire: The perceptions of instrumental and vocal teachers. *Psychology of Music, 36*(2), 215.

Guadagnoli, M., Holcomb, W., & Davis, M. (2002). The efficacy of video feedback for learning the golf swing. *Journal of Sports Sciences, 20*(8), 615–622.

Hebert, E., Landin, D., & Menickelli, J. (1998). Videotape feedback: What learners see and how they use it. *Journal of Sport Pedagogy, 4*(2), 12–28.

Hughes, G. (2011). Towards a personal best: A case for introducing ipsative assessment in higher education. *Studies in Higher Education, 36*(3), 353–367.

Jørgensen, H. (1998). *Planlegges øving? [Is practice planned?]*. Oslo: Norwegian Academy of Music.

Jørgensen, H. (2000). Student learning in higher instrumental education: Who is responsible? *British Journal of Music Education, 17*(01), 67–77.

Jørgensen, H. (2004). Strategies for individual practice. In A. Williamon (Ed.), *Musical excellence: Strategies and techniques to enhance performance* (pp. 85–103). New York: Oxford University Press.

Karlsson, J., & Juslin, P. (2008). Musical expression: An observational study of instrumental teaching. *Psychology of Music, 36*(3), 309.

L'Écuyer, R. (1990). *Méthodologie de l'analyse développementale de contenu: Méthode GSP et concept de soi*. Sillery: Presses de l'Université du Québec.

Magill, R.A. (2001). Augmented feedback in motor skill acquisition. In R.N. Singer, H.A. Hausenblas, & C. Janelle (Eds.), *Handbook of sport psychology* (2nd ed., pp. 86–114). New York: Wiley.

Masaki, M., Hechler, P., Gadbois, S., & Waddell, G. (2011). Piano performance assessment: Video feedback and the Quality Assessment in Music Performance Inventory (QAMPI). In A. Williamon, D. Edwards, & L. Bartel (Eds.), *Proceedings of the International symposium on performance science 2011* (pp. 503–508). Utrecht, Netherlands: European Association of Conservatoires (AEC.

McPherson, G.E., & Renwick, J.M. (2001). A longitudinal study of self-regulation in children's musical practice. *Music Education Research, 3*(2), 169–186.

McPherson, G.E., & Renwick, J.M. (2011). Self-regulation and mastery of musical skills. In B.J. Zimmerman & D.H. Schunk (Eds.), *Handbook of self-regulation of learning and performance* (pp. 234–248). New York: Routledge.

McPherson, G.E., & Zimmerman, B.J. (2002). Self-regulation of musical learning: A social cognitive perspective. In R. Colwell & C. Richardson (Eds.), *The new handbook of research on music teaching and learning: A project of the music educators national conference* (pp. 327–347). New York: Oxford University Press.

Nielsen, S.G. (1999). Learning strategies in instrumental music practice. *British Journal of Music Education, 16*(03), 275–291.

Rikli, R., & Smith, G. (1980). Videotape feedback effects on tennis serving form. *Perceptual and Motor Skills, 50,* 895–901.

Saldaña, J. (2009). *The coding manual for qualitative researchers.* London: Sage.

Selder, D.J., & Del Rolan, N. (1979). Knowledge of performance, skill level and performance on the balance beam. *Canadian Journal of Applied Sport Sciences, 4*(3), 226–229.

Van Wieringen, P., Emmen, H., Bootsma, R., Hoogesteger, M., & Whiting, H. (1989). The effect of video-feedback on the learning of the tennis service by intermediate players. *Journal of Sports Sciences, 7*(2), 153–162.

Winne, P.H. (1995). Inherent details in self-regulated learning. *Educational Psychologist, 30*(4), 173–187.

Zimmerman, B.J. (1995). Self-regulation involves more than metacognition: A social cognitive perspective. *Educational Psychologist, 30*(4), 217–221.

Zimmerman, B.J. (1998a). Academic studying and the development of personal skill: A self-regulatory perspective. *Educational Psychologist, 33,* 73–86.

Zimmerman, B.J. (1998b). Developing self-fulfilling cycles of academic regulation: An analysis of exemplary instructional models. In D.H. Schunk & B.J. Zimmerman (Eds.), *Self-regulated learning: From teaching to self-reflective practice* (pp. 1–19). New York: Guilford Press.

Zimmerman, B.J. (2000). Attaining self-regulation: A social cognitive perspective. In M. Boekaerts, P.R. Pintrich, & M. Zeidner (Eds.), *Handbook of self-regulation* (pp. 13–39). San Diego, CA: Academic Press.

Zimmerman, B.J., & Schunk, D.H. (2011). Self-regulated learning and performance: An introduction and an overview. In B.J. Zimmerman & D.H. Schunk (Eds.), *Handbook of self-regulation of learning and performance* (pp. 1–12). New York: Routledge.

Mathieu Boucher is a doctoral student in instrumental pedagogy at the Music Faculty in Université Laval, Québec, Canada. His thesis focuses on video feedback and the self-regulation skills of musicians and was funded by the FRQ-SC. He is a junior Lecturer in instrumental pedagogy at the music faculties in Université Laval and Université de Montréal, as well as being the coordinator of the *École préparatoire Anne-Marie Globenski de l'Université Laval.* He also teaches classical guitar at CÉPEG de Sainte-Foy.

Francis Dubé is a full Professor of Instrumental Pedagogy at the Music Faculty in Université Laval, Québec, Canada. His research projects, funded by various grants from the governments of Quebec and Canada (SSHRC; FRQ-SC; CFI; Global Affairs Canada), focus on music technology, musical creativity, informal teaching approaches, and other topics associated with instrumental pedagogy. As a regular member of the OICRM, he is the head of the *Laboratoire de recherche en formation auditive et didactique instrumentale* (LaRFADI), the *Centre d'excellence en pédagogie musicale de l'Université Laval*, and the *Équipe de recherche interdisciplinaire sur les pratiques et pédagogies musicales* (ERIPPM).

Andrea Creech is a Professor in the Music Faculty, Université Laval, Canada, and Canada Research Chair in Music in Community. Andrea was awarded a PhD in Psychology in Education. Since then she has led extensive funded research and published widely on topics concerned with musical learning and participation across the lifespan. She is a Senior Fellow of the Higher Education Academy and Graduate Member of the British Psychological Association. Andrea is co-author of *Active Ageing with Music* and co-editor of *Music Education in the 21st Century in the UK*.

CHAPTER 11

Compete With Yourself (CWY): Maximising Learning Gain in Schools

Sunita Gandhi

INTRODUCTION

Using assessment information for summative purposes can have the effect of hindering rather than supporting the learning of some, and in certain cases, all students. The negative effects of assessment for summative purposes on the learners include lowering the self-esteem of the less successful students which can reduce their effort and image of themselves as learners (Davis and Brember 1998; Johnston and McClune 2000; Leonard and Davey 2001; Reay and Wiliam 1999).

This chapter investigates the influence of CWY assessments that are based on the principle of ipsative or self-referential assessment. The term 'ipsative' assessment means comparison with a previous performance, or a self-comparison, rather than with a norm (Hughes 2014). Hughes explores this through two key arguments: (1) that competitive assessment with external standards is not conducive to motivation and learning for all learners, and (2) that the self-referential standards and goals delineated by

S. Gandhi (✉)
Global Classroom, Lucknow, India

Council for Global Education, Ashburn, USA
e-mail: sunitag@globaleducation.org

© The Author(s) 2017
G. Hughes (ed.), *Ipsative Assessment and Personal Learning Gain*,
DOI 10.1057/978-1-137-56502-0_11

221

ipsative assessment sustain motivation and progress for all learners (Hughes 2011). The CWY assessments do not emphasise comparisons for the individual pupil such as summative averages, norm-referenced percentile scores or age and grade equivalents. Relative comparisons such as these, though useful to a policy maker, administrator and teacher, can be damaging to a pupil's psychology. Evidence suggests a pupil does not put in more effort just because s/he is good or poor in performance in relation to others. The hypothesis this chapter explores is that CWY produces greater excellence than making a distinction relative to the standards of other pupils and school, or national norms.

The CWY assessments provide a snapshot of a class taken at any point of time, or as and when required. The reports provide valuable information that helps personalise learning for every pupil. Teachers undertake corrective action, and they measure their pupils' progress in the next assessment, either whenever the class is ready, or when the individual pupil is ready. The process continues like the double-helix of DNA. When progress between two similar topics or skills is measured, the first assessment serves as a baseline on the basis of which each pupil receives personalised reports and support. The pupil uses these to improve her/his performance using differentiated skills units called Perbooks. Progress assessments that measure every pupil's progress against their personal baseline may be taken using paper and pencil or online, but all CWY reports, personal work plans and selection of personalised study materials are generated on a computer.

The objective of CWY assessment is not classification or judgment of a pupil's ability. The primary purpose is to get objective information at the level of the skill or concept about each pupil so as to help each one succeed even more, not by competing with others, but by competing with themselves. The chapter reports on comparisons of experimental and control groups using CWY methods and tools. The greater increase in class average marks of experimental groups over control groups suggests CWY works better than traditional learning methods and enables pupils to make greater progress.

Doing Away with Summative Assessment?

Is our purpose in assessing pupils to identify talent or develop it? In present education, a derivative of the 19th century, we still suffer from the belief that grades should be used to identify talent. Though at the face value this seems harmless, the implications of this belief are significantly negative.

Summative assessment has become for most students in many countries not a once-a-year event which in comparison with daily interactions with teachers might be considered to have a minor role in determining their 'faith in themselves as learners' (Stiggins 2001, p. 46), but rather a frequent experience which may have an undesirable effect on motivation for learning. Moreover, research shows that this effect is greater for the less successful pupils and thus tends to widen the gap between higher and lower achieving pupils (Madaus 1991).

There are so many reasons why a pupil puts in less effort, does not want to study or gives up too soon. It is often assumed that a pupil with a poor grade is less capable, or even less intelligent. Differences in learning may not relate to a pupil's innate ability at all, but may be a result of poor teaching, prior experiences, home or classroom environment and the like. These can create a lack of motivation, or the will to put in effort. Harlen and Crick (2002) synthesised nineteen studies and found that with the introduction of the national curriculum tests in England, low achieving students tended to have lower self-esteem than higher achieving students. Prior to the tests, there had been no correlation between self-esteem and achievement. These negative perceptions of self-esteem often decrease students' future effort and academic success.

Evidence indicates that grades and other reporting methods affect pupil motivation and the effort pupils put forth (Cameron and Pierce 1996). No convincing research supports the idea that low grades frequently prompt pupils to try harder. More often, low grades prompt pupils to withdraw from learning. To protect their self-image, many pupils regard the low grade as irrelevant or meaningless. Others may blame themselves for the low grade but feel helpless to improve (Selby and Murphy 1992).

If the only instrument we have is a ruler, it would be at best an approximation to measure the volume of a bottle using it. What meaningful information would we get by adding the measures of length, weight and volume and by dividing these by three to get their summative average? Similarly, what would a summative average for English grammar, speaking and writing skills mean, all of these requiring a different set of skills. How would combining the averages of all these diverse skills in mathematics and English into one single measure yield any useful information, especially if the goal is learning? The 'hodgepodge grade' is hard to interpret and therefore limited in its potential to help a pupil improve (Brookhart and Nitko 2008; Cross and Frary 1996). Summative averages often de-motivate the majority who are not on the top rungs of a class. So many pupils give up very early thinking that they are just not good enough in relation to others in their class, and that in spite of their best efforts, they can never make it. They stop trying. Both the individual and society lose out.

The summative average, despite its potential usefulness to a policy maker, administrator or teacher, is more often meaningless for the individual pupil. It reduces a pupil to a number that is not only a poor estimation of his/her ability; it also potentially impedes growth and impacts negatively on a pupil's psychology. It is clear we must do away with the summative for the pupil, or use it judiciously as a measure of learning gain.

CWY: New Gauges of Success

Learning is a continuum along which every pupil moves, regardless of their relative position along the continuum. Every pupil has an innate capacity to grow and develop, even as each one progresses from one learning objective to the next. CWY helps speed up progress of all pupils, whatever their starting point. This is because the personalised CWY reports empower pupils with self-knowledge about their personal areas of strength and improvement.

Progress against oneself is the only true measure of success. Ultimately, a pupil cannot be pushed beyond her/his capacity, neither should another pupil be held back because others need to catch up. Every pupil in a class needs to be challenged and supported at her own level. The most important gauge of success, therefore, is whether every pupil in a class is making the best possible progress against their own potential. These new gauges of success give more importance to progress over performance.

The three most important set of questions to ask a pupil in the CWY system, therefore, relate to effort, quality and progress:

1. Is the pupil putting in his/her best effort? (Could you have done more?)
2. Can the pupil improve what she/he has done? (Could you have done this any better? How? In what ways?)
3. Is the pupil making progress? (What do you need to do next to progress beyond the present?)

Such questions lead to critical self-analysis such as how to improve on one's own past performance. They help pupils better articulate what they need to do next, and not to be satisfied too easily. If a pupil is able to articulate if she/he is progressing against his/her own past performance then, this is an important gauge of the effectiveness of CWY.

The next set of questions to ask a pupil in CWY relate to challenge, self-direction and self-regulation:

1. Is the pupil challenging herself/himself? (Do you self-study beyond the given assignments? How much? How often?)
2. Is the pupil able to set goals and direct his/her own learning? (Do you study according to the feedback provided? Do you set personal goals?)
3. Is the pupil able to exercise self-regulation? (Are you able to implement set goals and complete what you set out to do?).

Being able to set goals and self-regulate are necessary aspects of a pupil's self-assessment. CWY reports make it easier for pupils to answer the question: 'What next?' They help pupils better direct their own studies to those areas that need attention. They encourage pupils to set goals, put in greater effort and challenge themselves to do better than before.

CWY: A BEGINNING IN ICELAND

In 2001, Íslenskumenntasamtökin (ÍMS), a non-profit education society I founded, won the bid to run Iceland's first two charter schools in the city of Hafnarfjordur: Tjarnaras, a pre-school, and Áslandsskoli, a K-12 school (for ages 6–18). I asked the question: 'Is it possible to maximize the potential of every pupil in a whole classroom, or is this an oxymoron?'

To answer this question, Áslandsskoli provided the perfect setting for implementing several new approaches to teaching and learning, among them the pilot of the first CWY Assessment. In this, a pre-test was followed by all pupils receiving their personal CWY reports, followed by a progress assessment.

Both pre-test and progress assessments were criterion-referenced and scientifically similar. They were identical in the skills covered, the types of questions asked and the level of difficulty of the questions. I wanted to make these scientifically equivalent to be able to measure progress in the same exact skills, at different points in time, in the same academic year, on the same criterion, for the same individual. This was the beginning of assessments based on the principle of CWY.

After initial developments in Iceland in the period 2001–2004, CWY was implemented from 2005 to 2007 for 12,000 pupils of Grades 1-V at City Montessori School (CMS), Lucknow. This was followed in 2007–2009 for over 4,000 pupils at three other schools in India: Sharada Mandir School,

Goa, WH Smith Memorial, Varanasi, Sanskriti and the Gurukul, Guwahati. CWY was further replicated for some 1000 KS1 and KS2 pupils at six government schools in the UK in Greater London, Middlesex and Nottinghamshire in the session 2007–2008 in collaboration with the Innovations Unit of the Department for Education and Science.

Currently, there are some 40,000 students in 200 schools across 19 States of India and in Kathmandu, Nepal, who are using the CWY reports for all core subjects. A new pilot for KS2 and GCSE mathematics is also underway in the UK.

CWY Pupil Reports

Figure 11.1 has data from a pupil's CWY report from the first pilot in Iceland. Such a report provides much more information than a pupil is likely to get from a typical summative report which shows marks out of 10 or a 100. The CWY reports are also different from most diagnostic reports in subtle but important ways. A typical diagnostic report is a binary report. It tells what questions the individual pupil got right or wrong (with 1 or 0, ticks or crosses).

Most diagnostic assessments are norm-referenced and provide percentile scores, but CWY assessments and reports positively and consciously avoid the percentile and summative which compare a pupil with others. Regardless of whether this is useful information for the teacher and management, the overall score is not as relevant to the individual pupil, and clearly avoidable in a pupil's report.

A CWY report also acts as a personal work plan for the individual pupil following each assessment. The pupil in Fig. 11.1 had an average of 3.5 out of 10 in her baseline assessment taken in December 2003. A progress assessment of the same pupil and her class was taken in May, 2004. By May, this pupil's average performance in English had improved from 3.5 to 6.9 out of 10. Even with the higher average of 6.9 out of 10, this pupil was not amongst the top in her class in English.

The CWY reports are not binary; they present information in different bands according to confidence. The report shows areas of strength and improvement in at least three confidence bands:

1. Well done: Concepts or skills for which the pupil has a good understanding

WELL DONE: Maintain with Practice	
Picture Comprehension	10
Picture Comprehension	10
Word Meanings	8
Writing	8
NEARLY THERE: Consolidate	
Reading Comprehension 1	7.5
Spelling	7
Reading Comprehension 3	6.3
Reading Comprehension 4	5.7
Listening	5.4
Reading Comprehension 2	5
NOT YET: Start with simpler tasks first	
Speaking	4
AVERAGE	**6.9**

Progress in ENGLISH for the Pupil above	
Baseline Average in December, 2003:	3.5
Progress Average in May, 2004:	6.9
Progess points (6.9–3.5)	**3.4**

Fig. 11.1 CWY report for a pupil, grade 7, Aslandsskoli, Iceland

2. Nearly there: Concepts or skills for which the pupil has a moderate
   level of understanding
3. Not yet: Progress required

Besides a comparison of averages to indicate overall progress, progress was
reported for each item in the table. When we first gave out the CWY
reports that included summative grades, all attention went to the summative averages. When we removed the summative grade, we found that
everyone's attention shifted to the details, and hence benefited the pupil
more. By everyone we mean the three main stakeholders: the pupil, the
parents and the teacher. Such detailed information about performance
propels every pupil forward. The pupil sees in the CWY formulation of
his/her own progress just waiting to happen, only if she/he puts in the
effort. Greater intrinsic motivation begins to build, and a greater level of
effort is observed.

Most pupils in the typical assessment regimes are not privy to such
detailed information about their own performance, and therefore cannot
clearly articulate their own areas of strength and improvement. Before
handing out the personalised CWY reports, I have asked pupils in different
classrooms to share on a piece of paper three to four concepts they think
they are best in, and three to four concepts they find the most difficult in a
subject. After handing them their personalised CWY reports for that
subject, I have taken their feedback. Many pupils are surprised to find
that their hunches about perceived areas of strengths and weaknesses have
not matched their personal reports.

More recent versions of the CWY report (UK pilot in 2007 and 2016),
Nepal (2013–2016) and India (2004–2016), are of a similar nature. These
reports do not knowingly prejudice a pupil's view of his/her capacity by
comparison with others. Instead, baseline data is used to help him/her move
more efficiently towards the next set of goals that help him/her improve
from the present level. The focus shifts away from comparison with others to
competition with self.

Importance of Instant Corrective Feedback

Feedback is one of the most powerful influences on learning and
achievement, but this impact can be either positive or negative.
Effective feedback must provide feedback, and feed forward (Hattie
and Timperley 2007). Grades with comments are better than grades

alone (Gersten et al. 1996). Teachers can teach and pupils can learn without grades. Checking and commenting is diagnostic. Grading is evaluative in which the teacher is a judge. A standards-based report card, with comments as below, breaks down each subject area into specific elements of learning to offer parents and educators a more thorough description of each pupil's progress toward proficiency (Page 1958).

A Excellent! Keep it up.
B Good work. Keep at it.
C Perhaps try to do still better?
D Let's bring this up.
F Let's raise this grade!

Stewart and White (1976) replicated Page's (1958) study and reviewed 12 other replication studies. They concluded that teacher comments, such as above, had little or no effect on pupil performance. Story and Sullivan (1986) found that while teacher comments had no significant effects on the continuing motivation of pupils, the combination of comments and an easier task were effective in motivating girls to return to the same task.

When feedback is combined with a correctional review, the feedback and instruction become intertwined until: "the process itself takes on the forms of new instruction, rather than informing the pupil solely about correctness" (Kulhavy 1977, p. 211). To take on this instructional purpose, feedback needs to provide information specifically relating to the task or process of learning that fills a gap between what is understood and what is aimed to be understood (Sadler 1989). Specific goals are more effective than general or nonspecific ones, primarily because they focus pupils' attention, and feedback can be more directed (Locke and Latham 1990).

The CWY reports are supplemented with personal work plans, such as the one below for mathematics, translated from Icelandic and it provides more specific comments, such as:

1. Practice multiplication tables: 4–9
2. Learn about halving of numbers
3. Practice breaking down images into 1/3rds
4. Simplify algebra characters that stand for a number

CHARACTERISTICS OF A CWY REPORT

There are at least three aspects of the CWY reports that make them distinct and different from summative assessment reports:

1. Reports are personalised for each pupil and presented in three-bands. In place of right and wrong by question, three bands (well done, nearly there and not yet) represent a pupil's confidence level in each skill. Different colours are used for the three bands. The reports are visual and easy to understand.
2. The stress is put on strengths. The report begins with 'well done'. Seeing the positive first has a different, more positive impact on a pupil's psychology. The reports serve the purpose of smart work plans for the individual pupil.
3. The reports focus attention on the detail. Reports purposely avoid giving summative averages and percentile scores. The focus invariably shifts to the detail.

It is clear that these reports act as a powerful medium of communication to the pupil that says:

> You are capable of progress, and here is the information you need to improve on your own previous baseline. It does not matter how others have done, where you have been, or are at in the present. It matters where you are going now.

DIFFERENTIATION AT THE LEVEL OF THE TABLE AND ABILITY GROUPING

There is overwhelming evidence that, in spite of all the hard work that goes into it, differentiated instruction at the level of the table does not work. Hattie's (2009) meta-analysis suggests that ability grouping has an insignificant effect. All differentiated instructional methods acknowledge the fact that pupils differ in their skill level not only across different subjects but also within a subject. A pupil may be good in mathematics and poor in language, or vice versa, but also weak within a subject in certain areas, for example, weak in geometry that requires spatial thinking, and strong in algebra that requires more analytical skills. A pupil's reality is also dynamic and may change quickly. One minute a pupil does not know something, the next minute she/he does. Differences among pupils may also be due to lack in preparation, motivation, effort, a non-conducive home environment and other factors, not simply notions of ability based on marks. A teacher spends hours finding the right material for each table, but more importantly, thinking about ability limits growth. By seating pupils on different tables by ability in a subject can create fixed mindsets about capacity that can be potentially damaging. For these reasons not only should any comparisons of ability be discouraged, but also differentiation of teaching at a level of individual detail is needed.

Furthermore, according to a 2008 report by the Fordham Institute, 83 per cent of teachers in the US stated that differentiation was 'somewhat' or 'very' difficult to implement. Though there are a lot of arguments teachers give in favour, differentiation seems to be a promise unfulfilled, a boondoggle of massive proportions (Delisle 2015).

Perbooks: Differentiation at the Level of the Pupil

To support the process of differentiation of learning objectives within a class, Perbooks are used. We know it is better to improve per-pupil performance by differentiating at the level of pupil. However, when differentiating at the level of the table is so difficult, it is hard to imagine teachers differentiating learning materials for the individual pupil at the level of every concept. This is where CWY Perbooks come in.

The CWY Perbooks are short skill-based units, usually 16-page long worktexts that combine worksheet and theory, and that are easy to follow by a pupil at his/her level. The Perbooks are matched automatically by computer to every pupil's personal CWY diagnosis. The Perbooks fit individual needs at the level of detail, just like a glove to a hand. They provide the necessary support and challenge every pupil needs at his/her level.

Though selections are made online, the Perbooks themselves have been in the printed form only. Digital versions of the Perbooks are currently being beta tested for use on multiple digital platforms: tablets, iPads, computers and interactive whiteboards.

For the teacher, there is no longer hours of manual work to match study materials to individual table or pupil needs. Nor is it necessary to search for and duplicate stacks of worksheets. Ability groupings are also no longer needed, and pupils can sit anywhere they wish. While pupils work on their personal selection of Perbooks, in printed or digital versions, the teacher becomes more effective facilitator of learning. Once an initial level of a Perbook is determined for an individual pupil, the rest of the selections are intuitive. The Perbooks are graded along a continuum from one level to the next in natural progression.

Goal Setting and Personal Work Plans

Goal-setting is built in as an integral component of the CWY method. After they receive their CWY reports, the pupils often set their own goals and add their own objectives to the personal work plans provided. This is powerful. Not only do the pupils get to read and understand their own needs and capabilities, they are also likely to work harder when the commitment comes from them. Pupils have an in-built desire to push boundaries, as we have seen again and again.

Additionally, pupils have been quite innovative in designing visual logs of their effort that are displayed on the soft-boards inside their classrooms, that they colour in upon completion of each Perbook assigned to them. Pupils also often write down the dates they began and completed a particular Perbook. One main advantage of the visual displays is the tracking of effort. The teacher can tell at a glance how many Perbooks have been completed each week by the pupils. The teacher can thus intervene early to ensure effort is being made by all pupils.

As there is no similar program we are familiar with, it would be hard to make comparisons, but below is compelling evidence for the success of CWY and results of confidential surveys from teachers and parents using this method.

EVIDENCE THAT CWY IMPROVES LEARNING AND MOTIVATION

I wanted to learn whether the CWY improves performance of all or just some pupils, and whether this in turn increases their motivation and effort. Can the impact of this on progress of individual pupils be measured objectively?

CWY Survey Results from Iceland

Going back to when we began work on this in Iceland, the progress made by pupils between baseline and progress assessments at Áslandsskoli was highly encouraging, but how would we know for sure that this impact was not due to some other factors? We got opportunity to implement the CWY at another school nearby, Ingunnarskóla. This allowed us to create both experimental and control groups. Students in the experimental groups used the CWY reports. These were not given to pupils in the control group.

Figure 11.2 below is a Principal's Report in the form of a class-wise summary of results at Ingunnarskóla. The baseline assessment at this school was conducted in December 2003 and progress assessment in May, 2004. A total of 87 pupils in Grades four, five and six became the 'control group'. Looking at the progress out of 10 points, the average performance of the 140 pupils in the experimental group (remaining grades) improved significantly more than those in the control group.

Here is a comment from the eighth grade teacher at Ingunnarskóla:

After attending the seminar on individualized mathematics...which was organized by ÍMS, I was quite convinced with the idea of CWY, the baseline assessment. I went back to my class and carried out last year's Samræmdpróf (annual examination) on my 8th graders who did this same test a year ago. I was quite surprised to find that some pupils had not advanced at all in this one year. Now, I am proceeding with a more detailed analysis, as per CWY using Námsmatsstofnuns guide (how to evaluate and so on), to prepare individualized plans for my pupils. I find these ideas to be very helpful and useful for me as their teacher.

A School's Self-Analysis of CWY from India

In India, a 'control group' within the same school was created by Aggrasen Public School in Haryana. The school wanted to know if pupils using the CWY and study materials we provided that are similar to Perbooks in their school made greater progress than those who were admitted to their school in 2014 from other good schools of the city that were not using CWY methods. There were 135 pupils in the experimental group and 36 students in the control group. The school gave an unannounced test to both groups and the results of their study were provided to us as follows (Table 11.1):

The data are quite compelling in that the CWY group had more high performers and fewer low performers than the control group. The school has been implementing CWY till Grade V. They wanted to know how

Grade		Dec. Baseline corrected for Demo	May End of Year Survey	Progress out of 10 points
Grade 1	Average	5.50	8.83	3.32
	Median	5.63	9.20	3.57
Grade 2	Average	4.48	8.13	3.64
	Median	4.35	8.37	4.03
Grade 3	Average	4.06	6.87	2.81
	Median	3.80	6.75	2.95
Grade 4	Average	3.03	4.31	1.28
	Median	3.08	4.50	1.42
Grade 5	Average	4.18	6.25	2.07
	Median	3.90	6.17	2.27
Grade 6	Average	2.73	4.35	1.63
	Median	2.69	4.07	1.39
Grade 7	Average	4.63	8.01	3.38
	Median	4.32	8.42	4.10
Grade 8	Average	3.50	6.63	3.13
	Median	3.55	6.72	3.17
OVERALL	Average	4.25	7.04	2.79
	Median	4.17	7.39	3.22

Fig. 11.2   The CWY principal report, Ingunnarskóla, Iceland, 2004

Table 11.1 School's self-analysis of CWY, Aggrasen Public School, Haryana, 2014

	CWY (% of pupils with marks above 60 %)	Control Group (% of pupils with marks above 60 %)	CWY (% of pupils with marks below 40 %)	Control Group (% of pupils with marks below 40 %)
Grade IV	77.0	19.0	1.6	28.6
Grade V	62.4	11.8	7.8	41.2
Grade VI	46.4	9.0	14.8	28.0

their pupils would survive a traditional system in Grade VI after having completed two years in the CWY and it seems that although the difference between control and CWY groups is less marked at Grade VI, the benefits have continued.

Teacher and Parent Views of Perbooks (India)

A confidential survey of 236 teachers of Primary Grades I–V at City Montessori School in Lucknow, India, is summarised below:

- 92 % of all the teachers felt that the pupils have liked the Perbooks and think they are excellent or very good.
- 87 % of all the teachers felt that the parents have liked the Perbooks and think they are excellent or very good.

Comments made frequently by the teachers included the following:

The CWY Perbooks have worked out very well. The pupils come up with their problems and we work together.

The approach towards Perbooks encourages self-study. So, this has gained popularity.

They enjoy the Perbooks as they are easier to understand and doing the Perbooks is not a burden for the pupils.

The Perbooks are creating self-confidence in the pupils giving them the knowledge of the subject more clearly.

Similarly, in a confidential survey of some 12,000 parents after 1 year of implementation of the CWY at CMS, Lucknow, the parents reported that they liked the Perbooks (95 %) followed by CWY reports (92 %). The parents reported that Perbooks were good for:

- self-study (92 %)
- parents' greater ability to help their children (89 %)
- goal-setting (86 %).

Perbooks and Motivation, Effort and Progress

Impact of summative assessment on students' motivation for learning can be both direct and indirect. A direct impact can be through inducing test anxiety and the effect of low scores on self-esteem and perceptions of themselves as learners; an indirect impact can be through the effect on their teachers and the curriculum. Any negative impact on motivation for learning is clearly highly undesirable, particularly at a time when the importance of learning to learn and lifelong learning is widely embraced. Thus it has been argued that testing may be accompanied by unintended negative outcomes which have serious consequences for current generations of students (Harlen and Crick 2002).

Meanwhile, intrinsic motivation concerns the performance of activities for their own sake, in which pleasure is inherent in the activity itself (Deci 1975; Eccles et al. 1998). Working in the Perbooks becomes a satisfying activity. Intrinsic motivation is one of the main outcomes of CWY.

Data shows pupils that complete more Perbooks make greater progress. When pupils witness the impact of their own effort on progress, this motivates them to do more. The more effort a pupil puts in, the more progress she/he is likely to make, and the more progress she/he makes, the more motivated she/he is likely to feel. Effort becomes a proxy for progress. Progress against one's personal baseline builds intrinsic motivation and creates an inner desire to excel.

CHALLENGES OF CWY AND HOW TO ADDRESS THEM

A teacher saves time when Perbooks are used in place of differentiated study materials. However, the quantum of effort by the pupils increases tremendously. This can create a counter problem. Teachers can get overwhelmed by the quantity of work coming in for correction.

Teachers have nevertheless been able to find creative ways to deal with this. For example, instead of the usual homework, they assign Perbooks as personalised homework. Teachers save time by using self- and peer-checking methods to correct Perbooks in the class itself. This has other benefits: instant feedback followed by immediate corrective action has one of the highest effects according to the meta-analysis of education research by Hattie (2009). Despite all the hard work teachers do in correcting work outside of the class, feedback within the class is far more effective.

Self-diagnostic reports are provided along with assessment booklets in the recent paper and pencil version of the CWY assessments. These reports are hand-filled by the pupils themselves. Therefore, neither teacher correction nor data entry is required. Pupils peer-check each other's work and enter the scores. The purpose of assessment shifts from the collection of marks to understanding needs and learning from the assessments. When pupils feel safe that they are not being judged by the marks, they enjoy the learning involved in the correction process and do not cheat. The alternative is for teachers who prefer to check the assessments themselves to enter marks to generate all the necessary reports and work plans.

Using Technology to Deal with Teacher Workload

Perbooks can also be online and interactive. When assessments are conducted online, there is no need to enter data. The reports and Perbook allocations are automatically made by the computer to match individual diagnosis. The use of tablets and mobile technology further accelerate learning and reduce teacher workload. Armed with the reports that provide information for each pupil and the class at their fingertips, the teachers are better able to track per-pupil progress, and better differentiate for their individual needs, without dividing the class into groups. Overall, teachers save time, and become more effective in the goal of ensuring the maximum progress of the individual pupil and the class as a whole.

FURTHER DEVELOPMENTS IN THE USE OF IPSATIVE ASSESSMENT

Progress can be a vague term when we consider how it has been used at times, for example in the UK, assessments and reports using 'levels' have been used for over a decade and a half. Yet, in 2014 it was realised that levels were holding back individual potential and in-depth learning. Now assessments without levels are being mandated from 2016. In this case the onus of carrying out the assessments has shifted to the teacher, they are free to innovate and CWY is a possibility.

Making Case for CWT

We can all agree that the overriding principle of a good assessment is that it is clearly tied to its intended purpose. If progress of every pupil is the intended purpose as in ipsative assessment, then we need to go back to the drawing board and think a lot more radically about assessment.

Good formative assessment ranges from the probing questions, quick recap at the opening of a lesson, scrutiny of pupils' work, right through to formal tests with the explicit purpose of getting feedback that can be used to improve learning outcome. At all stages, assessment needs to be about the individual pupil, how to motivate him/her to make progress at each step, and how to support him/her in this process. Anything that distracts from this objective is unnecessary for the pupil.

As mentioned in Chap. 1 of this book, ipsative assessment is assessment for learning and is therefore formative, but also can be an assessment of learning requiring a measurement or judgement of learning gain at the end of a period of study (Hughes 2014). CWY is first and foremost a formative assessment used to modify instruction and guide the use of different interventions with the explicit purpose of improving a class' performance. It makes early intervention possible. It is also a tool for capturing real time data, checking on-going effort by a pupil and for measuring progress of every pupil, class and school.

The per-pupil data collected each time an assessment is taken, especially when standardised national tests are conducted as part of the CWY, have the potential to provide real time valuable information to the policy-maker at different levels: school, local, regional and national. With the support of technology, it is possible to get massive amounts of useful information without the need for separate summative assessments that governments use to hold schools accountable.

Teacher Incentives

If progress is the main objective, teachers need to get incentives for maximising the progress of their pupils. While there are proxies for performance-related benefits in the corporate sector, there are not many equivalents of this in education. Lack of incentives is due in part to lack of objective information and satisfactory measures of a teacher's success. CWY may be used to incentivise teachers based on the progress their pupils make. In the future, teachers may be held accountable for one goal only—the progress of their pupils. A focus on progress is also likely to motivate the teacher to become more meaningfully engaged and more intrinsically motivated.

SUMMARY AND CONCLUSIONS

Education's role is to ensure that all pupils maximise their personal potential. Overall comparisons of ability can be damaging to most pupils. A pupil who feels 'I am not good enough, I will never succeed, others are so much better than me' is less likely to progress than a pupil who feels his/ her efforts will make a difference. Poor performance in the past does not have to mean poor performance in the future. All relative distinctions, norm-referenced percentile scores and summative averages, though useful to the policy maker, need to be banished from reports for the individual pupil, except to report on any learning gains. Age, cohort and grade comparisons can be viewed as a double-check on a pupil's accomplishment but do not necessarily lead a pupil towards greater effort which is a prerequisite for progress.

Ipsative assessment, or improvement against one's own past performance, is, however, a reliable predictor of progress, not age and grade level performance or relative comparisons. When progress against self is considered important, 'A' is for effort and for doing one's very best, not for topping in a class, or for getting high marks. Measuring the difference in performance between pre-test and progress assessments provides useful and valuable information by which a teacher can gauge the success of his/her pupils and of his/her own efforts. The same data, presented in the summative format can be used by principals and policy makers to make policy level interventions at the school, local, regional and national levels, providing measures are scientifically equivalent, or the same.

The main purpose of the CWY is to help individual pupils develop greater confidence and build skill, while reinforcing the importance of effort and improvement and comparison with self. The CWY puts a pupil's assessment in the dynamic cycle of competition with oneself that, data indicates, improves performance and maximises progress.

There are many factors that contribute to such learning gain. The CWY not only empowers every pupil with self-knowledge about their personal areas of strength and improvement, it also provides them strategies, personal work plans and individual support through personalised study materials called Perbooks. With personalised support at the level of the pupil, CWY improves the possibility of every pupil progressing more than when relative comparisons are made. It is far more important to know that every pupil is putting in the effort and therefore progressing than to know whether the pupil is succeeding in relation to others in the age group.

Even though the proposition of replacing conventional tests with ipsative assessment is rather radical at this stage, such a transition needs to be seriously considered if we are to make quantum leaps in the progress and self-esteem of all pupils. The evidence already shared in this chapter and the book is proof enough, and there is a growing body of research in its support. The costs of implementing ipsative methods are also likely to be far less than the opportunity costs of wasted human potential in a prevailing age-based regime of the summative that reduces pupil potential to a mark out of 10 or a 100.

When countries can be held hostage for decades to reforms that do not make sense as acknowledged now in the UK in the abandonment of levels, it is definitely worth trying out the ipsative approach, with all the indicators of its potential for impact on learning gain. At a minimum, it may be worth a bigger trial and a much larger scale implementation with a third-party evaluation built-in, to provide further evidence of its efficacy to those as yet sceptical about its potential. Given that schools have more autonomy now, such an implementation is more likely in the next few years, paving the way for the large scale adoption of ipsative assessment. I believe these changes are entirely within the realm of possibility.

Acknowledgements I would like to most humbly thank all those who have helped me move along my own continuum of learning about CWY starting with Bodvar Jonsson, Steinunn Gudnadottir, Hanna Ragnarsdottir, and other members of the Islensku menntasamtokin, IMS, Iceland. Many amazing people have helped shape my thinking. These include Bob Saunders, Co-Founder, Council for Global Education, USA, Bob Baratta-Lorton, Center for Innovation in Education, USA, Fred Mednick, Teachers Without Borders, USA, Deryn Harvey, former Director, Innovations Unit, DfES, UK, Helena Thuneberg and Mari Pauliina Vainikainen, University of Helsinki, Finland, Pirjo Koivula and Irmeli Halinen from the Finnish National Board of Education. I want to especially thank Gwyneth Hughes for all our interactions following a long Skype session some 2 years ago.

REFERENCES

Brookhart, S. M., & Nitko, A. J. (2008). *Assessment and grading in classrooms*. Upper Saddle River, NJ: Pearson.

Cameron, J., & Pierce, W. D.(1996). The debate about rewards and intrinsic motivation: Protests and accusations do not alter the results. *Review of Educational Research, 66*, 39–51.

Cross, L. H., & Frary, R. B. (1996). *Hodgepodge grading: Endorsed by pupils and teachers alike*. Paper presented at the annual meeting of the National Council on Measurement in Education. New York.

Deci, E. L. (1975). *Intrinsic motivation*. New York: Plenum.

Delisle, J. R. (2015). *Differentiation doesn't work*. Retrieved March 4, 2016, from http://www.edweek.org/ew/articles/2015/01/07/differentiation-doesnt-work.html

Eccles, J. S., Wigfield, A., & Achiefele, U. (1998). *Motivation to succeed*. New York: Wiley.

Gersten, R., Vaughn, S., & Brengelman, S. U. (1996). Grading and academic feedback for special education students and students with learning difficulties. In T. R. Guskey (Ed.), *Communicating student learning: 1996 Yearbook of ASCD* (pp. 47–57). Alexandria, VA: ASCD.

Harlen, W., & Crick, R. D. (2002). *A systematic review of the impact of summative assessment and tests on students' motivation for learning*. London: Social Science Research Unit, Institute of Education.

Hattie, J. (2009). *Visible learning; a synthesis of over 800 meta-analyses relating to achievement*. London: Routledge.

Hattie, J., & Timperley, H. (2007). The power of feedback. *Review of Educational Research, 77*(1), 81–112.

Hughes, G. (2011). Towards a personal best: A case for introducing ipsative assessment in higher education. *Studies in Higher Education, 36*(3), 353–367.

Hughes, G. (2014). *Ipsative assessment: Motivation through marking progress*. UK: Palgrave Macmillan.

Johnston, J., & McClune, W. (2000). *Selection project sel 5.1: Pupil motivation and attitudes, self-esteem, locus of control, learning disposition and the impact of selection on teaching and learning*. Belfast: Queen's University.

Kulhavy, R. W. (1977). Feedback in written instruction. *Review of Educational Research, 47*(1), 211–232.

Leonard, M., & Davey, C. (2001). *Thoughts on the 11 plus*. Belfast: Save the Children Fund.

Locke, E.A. & Latham, G.P. (1990). *A theory of goal setting and task performance*. Englewood Cliffs, NJ: Prentice-Hall.

Madaus, G. (1991, November). The effects of important tests on students: Implications for a national examination system. *Phi Delta Kappan*, pp. 226–231.

Page, E. B.(1958). Teacher comments and student performance: A seventy-four-classroom experiment in school motivation. *Journal of Educational Psychology*, 49, 173–181.

Reay, D., & Wiliam, D.(1999). 'I'll be a nothing' structure, agency and the construction of identity through assessment. *British Educational Research Journal*, 25, 343–354.

Sadler, R.(1989). Formative assessment and the design of instructional systems. *Instructional Science*, 18, 119–144.

Selby, D., & Murphy, S. (1992). Graded or degraded: Perceptions of letter-grading for mainstreamed learning-disabled pupils. *British Columbia Journal of Special Education*, 16(1), 92–104.

Stewart, L. G., & White, M. A. (1976). Teacher comment, letter grades, and student performance: What do we really know? *Journal of Educational Psychology*, 68, 488–500.

Stiggins, R. J. (2001). *Student-involved classroom assessment*. 3rd edition. Columbus, OH: Merrill Prentice Hall.

Story, N.O., & Sullivan, H.J. (1986). Factors that influence continuing motivation. *Journal of Educational Research*, 80, 86–92.

Dr Sunita Gandhi is the President, Council for Global Education, USA, and Global Classroom Pvt. Ltd., India. She is the Hon. Chief Academic Advisor, City Montessori School, Lucknow, India. She is an educator, author, innovator and researcher. She is the Founder of Council for Global Education (USA), Dignity, Education Vision International (India) and the Education Society of Iceland (Islensku menntasamtokin ses). She has travelled to and studied education systems in 38 countries. Dr Sunita Gandhi has set up experimental schools in the Czech Republic, Iceland and India. In Iceland, UK and India, she has piloted programs and implemented curriculum and assessments based on the principle of compete with yourself, being used by some 500 schools.

CHAPTER 12

New Directions for Ipsative Assessment and Personal Learning Gain

Gwyneth Hughes

INTRODUCTION

The opening chapters of this book made two key assertions that call into question current thinking. First, competitive testing tends to encourage pedagogies that produce quick wins. For example, teacher transmission and rote learning might be an effective way to achieve short-term successes. By contrast, ipsative assessment supports innovative pedagogies by shifting the emphasis away from externally judged outcomes and conventional marking onto assessment for learning that stretches over time. Second, measurement of learning gain or value-added is not necessarily helpful for everyone. Data are gathered about the performance of educational establishments throughout the world with an aim of continuously raising the educational attainment of students and to monitor educational standards. However, while learning gain data may generate a better indicator of teaching quality than student exit grades or marks alone, such large-scale and aggregated data is not accessible to learners and teachers. I argued that the concept of personal learning gain is much more useful for

G. Hughes (✉)
UCL Institute of Education, UCL, London, UK
e-mail: Gwyneth.hughes@ucl.ac.uk

© The Author(s) 2017   243
G. Hughes (ed.), *Ipsative Assessment and Personal Learning Gain*,
DOI 10.1057/978-1-137-56502-0_12

practitioners to self-monitor their teaching and for helping students into the driving seat for their individual planning and progression.

This chapter aims to bring together the diverse set of case studies that support these assertions and draw out some meaningful conclusions that might take us beyond this book. I do not underestimate the challenge of this task. There may be no shared themes and areas of overlap between the case studies, or the findings from different studies might be completely at odds, yet any edited collection is expected to weave together threads of commonality. In this chapter I will revisit the themes and questions posed in the opening chapter and I will be mindful of areas of dissonance and difference as well as congruence. Nevertheless, I am confident that the final cloth that I weave will not be too threadbare and the power of ipsative assessment to expose and overcome inadequacies in conventional assessment will hold the collection together. As a reminder here are the themes again:

- Enhancing learning through ipsative feedback
- Advantages of measuring personal learning gain
- Practical challenges of implementing ipsative assessment and measuring personal learning gain
- Combining ipsative assessment with criteria-referenced summative assessment or examinations.

I am also conscious of the variability in the robustness of the examples of practitioner research presented in this collection. Practitioners may not have access to suitable data and the studies range from large-scale research to small scale evaluations of practice with evidence that is bordering on the anecdotal. However, practitioners are immersed in their practice and I give their evaluations and knowledge about their practice a reasonable amount of credence. In such practitioner pedagogical research, that is often a form of action research, knowledge that is generated through a reflexive project can contribute to a theoretical discussion.

> ... a good action research project contains three main elements: a good story, rigorous reflection on that story, and an extrapolation of useful knowledge or theory from the refection on the story. (Coghlan and Brannick 2010, p. 15)

The case studies provided the stories and reflections and this chapter will synthesise the results and I have included evidence from all the reflective case studies in this meta-analysis.

Finally, I view this whole collection as an ipsative project where there is development of ideas and evidence of change in practice that represents a professional learning gain for all the authors, including myself. I asserted in early chapters that the ipsative process is a long-term undertaking, and I finish the book by imagining some future scenarios built on ideas that have been presented to us in the case studies.

REVISITING THE THEMES OF THE COLLECTION

Theme 1: Enhancing Learning through Ipsative Feedback

As this is a collection emerging from those with an interest in learning and teaching, all the case studies addressed the enhancing learning theme. However, that does not mean it is easy to obtain clear answers about the value of ipsative feedback, particularly when evidence for learning enhancement is difficult for practitioners to obtain. Nevertheless, there are convincing early signs of three positive impacts of ipsative feedback in:

1. encouraging learning for the longer-term by rebalancing process and product
2. supporting the self-regulation of learning
3. motivating students to persist in their learning.

First, a cumulative or extended period of learning is a common theme to all the chapters in the book. Ipsative feedback provides information about the progress a learner has made from one assessment to the next or about development over a series of assessments. The feedback may refer to general skills such as an improvement in writing or the learning process itself (self-regulation), or it can be highly specific to a topic or learning outcome. For example, in Rattray's piece (Chap. 8) peer feedback was about development of critical thinking while Tilley and Roach (Chap. 7) gave an example of ipsative feedback on knowledge gained about the design of off shore wind farms. Effective feedback is always future-orientated but we have seen how ipsative feedback differs from outcomes-led feedback in that it refers to the next step as part of a learning trajectory towards a goal for that particular learner rather than how to reach an externally set outcome. This means that ipsative feedback ideally needs to be cumulative and to take place over a period of time and not be part of a 'one-off' event (Hughes 2014).

There was also evidence of resetting the balance between learning as process and learning as product when Zhao and Zang explored shifting Chinese student's language learning away from the product (examinations) and onto process. The change was achieved when rote learning of vocabulary was supplemented by applying the language to authentic situations which helped develop students' self-evaluation and reflection on learning. Ipsative feedback from the teachers was the cornerstone of this shift. Zhou and Zang sum up:

> The need to change was not imposed on them (students) by external requirements but was the intrinsic motivation emerging from a self-awareness process.

Rattray also explores how facilitating an unpredictable journey through a 'liminal' tunnel to master the essential, but often difficult, skills of critical thinking is better viewed as ipsative rather than outcomes-led. The whole process with all its messiness must be visible to students and looking for daylight at the end of the tunnel is not helpful. Students cannot be expected to understand what critical thinking looks like until they have got there. Peer assessment and ipsative self-assessment both help students identify for themselves what aspects of their thinking needs to change along the way:

> ... ipsative assessment, necessitating (as it does) self-assessment, does not only serve as a vehicle to support students' movement through the liminal space, as they explore their understandings of what they are learning and how. It tells us, moreover, about the strategies that they might use to help them move their thinking along.

Second, a longer-term goal may be to help the learner become self-regulating so that they can plan next steps for themselves within a context of support from peers or teachers or both. Zhou and Zang, Rattray and McIntyre all viewed ipsative feedback as feedback on learning strategies as well as learning content and this is what helps learners become more self-aware. The chapters also illustrated that to ensure that feedback is appropriate for an individual, the learners must be closely involved in the feedback process. Learner engagement and self-assessment could occur through a dialogue with peers or with an expert or both. In Chap. 3, Zhou and Zang provided evidence that students can be very successful in planning their learning of English through ipsative feedback arising from a set of interlinked assessment tasks. Even postgraduate students benefit from scaffolding to help them plan their learning for example in the use of the feedback response forms piloted by Hughes, Hawkes and Neumann in Chap. 6.

The case studies therefore support my previous assertion in Hughes (2014) that ipsative assessment methods encourage student dialogue with assessors, with peers or self-assessment (which could be viewed as an internal dialogue). While discussion of assessment and feedback can frequently occur verbally in class or in tutorials, the problem here is that there is no record of the dialogue for the student to take away and the value might get lost. Winstanley's cumulative coversheets in Chap. 4 facilitated a written dialogue and provided a permanent record of student progress over several assessments. This is a clear example of use of developmental feedback that is also ipsative because progress in relation to the feedback is recorded in some way. In a similar example, Rattray's students wrote responses to peer feedback as part of an ongoing dialogue that supported their development of critical thinking. Tilley and Roach in Chap. 7 also illustrated how ipsative feedback and prompts to encourage reflection on progress encouraged students to self-assess ipsatively. Students particularly reflected on development of generic skills such as team working that were not formally assessed, but could be invaluable for employment and future learning, as well as their progress towards the assessed criteria, and so their reflection was not only about meeting the requirements of a marking scheme.

Third, the case studies support the argument I have made in Chap. 1 that ipsative assessment motivates students to fully engage in their learning activities. For example, group work can be challenging and not necessarily motivational especially if the group is underperforming (Baron and Kerr 2003; Hughes 2010). But, Tilley and Roach describe the motivational effect of ipsative self-reflection for groups:

> ...the competencies that the students have reflected on were not assessed and no marks were allocated for competencies. It is clear, however, that the students have understood that effective team working is an essential skill that they need to develop in order to meet the standards required of them. This is a major breakthrough for the IE Design module.

McIntyre showed how teacher's use of the cognitive enhancement methods of Feuerstein – Mediation – combined with an emphasis on progress rather than competition with others motivated both staff and students.

Thomas understood the need to link relationships visually and use a system in his tasks. His growing confidence was clearly evident. His self-image noticeably changed with the undeniable evidence of his increased successes and results.

As a Mediator you are in a state of high interest throughout the process which improves task satisfaction for both parties.

However, any view that ipsative assessment motivates all learners should be treated with some caution. Hughes (2014) provided some evidence that students who are successful in competitive assessment may be wary of a shift towards assessment that focuses on distance travelled. There was some evidence from Winstanley that students believe that those who start from a strong position are disadvantaged in an ipsative scheme because it is more difficult for them to demonstrate learning gain. This may be an unfounded fear as other students showed pride in their progress and in any case ipsative assessment could be used to stretch high performing students. Nevertheless, innovators will need to listen to student concerns.

It is also worth noting that ipsative feedback can be captured systematically in many ways using a range of technologies. Methods of supporting ipsative feedback in this collection include the following:

- Reflective tools, for example, cumulative coversheets (Winstanley) and a feedback response form (Hughes, Neumann and Hawkes)
- Video feedback of performing on a musical instrument (Bucher, Dubé and Creech)
- Reflective journals (McIntyre, Zhou and Zang)
- Written response to peer feedback (Rattray)
- Formal written ipsative feedback from assessor/expert (Zhou and Zang, Tilley and Roach)
- Structured review meetings for group assessments (Tilley and Roach)
- Detailed progress reports (Gandhi).

However, this list is not exhaustive and there may be many more methods – indeed I would suggest that any feedback procedure currently in use can be adjusted or modified so that it encompasses an ipsative process by simply changing the emphasis away from externally driven outcomes and onto individual learning trajectories.

THEME 2: ADVANTAGES OF MEASURING PERSONAL LEARNING GAIN

To judge the value of learning gain measurement we must recognise that learning gain data can be obtained for individuals or aggregated for a cohort and these datasets may have different uses. I will explore several examples below.

Cohort learning gain data might be useful in comparing different teaching approaches. For example, student-led and teacher-led feedback methods were compared by Hoo and Hughes showing little difference in the performance outcomes. If the two pedagogies produce the same learning gains for students then the decision on which approach to take can then be based on other factors. Teacher workload or the non-assessed learning benefits of peer assessment could each in turn favour peer assessment, for example.

Personal learning gain data can be used by teachers to help tailor learning materials for individual needs to good effect. In Gandhi's work (Chap. 11), primary school teachers used learning gain information on a range of key skills to enable students to target areas of need through 'Perbooks'. Gandhi provided evidence that her 'Compete With Yourself' methods produce better results in standard tests than more conventional approaches although there may be other factors at play if the cohorts tested were not identical. In the study by Hughes, Hawkes and Neumann, doctoral students' learning gain was captured quantitatively and qualitatively in a synoptic portfolio.

Personal learning gain data can also be used to supplement summative judgements in borderline cases which have high stakes. Making pass or fail decisions about the continuation of struggling students can be made at a cut-off point or there can be wriggle-room. Having a fixed threshold so that students are immediately excluded when they do not meet the threshold may not give a full picture. Students who are just under the threshold and may possibly succeed in future and students who are well below and without any hope of success have the same outcomes. Unnecessary exclusions may be avoided if ipsative data are available which indicate when the student is close to the threshold or is on a trajectory towards meeting requirements. There was an example here from Hughes, Neumann and Hawkes where decisions on doctoral student progression for those who did not meet the grade requirement for the next stage were informed by the quality of student responses to feedback, and thus their potential to progress.

Learning gain data is not usually collated after teaching has ended, but evaluating the longer-term effectiveness of learning could be interesting and indeed very revealing. In the Hoo and Hughes case study it was rather worrying to see that although learning gain peaked after several assessments, a few weeks after the teaching on the topic had ended the learning gain virtually disappeared. It seemed that the students had used feedback to perform for the test but there was little permanent change in their learning. If learning attrition is common then the implications are significant; when learning is so easily lost what is the purpose of assessment other than selection of students based on a performance on a single occasion? However, such aggregated cohort data may mask individual trends and in a case like this individual learning gain data could be invaluable to show whether some students retained knowledge and skills more than others, and if so why this might be.

In the above three examples, numerical learning gain data was formally captured which gives these an advantage over other case studies such as Winstanley, Tilley and Roach and McIntyre which relied on a small number of descriptive learning gain evaluations from students themselves. We could argue that precise numbers are necessary for making important decisions, such as pass or fail, based on learning gain or lack of learning gain. However, marks and grades that are formally recorded for students may not provide sufficient detail for judging gain over time. Tests may not be equivalent or a detailed breakdown of how marks were obtained in a school public examination or university end of year examination may not be available to learners. Even if the marking scheme is visible, learners may not have the capacity to understand it. Without a method for systematically recording personal learning gain with descriptive information on exactly what the numerical data refers to such as provided in Gandhi's work, teachers and students will have to rely on memory of past performances to make meaningful learning gain judgements. There are no short cuts here.

There is, however, a role for digital technology in capturing learning gain and making it visible to users. Technology was discussed by Hughes, Hawkes and Neumann in the form of a feedback history tool for taught doctoral students which provided easy access to both grades and feedback for assessors and students. Video technology was also used by Boucher, Dubé and Creech to help music students compare current and past music performances and they demonstrated that without the video recordings ipsative self-assessment was much more limited. Based on current trends, technology is increasingly likely to be used to support assessment and potentially provide much wider access to data across a range of stake-holders. Hughes, Hawkes and Neumann refer to the increasing use of learning analytics in higher education to track student online behaviour, for example whether or not they have accessed digital feedback. Questions about who benefits from such learning analytics have yet to be answered.

Nevertheless, the value of measuring personal learning gain has some support from the case studies. But still a fundamental question has to be asked: who gains from knowing about learning gain? Not necessarily everyone. I demonstrated in Chap. 2 that continuous improvement is not always possible and learning gain could be zero or even negative. With this caveat also comes the possibility of repercussions for students who are not progressing and may be required to retake or leave their course, or a teacher may be unfairly exposed as underperforming by an accountability manager. This takes us to the next theme.

Theme 3: Practical Challenges of Implementing Ipsative Assessment and Measuring Personal Learning Gain

Practical challenges are to be expected for implementing any form of assessment that is outside normal practice. We might also expect these challenges to be highly context dependent. Some general problems discussed below include the following:

- student engagement with ipsative feedback
- students' perceptions of equity in ipsative assessment
- difficulty of making comparative judgements
- agreeing who should have access to ipsative feedback and/or learning gain data.

That students are not all engaging with feedback is a common complaint from teachers at all levels. There may be many reasons for this: not understanding the feedback, not agreeing with the feedback, lack of time to engage, or not believing that there are any benefits to be had from engaging (Price et al. 2010; Price et al. 2011). While all these may apply in an ipsative assessment too, we might expect that the personal and motivational aspects of ipsative feedback would encourage greater engagement. However, Winstanley observed that even when the feedback is ipsative and we might hope more personally relevant, that does not guarantee that all students will cope with formative or summative assessments.

In some instances, the areas they aimed to improve were too nebulous or too ambitious and became impossible to fulfil. Help with identifying clear, realistic enhancements was appreciated in these cases. In some instances, they felt demoralised by the sheer number of comments and by the amount of work they felt was needed.

Continuous improvement may not be a goal for all students: some may wish to remain in a comfortable position and coast through their studies or avoid assessment overload, some may have good reason not to progress, while others may expect to fail and no amount of encouragement will help. The social and environmental issues behind these individual positions cannot be addressed through the teaching and learning processes alone (Hughes, 2010). For example if a student is ill or struggling financially then no amount of feedback on progress will enable that student to continue to thrive. There may be times when an upward learning trajectory is not appropriate. Such situations do beg the question about whether the student should continue on the programme of study. I have indicated previously that sustained lack of progress without good reason should certainly trigger a discussion on future options in the same way that any failure to meet externally set standards requires students, parents and tutors to look at the possibility of resits or other options (Hughes 2014).

The next challenge is about perceptions of fairness and equity. In my previous work I have considered the possibility that under an ipsative regime students might deliberately start from a low base to ensure that they could produce a substantial learning gain, but I concluded that this is unlikely. Indeed there was not any evidence of such practice in these case studies. However, there was some concern from high achieving students that weaker students have an advantage because they have more ground to gain as Winstanley noted in her study:

> ...some students felt they were required to make more complex improvements than their peers; they perceived the personalised nature of the comments as unfairly weighted in favour of students with weaker work in the first instance.

This might be more of a problem if ipsative grades make a substantial contribution to a competitive award. We might also ask: when does benign self-monitoring become obsessive self-surveillance? Asking students to track their own progress is not necessarily easy to do and students could as equally underestimate as overestimate their performances. However, ipsative marking is a distant possibility and not likely to disrupt current practice in most contexts, but it is useful to anticipate such difficult questions.

The problem of comparing two or more assessment results to produce a learning gain measurement was documented in Chap. 2. Unless the same test is repeated with the same students under the same conditions, any comparison may not be valid. In most cases of learning gain measurement students will sit different tests that are judged to be equivalent and statistical methods can be used to ensure equivalence at scale. The validity of comparisons at the classroom or individual level also needs addressing, but it is not easy to distinguish between trends in learning gain and anomalies. Hoo and Hughes explored the issue of unpredicted anomalies in data arising from one of the assessments being more difficult than the others. The point that ipsative assessment requires equivalent or repeated assessments was also mentioned by Tilley and Roach. If students are working on a longer-term piece of work as in the engineering group projects of Tilley and Roach or in the example of the repeated performances of the same piece of music in Boucher, Dubé and Creech, then improvements are relatively straightforward to see. However, if the assessments are of a different form or content then identifying exactly the areas in which a learner has progressed is not easy and time constraints for teachers may make this kind of comparison near impossible.

However, in both the case studies above, the assessment was low stakes, so the precision of the comparison did not cause contention, and use of self and peer assessment spreads out the workload. Nevertheless, Winstanley expressed some concerns about the teaching resources required when ipsative formative methods are applied to large groups of students – in this case cumulative cover sheets. Gandhi also noted that some teachers found 'Compete With Yourself' time consuming because:

> ... the effort by the pupils increases tremendously ... Teachers can get overwhelmed by the quantity of work coming in for correction.

As mentioned earlier, digital technology can be used to capture and make learning gain and feedback information more widely available than the print systems of the past and so might provide some efficiency saving. However, use of easy-to-access digital systems raised interesting questions about who should have access to learning gain information. Hughes, Hawkes and Neumann have suggested that this issue needs much more exploration and visibility of data is likely to become a key consideration in future as assessment becomes more and more technologically mediated. Ethical questions arise such as should learners always have access to any information that is recorded about their progress? There was a hint of a concern from students that an assessor's knowledge of past performance gleaned from the digital feedback history tool might lead to marking bias. How much of an individual assessment history should be available to assessors and for whose benefit? How far does the standardisation and management of assessment that technology supports benefit learners? Or teachers?

Answers to these questions depend on the purpose of ipsative assessment: as a teaching tool or as a component of a competitive measurement of performance. While many would support transparency of process in teaching and learning, for the latter purpose ipsative assessment is likely to be contentious, especially when the stakes are high. This takes us to the final theme: the consideration of the relationship between ipsative assessment and conventional summative assessment and examinations.

Theme 4: Combining Ipsative Assessment with Criteria-Referenced Summative Assessment or Examinations

In my previous work I predicted that there would be friction between ipsative assessment practice and well-established criteria-based assessment that is outcomes focused (Hughes 2014). Combining two assessment systems presents challenges for many stakeholders. For example, students may be strongly guided by grades and view learning gain as evidenced only by an increase in grades or marks. Qualitative evidence of learning through feedback may be considered of secondary importance and may even be disregarded. High achieving students who do well out of conventional and competitive assessment may also be reluctant to embrace new entrants into the system who are on a trajectory to succeed but may not be achieving as highly as they do. Notions of 'fair' competition for scarce jobs or places on prestigious courses may be seen by some to be compromised.

Those responsible for maintaining standards for selective assessment may also be wary of ipsative measurements that may advantage learners who start from a lower base and give them more parity with high fliers. There is a view that an assessment should be objective and independent of knowledge about the learner or the learning process. A more equalitarian assessment does not sit easily with meritocratic ideals of selection of the 'best' for employment or higher level of study where performance in an examination or assessment at a particular time matters more for predicting future potential than evidence of a learning journey.

Despite these concerns, the relationship between ipsative and conventional assessment appeared surprisingly unproblematic in many of these case studies. Of course this may be because these are small-scale innovations which do not challenge established assessment regimes to any great extent. We do not know the experiences of assessments of these students in other contexts, but it is very likely that the case study methods are atypical of their experiences except perhaps in McIntyre's New Zealand school. In addition, the ipsative component of the assessments in the case studies was low-stakes. I have argued in Hughes (2014) that the extent of ipsative assessment might be significant and that there might be some tolerance of small quantities of ipsative feedback and the case studies support this.

To explore the findings of the case studies in more detail it is important to be clear about the different ways in which ipsative and conventional assessment can be pedagogically combined. There were several different methods proposed or tested for combining ipsative and conventional assessment. These fall in to two categories.

1. Ipsative feedback combined with outcomes-directed feedback.
2. Learning gain measurements or ipsative grades combined with conventional marks in a summative assessment.

Feedback on progress (or self-evaluation of progress) in combination with developmental feedback towards external goals was a theme in many of the case studies including those by McIntyre (external school tests), Boucher and colleagues (musical performance), Zhou and Zang (learning English vocabulary), Tilley and Roach (engineering design project assessment criteria). Ipsative feedback as a marginal activity did not appear to present any problems. However, Tilley and Roach who combined ipsative feedback and conventional grades gave some hints that the ipsative approach had a lower status and might be ignored. They recommend that:

> . . . academics need to be comfortable with giving feedback on progress, not just criteria based content, in live meetings with students through dialogue. For the students, it is essential that the ipsative feedback and formative assessment is clearly linked to the summative assessment.

There is a danger that in a competitive assessment system, students value 'quick fix' feedback that can help them with short-term performance goals rather than longer-term progression goals where the benefits are less clear (Hughes 2014; Orsmond and Merry 2011). Modular courses in particular may be designed as a series of largely independent hurdles for students to jump and it is not surprising if students then want information on how to obtain a better grade or mark or a pass mark in the next assignment rather than information on how to develop disciplinary attributes and skills over time (Hughes et al. 2015).

It is also difficult to judge the balance between the ipsative component of the feedback and the outcomes-directed component of feedback because the quotes presented in the case studies are likely to have been carefully selected and ipsative feedback may not be that common. The literature on feedback practice in higher education indicates that praise and error correction or critique are more prevalent than feedback that is clearly developmental (Orsmond and Merry 2011; Molloy and Boud 2013; Walker 2009). My previous studies of ipsative feedback have suggested that references to progress and future development are overshadowed by praise and/or critical feedback that refer only to the current piece of work (Hughes 2014; Hughes et al. 2015). Some students may of course be able to apply praise and critique to future learning and take an ipsative approach without any explicit guidance. However, Hughes, Hawkes and Neumann demonstrated that even doctoral level students do not necessarily draw on feedback to develop future work without some prompting, in this case using a reflective assignment cover sheet. It seems likely that most students at other levels will also need assistance with building their learning gain trajectories through feedback dialogue with peers and/or teachers or through self-reflection. For example, Boucher, Dubé and Creech discussed how music students were able to self-judge their progress through viewing video recordings – but there were indications that the weaker performers might need additional support and guidance. All in all, ipsative feedback appears not to be contentious as a marginal activity when these activities are low-stakes and occur below the assessment horizon.

For the second category of combing learning gain measurement and conventional summative assessment, there were some different approaches to be found in the case studies and here there were more hints of tensions between the two assessment approaches. One method is to combine ipsative and criterion-marked components and give each component a clear weighting which will be used to calculate an overall grade or mark. Winstanley describes how an assessment included 20 % of the overall grade for progress and this low weighting did not appear to be controversial initially, although the practice has now been discontinued.

A somewhat different approach is to include ipsative criteria in a progression decision. Hughes, Hawkes and Neumann discussed how a pass for a portfolio of work during the taught doctoral phase depended on not only achieving good grades, but also on demonstration of the ability to learn from feedback. Such a combination of traditional and ipsative assessment may be possible because doctoral study easily fits into a 'dual system' (Hughes 2014) where a developmental phase that is ipsatively assessed is separate from a summative phase where external standards and criteria are applied to assess the final doctoral thesis. In the developmental phase, ipsative data can be used to make important progression decisions in borderline cases.

However, in other cases applying ipsative assessment criteria may be unacceptable. For example, Zhou and Zang's vision for fully ipsative criteria or grading was not realised as the selective purpose of assessment required numerical scores and it was considered too difficult to give numerical scores for self-evaluations of progress.

The extent to which self-referenced criteria could be incorporated is questionable. The introduction of this chapter describes the faculty leader's aim to take into account student individual progress when giving their final grades. This aspiration was not fulfilled in reality. Tutors were worried that the presence of 'self' in summative assessment might be perceived as unfair by students and university administrators.

The most successful combination of ipsative and conventional testing was described by Gandhi in primary schools where both learning gain and performance marks were recorded but attention was mostly given to the ipsative assessment to direct a pupil's future learning. So, assessment using personal learning gain measurement may be acceptable in some circumstances, but not as the dominant practice. With deeply ingrained views that competitive outcomes are more important than the learning journeys of students, ipsative assessment will be difficult to promote. But that does not mean that it is a waste of effort as every challenge to the tyranny of competitive marking and qualifications gives students and teachers optimism about the joy of learning.

CONCLUDING COMMENTS

It is heartening to find so many examples of ipsative assessment in a range of educational settings. We might speculate that there is considerably more ipsative assessment taking place than is currently recognised and that students world-wide may be benefiting from this practice.

However, while it remains in the shadows of assessment regimes that value competitive performance, ipsative assessment will be limited to pockets of interest and remain on the margins of assessment activity. Learning gain is also becoming a useful tool in evaluating the quality of teaching provision in schools and now higher education, but its application for personal learning is yet to become widespread. There is much potential here for gradually shifting the emphasis from large-scale learning gain data gathering to personal learning gain measurements and making this data more visible to both teachers and students with the aid of a growing array of accessible digital technologies. Tracking one's progress in fitness and sporting activities through electronic devices such as digital pedometers is becoming popular and there seems to be no reason why detailed tracking of progress in academic matters could not become standard practice.

All the contributors have expressed their concerns with competitive assessment and have offered alternatives and the main theme of this collection is a call for the rebalancing of ipsative and externally mediated assessment. Incremental change could be achieved by including small components of ipsative assessment into existing assessments or by giving students and assessors feedback on past learning to inform next steps. The image that comes to mind here is a gentle cascade of sparks from ground-based fireworks. As assessment becomes more and more attuned to student learning, is a compromise of keeping ipsative assessment under the radar acceptable? Perhaps while it becomes established this is the only realistic scenario for ipsative assessment, but there are whispers in these stories of a more radical vision.

A stronger scenario might be one in which ipsative qualitative assessment and personal learning gain measurement becomes become the norm in assessment with at least equal recognition to conventional competitive methods. To achieve this point the path may more resemble the flaming trail of a rocket going up with some force accompanied by cries of astonishment. I described assessment transformation in my previous book as a 'feasible utopia' (Barnett 2013) – the idea is utopian and speculative, but it might just happen if the conditions are right. Perhaps there is more possibility when teachers design assessment and assessment is not heavily regulated through national testing, in other words conditions are more favourable in primary education and post-compulsory education than in secondary education. These case studies have indicated that the bedrock for a major shift in assessment is being laid down, albeit in a fragmented and unsystematic way, and these practitioners are among the pioneers. Bringing these case studies together might enable more examples of ipsative assessment from readers to be made visible and the book has outlined some future trajectories for researchers, educational leaders and policy makers for developing larger-scale, consistent and integrated systems for applying ipsative assessment and recording of personal learning gain.

REFERENCES

Barnett, R. (2013). *Imagining the university.* London: Routledge.

Baron, R., & Kerr, N. (2003). *Group process, group decision, group action.* 2nd edition. Maidenhead: Open University Press.

Coghlan and Brannick. (2010). *Doing action research in your own organization.* 3rd edition. London: Sage.

Hughes, G. (2010). Identity and belonging in social learning groups: The value of distinguishing the social, operational and knowledge-related dimensions. *British Educational Research Journal, 36*(1), 47–63.

Hughes, G. (2014). *Ipsative assessment: Motivation through marking progress.* Basingstoke: Palgrave Macmillan.

Hughes, G., Smith, H., & Creese, B. (2015). Not seeing the wood for the trees: Developing a feedback analysis tool to explore feed forward in modularised programmes. *Assessment & Evaluation in Higher Education, 40*(8), 1079–1094.

Molloy, E., & Boud, D. (2013). Changing conceptions of feedback. In D. Boud & E. Molloy (Eds.), *Feedback in higher and professional education: Understanding it and doing it well* (pp. 11–23). London: Routledge.

Orsmond, P., & Merry, S. (2011). Feedback alignment: Effective and ineffective links between tutors' and students' understanding of coursework feedback. *Assessment & Evaluation in Higher Education, 36*(2), 125–126.

Price, M., Carroll, J., O'Donovan, B., & Rust, C. (2011). If I was going there I wouldn't start from here: A critical commentary on current assessment practice. *Assessment and Evaluation in Higher Education, 36*(4), 479–492.

Price, M., Handley, K., Millar, J., & O'Donovan, B. (2010). Feedback: All that effort, but what is the effect?. *Assessment & Evaluation in Higher Education, 35*(3), 277–289.

Walker, M. (2009). An investigation into written comments on assignments: Do students find them useable?. *Assessment and Evaluation in Higher Education*, *34*(1), 67–78.

Gwyneth Hughes is Reader in Higher Education at UCL, Institute of Education, London, UK. She leads and teaches on Masters programmes in higher education and supervises doctoral students. She is on the editorial board for the journal *London Review of Education*. She has researched and published widely on learning and teaching in higher education and she specialises in both assessment and e-learning. She is co-author of *Learning Transitions in Higher Education* (Palgrave Macmillan, 2014). Her latest book *Ipsative Assessment: Motivation through marking progress* was published by Palgrave Macmillan also in 2014. She is a Senior Fellow of the Higher Education Academy.

Index

Printed by Printforce, the Netherlands